PERFECTING THE SOUL

Remembering Who You Are

Perfecting the Soul

Remembering Who You Are

Inspirational Nonfiction
by

DAWN ELY

Adelaide Books
New York / Lisbon
2020

PERFECTING THE SOUL
Remembering Who You Are
Inspirational Nonfiction and Self-help Book
By Dawn Ely

Copyright © by Dawn Ely
Cover design © 2020 Adelaide Books

Published by Adelaide Books, New York / Lisbon
adelaidebooks.org
Editor-in-Chief
Stevan V. Nikolic

For any information, please address Adelaide Books
at info@adelaidebooks.org
or write to:
Adelaide Books
244 Fifth Ave. Suite D27
New York, NY, 10001

ISBN: 978-1-953510-59-4
Printed in the United States of America

Contents

Introduction

Perfecting the Soul: Remembering Who You Are, along with its Companion Workbook and Audio, illuminates the *source* of our individual and collective consciousness that leads us to experience and express fear, anger, hate, judgment, and conflict. That source of our conflict and suffering is *the ego.* The ego is not, as many may believe, just the source of egotistical, or arrogant, thoughts and behaviors. Instead, the ego is the operating system of being human. When that egoic system overreaches beyond its intended function, it can lead to devastating effects of dysfunction and imbalance. Each day, most of us experience this egoic dysfunction, and we see it happening in others around us. The only way we can achieve balance and heal the dysfunction in ourselves and in this world is to regain control over our egos.

When our egos are in control, our thoughts, emotions, behaviors, and perspectives become imbalanced and we experience overwhelming suffering and conflict. We cannot master our egos when we are unaware of what our egos really are, and how they operate. When we are not mastering our egos, they go unchecked, becoming unruly and destructive, like an undisciplined child. Ego management and mastery is not just for those with domineering, controlling, arrogant, or self-centered thoughts and behaviors. The ego affects every single human being. We all have to play tug-o-war with our egos every day – more than we realize. What state of consciousness any person is in affects not only themselves, but those around them. There are no bystanders. This is why every human being needs to understand their ego, how it works, how to recognize it, how to master it, and how to choose differently than its knee-jerk default reactions.

This book is not just an intellectual exercise in understanding the ego. When combined with its Companion Workbook and Audio,[1] it is additionally, and most importantly, an intensive experience in your ego. By reading this book, you will learn in layman's terms and from common experiences the depth and breadth of the ego, its shadow, and how both operate. Even more importantly, through your personal work with this book's experiential guides, you will be able to see, feel, and experience how *your own unique ego and its shadow are central to your own suffering and struggle.* You will learn further how your own ego and its shadow are working both in yourself and others with sabotaging effects on your relationships and life experiences. Through the lessons and experiences of this book, you will be able to gain control of your ego, end your own struggles and suffering, while learning further how you can help to de-escalate conflict when others are imbalanced in their egos. This book's discussion on the ego is intended for everyone, regardless of their culture, philosophy, spirituality, religion, or any other view of life.

What is essential to benefiting from the information in this book is the recognition of—or at least an openness to—the fact that there is more to us than only our ego and its egoic

---

[1] The Companion Audio exercises can be found at http://dawnely.com/ perfecting-the-soul. The Companion Workbook can be found at the end of this book.

thoughts and desires. The part of us that is distinct from our ego is what I call our *higher self*. This higher self is our *true self*, which has different names, depending upon your belief system. Those whose perspectives are more based in agnostic, atheist, or scientific materialism may simply call it the *conscience*. Those with a penchant for New Age beliefs may call it the "I AM" presence. Those of other spiritual beliefs may call it the divine self or the spirit within us, while others of various religious affiliations may call it the Christ Consciousness, Krishna Consciousness, the Divine Consciousness or the Buddha Nature within us. All of these beliefs are incorporated and respected in this book's discussion. While some may think of the higher self as the soul, I believe there is a distinction between the soul and the higher self; however, that is a topic for another book. For the purposes of this book, viewing this higher true self to be the soul will allow a reader to absorb the teachings and self-mastery contained here. The key distinction I will make in this book, and what is most important for you, the reader, is to distinguish between the egoic self in all of us from our consciences, or higher, true selves, which speak to us about a more loving, compassionate, and balanced way of BEing and how we respond to life. Call that higher self whatever you desire, as long as you call upon it, while learning to recognize it as distinct from the ego.

In this book I describe in detail what the ego's function, operation, and impact is in all of us, as well as how to recognize it as distinct from our higher self. Much contained within this book will likely surprise you, as the ego is not only what is commonly viewed as simply being self-centered, egotistical, or arrogant. Since the ego is the operating system of being human, we don't see its tentacles running through us because it has become the background of all our thoughts, emotions, behaviors, and belief systems. How often do you see, hear, or recognize your Microsoft® Windows or IOS® operating system running separately from their applications? Likely not often, unless you are a well-trained computer expert who understands the nuances of the systems. This book is designed to make everyone expert masters of their own operating system.

Once we can recognize and see our operating systems functioning, the second part of this mastery will be to learn how to insert customized preferences and features of our higher selves, instead of relying on the default programming. We want to move from allowing the ego to drive to allowing the higher self to drive our thoughts, emotions, and perspectives in order to return the ego to a more balanced, supportive role, rather than the chaotic, oppressive ruler that it has become. The effects of managing the ego's tendencies to take over are that we will then BE our *true and best selves*, while breaking down the ego's stories of fear, lack, and separation into the illusions that they are. Seeing through our egos' illusions allows us to break out of the egoic boxes so that we can show up in truths instead of the ego's illusory stories. This clearer vision helps us to curb our suffering and struggles, and enables a deeper connection to ourselves and others. If you so believe, this self-mastery will also provide a deeper connection to whatever divine realm you may believe exists. Conversely, the impact of not understanding and mastering the ego results in an endless cycle of struggle, suffering, fear, frustration, disconnection, conflict, discontent, and discord. So, you must ask yourself, "Do I want to end my suffering and BE my best self?"

In the end, whether your motivation is to achieve a greater, deeper connection to your true and best self, to achieve enlightenment, to experience joy in life more regularly, or simply to avoid struggle and conflict, the result is the same. The path to achieving a deeper and broader joy, enlightenment, and abundance is the same path as short-circuiting the misery. Through mastering our egos, we empower our best and highest self, thereby putting an end to our struggling and suffering. Our society today is steeped in the ego and mired in the negative experiences of the ego. This egoic consciousness is currently pervading the collective mindset, and creating ripple effects that continue to grow and gain strength in perpetuating negative cycles. However, operating as our higher selves, too, has powerful ripple effects that create very different experiences. The ego is the source of our suffering. The higher self is the source of our joy. Each moment of every day, therefore, we must make choices between what is presented by default from our egoic self or consciously choosing our higher self and our higher self's way of life.

Each day, most of us walk around not realizing that we are making an unconscious choice by relying on our default programming, allowing our ego to make the choice for us. Because we carry energy that impacts others the default, unconscious, reactions, as well as the conscious choice responses, have repercussions. If you question this assertion, just think of the last time you were in a room with someone who was particularly happy, sad, angry, or grateful. What did that do to the energy of the room? We all impact each other, whether we realize it or not. As the saying goes, *hurt people hurt people*. The corollary is also true that, *healed people heal people*. We want to be one of the healed people helping to heal others. The thought of being one of the hurt people continuing to hurt people, I hope, motivates everyone to say, "I want something different." Even if you are comfortable with where you are in your current perspectives and constructed identities, having the knowledge, skills, and toolset to create something more for yourself, while helping to move our collective human consciousness to a more compassionate and balanced place, I hope, inspires you to seek to know more about how the egoic consciousness and energy works and BE more.

What is important to keep in mind as we move through this process is not to shame or condemn the ego. Instead, we want to think of the ego as a two-year-old child who is undisciplined, misguided, and ill-informed. Like an unsophisticated, sheltered, and indulged child, the ego thinks it knows all about the realities of life, and thus it tries to control and direct the action to get what it thinks we need and want. The ego's perspective is skewed, however, although well-meaning. So, instead of trying to bury, shame, blame, kill, or vilify the ego, we want to have compassion for it in its limited and skewed perspective that is often fearful and hurt with the sensitivity of a two-year-old child, believing that it has been abandoned to fend for itself in a cold, harsh world. We want to thank it for trying to help us, but without indulging it, and get our higher self into the driver's seat. A two-year-old driver is not going to be a reliable or safe driver, and cannot take us where we really want to go, despite how convinced that child may be that it knows what is best.

Where we really want to go is to a place of peace, joy, gratitude, compassion, courage, abundance, and love – both receiving and giving. For those seeking spiritual enlightenment and connection, there is no enlightenment without going through the ego's shadow and mastering the ego in its various expressions and functions. The ego will never be able to take us there, and your higher self can't get you there unless you have mastered the ego sufficiently to put it in the back seat and allow the higher self to drive. So, we must learn to notice when the ego slips into the driver seat and takes over so we can—through our higher, true self—regain control. Only when our higher selves are driving will we achieve more conscious choices about our thoughts, emotions, speech, behaviors, objectives, as well as the energy we project onto others in our environments. This is how we change our experiences and help our world evolve for the better. Our higher self is the only part of us that can lead us to our desired destination, and the path must be cleared to enable it to lead.

Regardless of which consciousness we are in—whether it be the ego or the higher self—when we interact with others from that consciousness, we trigger them to join us in that consciousness. This is why many of the great thought-leaders of humanity have said that in order to change the world, *"you must BE the change you wish to see in the world"* (Ghandi) and that *"change is an inside job"*. These oft-said axioms give much more meaning to the saying, *as within, so without*. As a result, embodying the saying that we must *lead by example* is critical. We have to do a U-turn on all the finger-pointing we do to others as the cause of our suffering. Instead of triggering each other into a deeper and wider collective egoic consciousness, we must all remember what it is to BE in the consciousness of our higher selves – our true selves — and learn how to stay there throughout our various life experiences and interactions with others. Who we really are is the being we are when we are in our higher-self consciousness. We've forgotten how to BE in that place, respond from that place, and use the coping skills of our higher selves, instead of our egoic selves, in dealing with the hills and valleys of life. Because the sayings that *hurt people hurt people,* and *healed people heal people* are both true, it is imperative that instead of continuing to participate in a downward spiral of hurt, with its pain, suffering, struggle, anger, hate, conflict, frustration, resentment, and blame, we have more healed people in the world to trigger an upward spiral of the collective healing.

Join me in this journey back to your higher self and re-membering who you truly are. Join me in making this world a better place. The journey starts with each of us as individuals.

SECTION I

THE OVERVIEW—SEEING THE FOREST THROUGH THE TREES

In this Section, I will present the mile-wide, inch-deep discussion of the basic nature of our ego, the stories and conditioning it creates, and its basic functioning. Within this discussion, I will include the identification of the ego's shadow along with its nature and how it shows up. The egoic and higher-self consciousness states will be compared and contrasted extensively for easy identification. The foundations of the ego and our higher selves that are described in this Section will be the basis for the mile-deep discussions that take place in the subsequent Sections.

Chapter 1

The Nature of Our Suffering

Why do some people seem to struggle and suffer more than others? Is it all based on circumstances? There is no denying that some people are born with more or less resources at their fingertips and have more or less circumstantial challenges to overcome. What is more important than our circumstances, however, is our *perspectives*. Our perspectives include what we value and desire, what our attitude is towards what transpires, and how attached we are to both our and others' attitudes, beliefs and outcomes. We all know people who seem to have a "This too shall pass" attitude to all that life throws at them, while others have, "Why me?" or "Nothing ever works out for me" defeatist attitudes towards even the smallest of inconveniences. It is often clear to see who is happy in life and who is miserable. The differences rarely have to do with life circumstances. As the saying goes, *10% of life is what happens to you and 90% is how you respond to it*. So, what determines your attitude and whether you let life beat you down, or you let the waves roll off your back? The short answer is your egoic versus your higher-self consciousness.

It is your consciousness state that determines your attitude, and it is your attitude that determines whether you are happy or suffering in life – regardless of your circumstances. Understanding from what your attitude arises is key to being able to change it and to make conscious choices for how you want to approach life. As an initial exercise towards this goal, look at the following suffering- and struggle-oriented perspectives, and consider what thoughts and perspectives might give rise to these sentiments about life circumstances:

"Why is this happening to me?"

"I don't deserve this!"

"I DO deserve this!"

"I just don't want to deal with this and need a distraction, so I don't have to think about it."

"I am not (or don't have) enough to do this, so why bother?!"

"She is out to sabotage me!"

"He is so (judgmental, hypocritical, inconsiderate, superficial, clueless, and so on)!"

"What is he thinking?! What an idiot!"

"I don't know what his problem is; I know I'm right!"

"I'm thankful I'm not like her! I'm so much better!"

"Nothing ever works out for me."

"I can't seem to ever do anything right or get ahead!"

It is easy to see the kinds of negative perspectives that underlie these statements and beliefs above. Imagine what thoughts about others and life are reflected in these statements. You can see the negative emotions those underlying thoughts and perspectives create. There is no trust, joy, or compassion for the self or for others, or even for life itself in these statements. Instead, the statements reflect mistrust, misery, and beliefs in lack. However, what if, instead of saying "Why me?" we said,

"I am not sure why this is happening, but I'll get through it—I always do." Instead of thinking "I don't deserve this?" what if we thought "I'm not sure I deserve this, but let me see how this plays out, and whether there is something better for me, or something I can learn that could help me in the future." It is easy to see the different perspectives about ourselves, others and life all of these statements represent. These different statements will generate different emotions as well. These instead statements create very different storylines, which are derived from very different thoughts and perspectives, which then engender very different resulting emotions. You can see from these examples that our thoughts determine our emotions. Thoughts elicit the emotions that align with those thoughts. Therefore, when we think negative thoughts, we elicit emotions that will be used negatively. In contrast, positive, constructive thoughts elicit aligning emotions that will be used constructively.

The source of our perspectives—our conditioning.

The key here is to recognize that it is our own thoughts and mental stories about a circumstance that create our emotions, and therefore our experiences of a situation. The thoughts running around in your head create storylines about you, others and your life. These thoughts are a product of our egos. The ego lives in the *thought-stream*. These egoic storylines, with their thoughts and engendered emotions, form our perspectives about ourselves, others and life. When we give our thoughts credence through our continued focus on them, we give them life as truths and *reality*. The continued focus we give to our thoughts continues to generate synergistic emotions, which then seem like a validation of our storylines because those emotions make the thoughts seem real, which we then view as *truth*.

This perceived *reality* that our ego fabricates, and continues to recycle repeatedly in our thoughts, are the storylines that create our *conditioning*, which then creates the expectations we have about ourselves, others and life itself. Through this conditioning, we establish habitual patterns of thoughts–emotions–behavior, which become like colored lenses we put in our eyes, distorting our views, making us see what we expect to see. As we see and experience what we expect, we then create self-fulling prophecies of our own egoic storylines. Depending upon your mental state and consciousness, you might default to an egoic story that elicits fear, sadness and despair, or, instead, you could allow your higher self to lead with its inherent knowledge and trust in you and life that produces courage and perseverance. Whether you allow your default ego to drive your consciousness, or instead choose your higher self, will determine whether you allow these storylines and conditioning to determine whether you view life with suffering and struggle or with your higher self's joy and acceptance. Both results are completely within your control, regardless of your circumstances.

In order to understand the genesis of our egoic perspectives that lead us away from an inherent trust of our higher selves, we must first return to the beginning of our life experiences in childhood. Everything about our egoic perspectives about life naturally starts in our childhood, as this is where our experiences of life began. Therefore, it makes sense that our conditioning began there as well. As we begin to experience life, we inevitably experience painful and uncomfortable circumstances. People may have treated us unkindly, didn't love us, made fun of us, didn't protect us, and hurt us. These are all painful experiences because they represent unmet or violated familial and social expectations. As children, we don't understand that there is anything other than love and compassion from life until we experience it. These unmet expectations and negative experiences create painful and uncomfortable thoughts. These uncomfortable thoughts, then, generate painful emotions when our egos replay the thoughts of disappointment and pain over and over, spinning the stories about *"What does this say about me?" "What does this say about you?" "What does this say about life?"*

Repeated attention to these stories results in the continued stoking of the corresponding emotions, which ultimately leads to self-fulfilling experiences, which then become belief systems that turn into habitual patterns. This pattern creates our conditioning. This conditioning, then, becomes the lens through which we see everything, coloring our experiences. If we've put yellow lenses in our eyes from our conditioning, we will never see the sky as blue; it will always appear green. We will think, "That's just how life is," because we can't see the edges of our lenses to see that we have tinted lenses in our eyes. Our conditioning, therefore, prevents us from seeing life as it really is. It prevents us from seeing ourselves as we truly are and others as they truly are. Because our conditioning puts these colored lenses in our eyes, it thereby puts our brains in a box. The result is we don't allow life to present itself any differently than what we expect to see based on our conditioned, colored lenses.

This illusory story creation and self-fulfilling experiences arises from our ego and its spin on our life circumstances. "Don't believe everything you think," is more than just a saying. It is the key first step to breaking the ego's grip, and getting yourself out of the ego's uncomfortable, limiting box that holds you back, sabotaging your life experiences. There is no box but the conditioned one in which you put yourself, and you put yourself there by looking at life through your ego's conditioned lenses.

Now, let's take a closer look at the thoughts that start this chain reaction and create our conditioned boxes. The thought-stream is the "motor mind" that continually runs in our heads with thoughts, stories, "what if's," the "why's," the "would's," "could's," and "should's" that convey opinions and judgments about who you are, who others are, and how life is. It is the home of the ego. The ego is the generator of the thought-stream and takes up residence there. The ego spins the stories that create these colored lenses. The ego's motor mind is not to be confused with the rational intellect, which is discussed in a later chapter. The stories that our ego spins about who we are, who others are, and how life is get repeated over and over in our motor mind. Our egoic thinking acts like a vice-grip over our mind.

Repeated attention to anything gives life to it, so by giving repeated attention to the stories and thoughts the ego spins, they become belief systems. These egoicly-spawned belief systems then create habitual patterns of our behavior, continuing to maintain and reinforce the egoic lenses that we've put in our eyes. The key here is to realize that, if we didn't give repeated attention to the ego's thought-stream, we could break the ego's grip right there and then. One of the main focus points of this book is giving you tools and techniques to see these egoic thoughts, and break this vice-grip the ego has over you.

When we are operating with our egos in the driver seat, which most people are most of the time, we experience little more than a projected view of our own egoic thoughts streaming through our head. We end up seeing what we expect to see, thus creating self-fulfilling experiences. Ask yourself how often others and life surprise you, or whether you seem to experience people and life the way you expect or the same way, most of the time. While an entire chapter in this book is devoted to projection, for now, think of projection as a film strip of thoughts and stories you have in your head illuminated outward on to a screen that you see in the outside world. This outside viewing screen just reflects the movie in your head that you watch unfold as you experience life. This reminds me of a saying that I've always detested, that "perception is reality." You can see now that perception is not reality; instead, it is merely YOUR *perceived* reality. I realize that you may *think* this is your reality, and so this means I must deal with you in *your* attachment to that perception, as you must deal with *mine*. This is where conflict originates.

The challenge in this conflict is to refuse to accept another's perception as your truth in a way that diffuses conflict instead of exacerbates it, recognizing that others don't always share your perspective because the lenses you each have put in your eyes are different colors. Therefore, people will each see the outside world differently, with different expectations and assumptions arising from their different conditioned lenses. Their behavior will simultaneously be in response to, as well as a reflection of, their own conditioned beliefs and perceived realities. There are many *realities* created by different perceptions, which are the foundations of our conflicts. Our egos then want to divide everyone into *us* and *them* groups, based on these different perspectives that create further separation and conflict through divisiveness. We all behave in ways consistent with our respective egoic conditioned beliefs, vilifying, or labeling, as *wrong* those with different conditioning. This is how we've created the collective consciousness of division, hate and conflict.

Since our behavior is an outward reflection of the thoughts and belief systems we hold inside our heads, we continue to see and experience what we expect to see and experience. We end up living lives of self-fulfilling prophesies, where we have written the play for us to now simultaneously act out and direct. The conflict starts when the parts we've assigned to others, based on our own aren't played by others as we – as the director – believe ___ be played. This conflict can be localized into particular relationships, or it can be a reflection of the larger *us* and *them* story lines that have divided us based on our different scripts viewed through yellow lenses versus green lenses versus red lenses or any other colored lenses through which people view life.

These egoic storylines - turned into belief systems – shape our attitudes, and then direct our behavior and language as we perpetuate and re-live them over and over. We end up on egoic auto-pilot, being driven by the navigational plan of the ego, giving up control, and allowing our egoic tail to wag our true self's dog. We cease being a conscious co-creator of our experience, and instead let the ego do all the work. How is that working for you? How well does your ego do in driving? Are you filled with joy and gratitude? Or are you filled with fear, anxiety, frustration, annoyance or anger? If you're filled with any of the latter, your ego has been driving. In order to take back the controls from our unbalanced ego, we must first take a step back from our belief systems to look at the individual thoughts that make up those belief systems.

If you question how our words and thoughts define our outer experience, let me give you a personal example from my own life: Around 2007 or so, once a week, I hosted a women's group of about six ladies at my house. One night, one of the ladies was a little preoccupied by an experience she had on the way to my house that night—an experience most of us have had. She was driving on the highway when another driver cut her off. As she was describing the scenario, she ended with, "and I was just so glad I didn't run into the back end of them." That sentiment immediately struck me like a brick in the face. She was expressing gratitude. Wow. That absolutely would *not* have been *my* reaction. My response probably would have involved a few four-letter words, combined with annoyance, blame, and maybe a little anger toward the other driver.

What was the difference between my usual reaction and hers? Was it that I had more egregious drivers on the road cutting me off than she had experienced? Doubtful. So, what was it? I started thinking back, dissecting my thought process in those moments. My thoughts were in the realm of "Who does that person think they are?! Running around the lanes as if they own the place, not paying attention, or being careful where they're going, acting so entitled and careless towards others, getting into *my* lane. . . ." What a minute . . . "*MY* lane"??? Who is the one with the entitlement problem here?? Again, I discuss projection in a later chapter; however, you can see the difference between my thoughts and hers producing completely different experiences. In contrast to mine, my friend's thoughts had no sense of road ownership, no entitlement, no judgment of the other driver, just gratitude for a safe outcome.

My friend experienced that uncomfortable circumstance with gratitude, while I had experienced similar circumstances with irritation, anger, and blame. You can see how it would be easier for her to view life with trust, being grateful for a good outcome after a close call. Conversely, it would be easier for me to believe life was full of careless, thoughtless, overly-entitled jerks who just get in my way, so you always have to be *on guard*. Who was going to have the more joyous life experience? Clearly, she would. The difference was not in our circumstances. The difference was in how we experienced them. The difference was in our thoughts and attitudes about what happened, and who others were. We had different lenses through which we viewed our circumstances. Therefore, you might want to ask yourself what perspectives and experiences you have when you get cut off driving on the highway. These different lenses and perspectives will necessarily produce a different set of experiences and relationships with other people because they color how we see others, the expectations we have of ourselves and others in our respective storylines, and when and how we blame and judge ourselves and others.

Impact of Words

When considering the thoughts we have that lead to our stories, emotions and experiences, we must also look at the words we use that make up those thoughts. The full meaning and energy behind our words are often expressed through the tone and way in which we use the words, in addition to the inherent meaning we give the words themselves. This meaning is essentially our intention, and intentions have energy behind them. Words define your experiences because they reflect your inner thoughts, which then inform and direct your outer experience. The same energy you express internally will be the same energy you express externally. *As within, so without.* I can't stress enough how important words are to our thoughts, and how they ripple effect into our experiences. Just as Albert Einstein and others' many scientific theories have shown that everything is made up of energy, there have also been scientific studies conducted on the energy behind the power of words.

One such scientist is Dr. Masaru Emoto, who has conducted several studies on the power of words on water, which was published in, *The Hidden Messages in Water.* One of his studies involved putting water into different containers, with different words taped to each container. A series of different individuals then walked by each container, saying the word that was taped on that container, essentially treating the water with the energy of what those words meant to them. Next, Dr. Emoto froze the water, and then chipped crystals off each container's frozen water and examined the magnified crystals. The water exposed to beautiful words and energy, such as "love" and "gratitude," formed beautiful crystals, while water exposed to negative energetic words and phrases, such as "you fool," or "you disgust me," did not form crystals. Given the high water content of our bodies[2], the impact of our words on ourselves and others is dramatic. Some pictures of Dr. Emoto's study, as reflected in his book, are included below:

You fool   *Thank you*   *Truth*

You disgust me   *Love and Gratitude*   *Wisdom*

Dr. Masaru Emoto water crystal study, as published in *The Hidden Messages in Water*. Reprinted with the express permission of the Office Masaru Emoto, LLC.

---

[2] Depending upon the part of the body, the age and the fitness level of an individual human body, the water content could be up to eighty percent. See https://www.usgs.gov/special-topic/water-science-school/science/ water-you-water-and-human-body?qt-science_center_objects=0#qt-science_ center_objects

What are you saying to yourself? Do you say things to yourself such as, "I'm so stupid," or "I can't do anything right," or similar things? The same is true of what we say aloud to others. Based on these studies and our biological make-up, it would seem to be physiologically unlikely for our bodies to be impervious to the thoughts we say to ourselves, the thoughts we receive from others, as well as the statements we make to others. What effects are you creating with your thoughts?

The energy of our thoughts, emotions, and actions

As we express our thoughts and emotions, we give off the energy of those thoughts and emotions. Thoughts are made up of both words and the energies of those words. Emotions themselves are just energies. *E-motion* is *e*nergy in *motion*. The emotions match the energetic resonance of and flow from the energy of our thoughts, as reflected in the words–taped–to– water crystal study by Dr. Emoto. We are either giving off the energy of the ego, with its fear and need to be right over anything else, or the energy of the higher self, with its love, compassion, and harmony. Like the Newton's Cradle of balls, when you lift one ball and let it hit the others, the energy flows through the balls to impact the last ball in the line, which then reacts with equal action to the energy input.

The Newton's Cradle[3]

[3] Credit: Public Domain

Just as the energy of our thoughts triggers corresponding emotions, the energy we exude from our thoughts and emotions also triggers energy in other people. When we put out the energies of the ego of fear, anger, and lack, we often trigger the same imbalanced egoic energy mirroring reactions both in and from others. This is a similar energetic reactive default as the Newton's Cradle. When you perceive someone judging you (whether actually happening, or just imagined by the ego), you will often react to the energy that you perceive with the same reactive energy in return—like the Newton's Cradle.

The key point here is that the energy we give off often triggers the same energy from others when there isn't a conscious choice made to change the typical default, programmed ego–to–ego reactions. This is what creates the collective negativity or positivity of a room, of a society, or even of a culture. If we are not maintaining our balance by mastering our egos, we are not making conscious choices. When we are not making conscious choices, we default instead into triggered, imbalanced egoic reactions. Then, we often trigger others' imbalanced egoic reactions, who may reject our storyline, pushing theirs instead, creating conflict. Just as the Newton's Cradle illustrates, the energetic flow can escalate as each person continues to respond with equal negativity towards one other.

This Newton's Cradle ping-pong effect of our egoic energies and consciousness states is the source of great conflict in personal, professional, social, and diplomatic relationships in our world today. When we can maintain the equilibrium of self-mastery, and not fall into our imbalanced ego, two benefits occur: First, we aren't taken off balance by anything externally going on from others, so we maintain our internal peace, wisdom, and conscious choice, thereby not reverting to our own egoic knee-jerk reactions. Instead, we stay balanced when another is interacting with us in their egoic consciousness, and our response can then be an aware, conscious choice. Second, we won't trigger others to fall into their imbalanced egoic reactions, thereby diluting and diffusing that person's egoic negativity. Both these energetic truths can be seen in the physics of the Newton's Cradle. When one side of the balls is engaged, if there is something on the other side that prevents the last ball in the line from reacting at the same energetic intensity, then the energy returned to the initiating ball also reduces by the same amount. Instead of escalating negativity, you end up with de-escalation.

The Newton's Cradle is an illustration of how energy flows. Our thoughts and emotions are forms of energy, just as many scientific theories have shown. Thus, the Cradle is an instructive visual of how our individual energies affect one another. When we consciously choose not to have knee-jerk reaction from our egoic storylines instead of creating or contributing to the collective egoic consciousness, we simultaneously contribute to de-escalating others' egoic consciousness, while also creating a collective higher energy and consciousness that is rooted in love, compassion, peace, and harmony. So, you see, there is no neutral ground here. Everyone is contributing to the collective energy of our environments. You are either responding in kind to egoic energies, thereby escalating egoic negativity, or you are maintaining your balance, and thereby contributing to a de-escalation of the ego and perpetuation of the higher energies of love and compassion. There are no bystanders.

The ripple effects of whatever energy you are exuding are both real and powerful. As an example, I'm sure you've experienced situations when someone was in a bad mood, and they walk into an interaction with others. Their irritable mood and energy prompts others, who may also not be well-controlled, to mirror short, snippy, and judgmental behaviors, with negative thoughts, emotions, and energy in response. You've likely noticed the change in the energy and feel of the room. This mirroring is in no way blaming, or a justification, for anyone's reactive behavior. Everyone is always responsible for their own thoughts, emotions, and behaviors. What I'm describing here instead is the default energetic mirroring ping-pong effect that occurs when people rely on their default egoic consciousness. I'm sure you've experienced this in the reverse as well when another is exuding positive, joyful, and compassionate energy, and how it makes others feel and react. When someone treats you with compassion and kindness, it immediately diffuses your negative thoughts and emotions, provoking a more in-balance, less angry, or irritable energy in you. Then, when you have more interactions with others, your mental and emotional states are in a better place, so your interactions with others go better, and you just overall feel better. The ripple effects are not just powerful—they are both deep and far reaching.

This gives new meaning to the concept of *pay it forward*. What are you paying forward? Whatever you are paying forward is your responsibility because it is your energy. You cannot engage in the blame game and say someone else made you angry. As discussed, with our own thoughts eliciting our own emotions, no one makes you anything—whether angry, sad, irritable, or happy. *You* engender your emotions yourself from your own thoughts and expectations. Therefore, you must retain responsibility for them. This does not mean that others aren't at times unkind; however, as discussed above, when others are unkind and acting out of their negative egoic consciousness, if you maintain your balance in your higher self, then you won't allow yourself to be pulled into an egoic thought, emotion and consciousness in a knee-jerk, reactive, fashion. Maintaining your own equilibrium and grounding requires you to be in conscious control and responsible for your own thoughts, emotions, and consciousness *at all times.* This is worthy of repeating: *You are responsible for your thoughts and emotions at all times, <u>regardless of the actions of others</u>.* Throughout this book and its exercises, I will discuss how to maintain this balance in the face of unkind treatment by others, and how to not take things personally.

Another truth about the ego is that because the ego is centered in the self, it takes everything that it experiences personally. To the ego, another's unkind treatment of us must mean something about us or that person's thoughts about us. As we've discussed, when the ego thinks, emotes, and reacts in life, it is a reflection of its own conditioning. Like the projector analogy, whatever anyone does, says, thinks, or emotes is a reflection of what is in their head, and where they are in their consciousness, and nothing more. Therefore, what anyone does or says has nothing to do with you. Conversely, what you do, say, and think has nothing to do with anything outside yourself either. Everyone is responsible for their own stuff. Blaming is just a tool of the ego to make itself feel validated. Blame is just another illusory storyline of the ego. (I discuss what is behind blame in a later chapter.)

This individual responsibility can be seen in the example of my friend's reaction versus mine to another driver cutting us off on the highway. My anger and irritation wasn't the fault of the driver, rather it was my own fault, based on what I was thinking and my own expectations arising from my own egoic lenses and conditioning. My friend's gratitude was not due to a friendlier, more gracious driver cutting her off, but instead originated from her own thought processes and consciousness.

She had been in the consciousness of her higher self. I had been in my egoic consciousness. What consciousness we are in as we experience life's circumstances determines how we react or respond, and how we perceive those experiences. How different would our world be if we all reacted out of the consciousness of our higher selves?

Characteristics of the Ego

The ego has many facets and reveals itself in our lives in many ways. The ego can be identified primarily through its beliefs in separation, fear, and lack. The ego has two primary useful functions: First, the ego can be useful for creating a foundation for humans as individual beings, each worthy of value as a unique expression of gifts and talents within humanity. Second, from an evolutionary perspective, the ego was instilled with a primal fear designed to ensure our survival. This fear ensures that we recognize imminent physical threats to our existence, such as threats posed by a prey-eating animal or falling off a cliff. We can see, then, that the ego is built on foundations of separation (through our individuation) and fear. Those are both precarious foundations, if not managed closely. When the ego is balanced within those strictly confined boundaries, the ego can be both functional and constructive. However, when the ego is allowed to go unchecked, it can quickly veer off the rails and become dysfunctional, destructive, and sabotaging. Today humanity reflects an off-the-rails egoic consciousness of separation and fear, believing there are limited resources in life for which we must compete. This egoic, fear-based belief in lack—lack of resources, lack of affection, lack of opportunity, and so on—underlies everything the ego values, perceives and attempts to achieve.

The ego's perspective on its experiences and circumstances naturally will be self-centered and focused on its survival. Survival, to the ego, requires obtaining, controlling, and dominating in what it believes is a world of competition in order to acquire what it believes are the limited resources and opportunities for its survival. These individual, self-centric, fear-based perspectives of the ego keeps the ego trapped in the anxiety of the "would's," "could's," and "should's." I call this the *if only trio.* The ego becomes both entrenched in the past and anxious about the future. The ego is constantly striving to shape and mold life to its desires. It is always spinning stories about its experiences, and what they mean about itself, others, and life, preoccupied with the past and anxious about controlling the future.

When you notice your own thoughts involving the *if only trio,* then you know that your ego is driving your current consciousness and is unhappy about what occurred in the past, fearful, anxious about and trying to control the future. This keeps you running on a human hamster wheel, around and around, split between the past and future, with little ability to live in and appreciate the present moment. Unless we are fully aware of and mastering our egos, our egos will be imbalanced, undisciplined, and immature default operating systems with uncontrolled thoughts of fear, separation and lack. I refer to our egos as being primarily unchecked and imbalanced in this book because our egos are predominantly un-mastered in our society today. Notwithstanding the predominance of imbalance in our egos today, we nevertheless do not want to vilify the ego. Like a typical two–year–old, it just requires boundaries, managing, and parenting with constructive tools, while showing it love and compassion without indulgence.

The nature of our egoic perspective

Because the ego's perspective is self-centric, based on lack and driven by fear, the belief systems and lenses of our egos will be based on a belief that resources are limited, that we must compete for everything, and that little is more important than obtaining the desired resources for ourselves. This spawns the belief that we must separate ourselves further from others through competition, controlling, winning, and dominating in order to gain access to what the ego believes are limited resources in every category: money, jobs, housing, material possessions, earthly resources, affection, and acknowledgement, and so on. The ego does not believe in or see abundance in anything.

This separation from others that the ego insists on creating results in a polarized perspective without balance, a middle ground, or a win/win positioning. The ego sees everything as right or wrong, good or bad, win or lose, and with everyone as part of either *us* or *them.* From the ego's perspective, if you win, that must mean I lose. If I am right, and we don't agree, it must mean that you are wrong. If we don't agree, you are therefore part of *them.* If we agree, then you are part of *us.* In order to create this perceived need for separation, the ego uses several tools to get its way, such as judgment, criticism, anger, bullying, threats, withdrawal, withholding, insistence on a win without compromise, and fear. As you might notice from this list, the ego uses tools that reflect an imbalanced approach to life's circumstances. The reason the ego uses these tools that are so out of balance is because the ego itself is nearly always coming from a place of imbalance, especially when it is un-mastered, and therefore not consciously integrated as part of a whole with our higher self.

Chapter 2

Imbalances of the Ego: Aggressive and Submissive Expressions

Because the ego is based in fear and lack with its focus centered on the self, its perspective and reactions are then both undisciplined and unbalanced. This imbalance will be either on the submissive side or the aggressive side of center. In contrast, to be balanced, the ego must be moderated by the higher self, with the higher self in the driver seat with the ego merely a passenger. The higher self helps to uphold the sense of self, balanced by the higher self's characteristics of humility, compassion, and generosity, as well as others (all of which are discussed in a later chapter). We can think of being "in balance" as, figuratively, in the middle. Like a seesaw, balance is when the weight distributes evenly, while the opposite ends are aligned at the same level. When you step to either side of the center, however, you create an imbalance, which is expressed as being either aggressive or submissive. On the aggressive side, there is a push outward externally, such as venting, an attempt at showing, shoving, or moving outward, often toward or against someone else. In the aggressive mode, you are fighting against and rejecting a certain thought, act, or an egoic storyline. In contrast, the submissive side can have the same degree of movement, but it is instead focused internally, reflecting thoughts and acts directed towards ourselves that submit to the egoic storyline. This submissive expression of the ego absorbs, reflects inward, pulls in against ourselves, believes the storyline, and thereby identifies with it. While the aggressive expression of the ego pushes outward, the submissive expression pulls inward and absorbs.

Both sides of these ego imbalances are based on the same egoic storyline fearing a lack of self-worth. Yet, each side responds to that fear differently. The aggressive ego expression of that storyline rejects and fights that unworthiness story, often venting with anger and thoughts of entitlement. In contrast, the ego's submissive expression of that unworthiness story submits to the storyline, pulling inward, often with thoughts and emotions of sadness, dejection, and insecurity. Because both expressions originate from the same fear, the dysfunctional anger and sadness that get expressed are often just the aggressive and submissive reactions to the same egoic storyline and circumstance.

We see these aggressive/submissive imbalances reflected in many persona archetypes that we create for ourselves and with which we label others. Some of these archetypes are discussed below.

Persona Archetypes[4]

As the ego creates storylines about our experiences, it creates and labels *persona archetypes* about who it believes we are and who others are, based on those stories. However, these persona archetypes are not archetypes of our soul or of our true selves, but are rather the personas of the egoic personalities and/or identities the ego adopts. These include personas such as the following:

- The Victim
- The Know-it-all
- The Wallflower
- The Dominator
- The Judge
- The Woe-is-Me

- The Passive-Aggressor
- The Bully
- The Whiner
- The Control Freak
- The Star
- The Gossip

The Victim. The persona archetype of the Victim does not refer to someone being victimized in terms of physical, mental, or emotional abuse. Instead, the Victim is a persona tool adopted by the ego as a result of an imbalanced egoic reaction to its life circumstances. However, if an individual does not process their traumatic experience in a healthy, balanced manner, their ego may ultimately adopt this persona archetype as part of their identity. The Victim, as an adopted egoic reactionary persona archetype, takes little to no responsibility for their acts

---

[4] The psychologist, Carl Jung, identified what he believed were four major archetypes (the Self, the Persona, the Shadow, and the Anima/Animus, along with twelve character archetypes, which primarily describe differing, yet innate, personality makeups. The persona archetypes outlined in this book, however, do not rely on Jung's categories, and instead refer to various imbalanced egoic expressions, as well as persona tools, identities, and tendencies that our egos adopt in reacting to life's circumstances.

or behaviors. Therefore, the Victim views life as just happening to him, while blaming others, as well as life, for his circumstances. Because the Victim refuses to take responsibility for his behavior and resulting life experiences, he acts as if, and believes, that he is powerless to change his circumstances, experiences or behavior. The Victim justifies and rationalizes his beliefs and behaviors as being natural, while blaming others for everything that occurs in his life. Instead of accepting responsibility, the Victim believes that his experiences are always the result of someone or something else external to him. The Victim is left with only default egoic reactions, instead of conscious choice responses, because he refuses to see his role, responsibility, and options for choices. The Victim demonstrates also a passive-aggressive or submissive-aggressive nature because this persona simultaneously, aggressively blames others, while submitting to the egoic storylines about his experiences.

The Know-it-all. The Know-it-all has a deep-seated belief in a lack of self-worth. This aggressive expression of acting as if he "knows it all" is an egoic reaction where he tries to hide what he believes to be his lack of worth, and instead shows others what he wants them to see by pushing his knowledge out into others' faces. The Know-it-all rejects and pushes back against the low self-worth storyline of the ego's making, wanting others to believe instead that the Know-it-all has a high worth through his knowledge. He both suppresses and rejects his thoughts and feelings of a lack of worth, taking on instead the aggressive form of imbalance by aggressively pushing his worth onto the external world. In many cases, the Know-it-all's reactions of talking over people, having to show that he knows more than others, is a knee-jerk reaction to the ego's story of low worthiness that he wants to reject. The Know-it-all sees many life circumstances as challenging his worth through his intelligence or knowledge. Since the ego always views itself in comparison to others as part of its need for separation and "winning," it must be perceived as knowing more than others. For the Know-it-all, to be knowledgeable is not only showing his worth, but also thereby trying to convince himself and others of the Know-it-all's value.

The Wallflower. The Wallflower is the opposite of the Know-it-all. The Wallflower has a similar sense of a lack of worth but reacts on the submissive, rather than aggressive, side by submitting to that storyline, believing it, and taking it on as part of his identity. Instead of aggressively pushing out into the world a sense of worth as the Know-it-all does, the Wallflower tries to make himself as small and unnoticeable as possible, believing he is not worthy of having attention or being valued. He wants to hide from attention, so others won't see how lacking in worth he believes he is.

The Dominator. The Dominator is filled with fear, fearing both what he believes to be a lack of resources in life in tandem with what he believes to be his own lack of worth or weakness. The Dominator fears that others will try to dominate, oppress, or control him because of what the Dominator fears is his weakness and ease of being dominated or oppressed. This can be one of the reasons why you often see individuals from a marginalized or minority group become especially oppressive if and when they come into a position of power or influence. The Dominator fears he will be dominated and oppressed in gaining access to a perceived limited pool of resources. As a result of these fears, the Dominator uses his fear to motivate him to an aggressively imbalanced need to dominate and oppress others in order to avoid being dominated and oppressed in order to gain access to the perceived limited resources. The Dominator's fears will not allow him to trust anyone, or even life itself. He believes that survival depends on an aggressive display of control, domination and oppression of others in a competition for limited resources, which could include affection, power, and influence.

The Judge. The Judge is another aggressively imbalanced expression of a belief in a lack of self-worth. As is typical of an egoic perspective, the Judge believes in polarizations of good/ bad, right/wrong, win/lose and us/them. The Judge must therefore label and characterize everyone into these polarized categories because the ego must believe it knows, and thus understands, both others and life. This results in the need to separate from others. The Judge uses these labels and characterizations to comfort itself that it has such knowledge under control and is therefore *better than* others. By judging others and putting them down, the Judge believes this puts himself in a higher place within the pecking order of worthiness, like a two-sided balancing scale. This is how the Judge attempts to fight and reject the egoic storyline of his own unworthiness.

The Woe-Is-Me. The Woe-Is-Me persona archetype has a negative storyline about many of his experiences due to an underlying distrust and distorted lens through which he views his experiences. The Woe-Is-Me is more of a pessimist because he doesn't trust others, life, or even himself. That mistrust always comes from an underlying fear that starts with a fear about our own weakness or lack, which then gets projected out in ways that express a fear of others oppressing us. The Woe-Is-Me can be viewed, in part, as the submissive version of the Dominator. The Woe-Is-Me's fear is understated when compared to the Dominator's; however, it is still there, and the Woe-is-Me's archetype is a suppressive expression of that fear. The Woe-Is-Me feels beaten down by life, and so sees the thorns instead of the roses. The Woe-Is-Me cannot see the pearls left by the ebbing tides, or the strength he gains by surviving the level-5 rapids of the flow of life. There is a strong element of the Victim in this persona as well, but not because the Woe-is-Me won't take responsibility for his circumstances. Instead, the Woe-Is-Me and the Victim both have cloudy lenses through which they view whatever occurs in their lives. There is a certain self-fulfilling validation or perverse enjoyment that the Woe-Is-Me gets from seeing his life play out according to his negative perspective. This is typical ego that would rather be *right* than have *success* or love. Like the Victim, the Woe-Is-Me thinks that his negative experiences garner him sympathy. Both archetypes need the validation of being a victim of life. They both relish the pity party.

The Victim believes he is a victim of others, whereas the Woe-Is-Me views himself as a victim of life. The Woe-Is-Me will make more of an effort to affect his circumstances than will the Victim, but his view will often be *"I don't know why I'm even bothering to try; it never works out for me."* Yet, he will often feel compelled to keep trying, feeling like a pack mule who is weighted down, constantly trudging up a steep hill, and always feeling oppressed and beaten up by life. The Victim, in contrast, will not usually try very hard, feeling more entitled about what *should* or *should not* be, believing he has simply been wronged by others as well as life. The Victim usually will be able to point to a *them* person to blame, but if that fails, he will fall back on life itself as being the oppressor. The Woe-Is-Me doesn't have the same edge of aggressiveness that the Victim has in his blaming and lack of taking responsibility. The Victim often has an anger (aggressive expression), whereas the Woe-Is-Me takes the sadness route instead (submissive expression).

The Passive-Aggressor. The Passive-Aggressor is an interesting combination of both the submissive and aggressive sides of imbalance. This persona is much like the typical passive-aggressive nature typically defined in mainstream psychology. In this discussion of aggressive and submissive expressions of the ego, it may allow you a deeper understanding of this persona. The Passive-Aggressor has an aggressive thought and perspective, but his behavior and response will be on the submissive side outwardly. He will appear outwardly passive and submissive, appearing to submit to the storyline, usually because he believes that expressing anger or engaging in conflict is *bad*. Since the Passive-Aggressor typically believes that disagreement would result in conflict, or would be a hassle, they simply don't care enough to engage. He would rather take the easy way out by rejecting others more indirectly. Instead of believing that he builds himself up by pushing others down, like the Judge, the Passive-Aggressor believes he builds himself up by avoiding conflict, ignoring others, and being free to do as he pleases on his own, regardless of what others want or think. This persona has an aggressive perspective because he doesn't really care what others think and feel, and he aggressively rejects the storyline or perspective of another without regard or respect to them. The Passive-Aggressor's passive outwardly response, however, will be on the submissive side, using submissive tools, by presenting a *go along with* behavior on the surface, while having aggressively-oriented plans to behave differently. The more a Passive-Aggressor views conflict as an interfering inconvenience versus being *bad*, the more disrespect or disregard the Passive-Aggressor likely has for others, and the more aggressive the person is within this archetype.

The Bully. The Bully, like the Dominator, has a fear about others dominating or oppressing him, along with an internal belief in his own lack of worth or other weakness. The Bully is an aggressive expression, combined with a sense of fear for his image and ability to thrive. Both the Bully and the Dominator personas have superficially built up their own self-worth by putting others down. Both also have a sense of entitlement, which is the aggressive form of a lack of self-worth. These two personas are very similar. The main difference between the Bully, Dominator, Know-It-All, and the Star (discussed below) is that the Bully and Dominator combine their lack of self-worth with a more extreme fear of being oppressed themselves. The Know-It-All and Star, however, mainly fear that their lack of worth will be seen by others and how that will impact their image and identity; however, they do not typically carry a primal fear of oppression for basic survival. In contrast, the Bully and Dominator both fear others will oppress or take advantage of them, but that fear is greater in the Dominator, who fears his own lack of power and a severe constraint on his access to limited resources for basic survival.

 Whiner. The Whiner is a hybrid archetype persona composed of characteristics of the Judge, the Victim, and the Woe-Is-Me. The Whiner judges everything, and nothing ever measures up. Instead of focusing this judgment on putting others down as the Judge and Gossip (discussed below) do, the Whiner's judgment is primarily funneled into a negative perspective about his own circumstance, like the Woe-Is-Me. The difference between the Whiner and the Woe-Is-Me is that, while the Whiner judges things to be *bad*, along with a certain sense of entitlement like the Victim, the Whiner simply can't understand why things aren't working out the way he thinks they *should*. Therefore, for the Whiner, things are not only always *bad*, but also *not good enough*. In contrast, the Victim doesn't feel as much of a need to judge things as *good* or *bad* as much as simply blaming all their circumstances on others. The Whiner has a more aggressive approach to his view and resentment of his circumstances (like the Victim) than the Woe-Is-Me. The Woe-Is-Me has more of a *grin and bear it* perspective, with his head hung low as he piles more on himself, like that of the pack mule climbing the hill, and then will look forward to the pity party later. The Whiner, however, doesn't want a pity party. Instead, he wants what he wants, feels entitled to receive it, and will complain until he gets it. The Whiner has some of the Passive-Aggressor in that he has a touch of the aggressive entitlement, while still submitting to the negative storyline, like the Victim.

The Control Freak. The Control Freak trusts no one and no thing. He doesn't trust others, life, and when it comes down to it, he doesn't trust himself. His distrust for everything outside of himself is just a reflection of the fact that he doesn't trust himself. Therefore, he controls, double-checks, triple-checks, and hovers to ensure nothing is ever left to chance or is uncontrolled, since, in his view, even life itself cannot be trusted. The Control Freak has a fear of the unknown combined with an attachment to everything matching exactly the view in their head. As a result, the Control Freak is unlikely to see any deviation as being positive, and so will fear deviations, changes, or anything not emanating from his own tightly-controlled intentions and actions. This attachment to every outcome leads to high anxiety levels for the Control Freak. This attachment and anxiety tendency is true also for the Dominator and other persona archetypes with trust issues.

The Star. The Star is an aggressive form of a lack of self-worth, similar to the Know-It-All. As previously discussed above with the Bully and Dominator, the Star is on the aggressive side, but usually does not carry the fear of oppression that the Bully and Dominator carry. Instead, the Star carries a fear of others' seeing and judging his perceived low value.

The Star has an unworthiness belief, and so instead of being the Wallflower, he reacts aggressively to try to create the view he wants others to have of him. The Star's reaction is an aggressive, *in–your–face* show of a manufactured persona that demonstrates the worthiness he wants, but which he believes he lacks in reality. It is through the external affirmation and adoration of others that he obtains his sense of worth because he doesn't believe it internally. For the Star, the value he tries to convey usually concerns his worth in areas such as his appearance, likeability, talent, personality, or another trait. For the Know-It-All, it is about his knowledge and intelligence. Each archetype values and pushes out to others the storyline of high value in relatively superficial egoic traits and characteristics that do not reflect their higher self.

The Gossip. The Gossip has an element of the Judge. Combined with a lack of self-worth he believes deep down, the Gossip also believes he can raise himself up by putting others down. In contrast, the Star and Know-It-All don't need to put others down to make themselves feel higher, they just need external affirmation. The Gossip, however, needs both the external validation as well as the internal validation that putting others down gives him in order to feel worthy. The Gossip feels his worth is comparatively raised when he pushes down others on the weighted scales, saying to themselves: "Look at that person; I'm *so much* better." This is the classic polarized ego positioning of a win/lose, or high/low perspective.

Our Addictions to our Personas

As discussed earlier, our egos adopt, consciously or unconsciously, a persona archetype that is based on the beliefs we have about ourselves. These personas are limited because they are based on false egoic stories and imbalanced expressions of these stories. We can adopt many of these personas, depending upon the circumstances and the storylines our ego creates. All personas, however, become boxes in which our egos operate in order to define our identities as to who we are or are not. These personas may not be conscious choices, but rather go-to tools and coping mechanisms of the ego. These conditioned persona boxes keep us confined within their walls, providing the basis for the limitations we place on ourselves. Our egos feel comfort in believing the illusion of the persona that tells us we know who we are, and who we are not.

We not only become trapped within these confined boxes, but we also become addicted to them. We cling to them because they are known. Our egos fear the unknown more than the suffering. With the known the ego feels in control, even in its pain. Loss of control, for the ego, is far more frightening and painful than the suffering that the ego's stories and persona archetypes create. We thus allow our egos to move us to fear that, if we aren't who the ego has defined us to be, we should feel anxious. Our egos want and feel safe only with the assuredness of definition, certainty, known entities, reliability, labels, and the belief of "I know this."

This ego addiction is like a Stockholm Syndrome, where captives become addicted to their captivity, while feeling a misplaced trust and affinity for their captors. The captors convince the captives of their intention to care for them, in between the captors' sabotaging treatment. This trust in, and addiction to, such abusive scenarios arises, in part, because the captives' circumstance becomes a known to which the captives and their psyches adjust, while incorporating this into their accepted existence as a coping mechanism. The captives want to believe in the captors' benevolence because that is an easier coping mechanism than to submit to the captors' storyline, as that suppresses and numbs the pain of the captivity, alleviating the fear of what might be otherwise. There is a similar degree of trust, comfort, and dependence the captives have in both the captors of the Stockholm Syndrome and the ego's boxed limitations and storylines. In both cases, there is a feeling of being protected and *cared for*, despite the extreme confines, limitations, and sabotaging limitations. The degree to which our egos fear the unknown and believe in the known limitations as a form of protection, is one of the greatest imprisonments we allow our egos to place on us.

Much of the psychology behind the Stockholm Syndrome is that the captor breaks down the victim's desire for freedom and independence, thus making the captive believe that they are more comfortable with, and can't survive without, the oppressor's protection and guardianship. The captor makes the captive think the captor is looking out for them, caring for them, having their best interests in mind. The captive then starts to trust the captor, believing he or she is, in fact, dependent upon the captor for survival, viewing the captor as his or her protector and benevolent guardian. This relation between captor and captive is like the type of relationship many of us have with our egos. Our egos confine us with distorted perspectives that they want us to believe are beneficially serving and protecting us. We then believe their illusory stories and the spin our egos tell us, and we soon become dependent—even addicted to—our egos' stories and belief systems. This is why our ego's conditioning is so powerful and entrenched. The known is always more comfortable than the unknown to the ego, and to the human psyche when we are operating out of, and reliant upon, our egos.

This discussion on the dysfunctional addiction to our egos is not to demonize the ego, but rather to allow us to recognize the dysfunctional relationship, as well as our addiction to, and reliance upon, the illusory storylines manufactured by the imbalanced ego as to what it says is in our best interest. The Stockholm Syndrome analogy, therefore, is intended to help us begin to see that the ego's stories are, in fact, a kind of prison that is more likely leading to misery and limitations, rather than to joy, comfort, happiness, or any other positive aspirations. In Stockholm Syndrome, while the captive is physically held hostage, with the ego the captivity is psychological. In both cases, however, the captor believes and behaves as if it is protecting the captive from a worse fate, while only serving the captor's own indulgences. In any case, both captives nevertheless remain confined.

When being held captive by the ego, it may not be immediately physically harmful; however, it is still every bit as psychologically harmful, as it keeps its captive in a mental box just as damaging. This mental box leads to emotional boxes, creating pain and suffering, which can and often does lead to physical effects. Since the ego truly does believe it is acting in our best interest, but its perspective is entrenched in an illusion of fear, lack, and separation, we cannot rely on the ego to be a reflection of truth or reality any more than we can rely on the perspective of a two–year–old child to guide us through life. Just as any captor has a distorted perspective of their benevolent protection, the ego is similarly distorted in its belief of its own knowledge and benevolence, even if it is well-intentioned in order to protect and provide for us.

As discussed earlier, we should view the ego with compassion, like we view a two–year–old child who truly believes their toddler-mind perspective is helpful, but simply does not have the sophistication, knowledge, skillset, or tools to truly be helpful. Therefore, the ego does not have the ability to offer us perspectives, belief systems, or solutions that are in our highest good. We may appreciate that a two–year–old believes it is doing what is best, but because it does not have the requisite knowledge, perspective, experience or skillset, it cannot offer us the best outcomes. As a result, we must show compassion and love for our immature ego without allowing it to run the show. In most cases, the ego is in pain because it is in fear, so we must acknowledge it, comfort it, and have compassion for it, but without indulging it. This is how we should think of our egos and its values, objectives, belief systems and suggested behaviors—to comfort our two–year–old egoic child with its fears and beliefs in lack, but do not allow it to run our lives from that place of fear, lack and separation.

Ego-Induced Conflict

Our egoic-conditioned stories, belief systems, values, and expectations become the colored lenses we put in our eyes, and each of our respective storied lenses are different from one another. My story is different from your story, which is different from his story, which is different from her story. These different storylines produce different expectations, values, and belief systems. Because our egos don't see these stories as subjective, but instead see them as truths, when we allow our egos to drive our thoughts and behaviors, we see these storylines as truths that *must* be true, not just for ourselves, but also for others, and even for life itself.

The reality is that there are many different colored lenses represented in our communities that represent different perspectives on what are life's *truths*. I may have a red lens, while you have a yellow lens, while another has a brown lens. As we each look up into the sky, I see a purple sky with my red lens, while you see a green sky with your yellow lens, and another sees a midnight dark blue sky with their brown lens. We each see something different because our lenses through which we look at the world are different. Each view of the sky seems to be absolute, with our perspectives on the color seemingly a truth, because we cannot see the borders of our lenses. In other words, the ego cannot see itself. So, when we are living life through our ego, we cannot see that we have a colored lens in our eyes preventing us from seeing truths. No egoic story- just as no tinted lens - sees the truth, however.

When our egos are driving our thoughts and behaviors, not only are we *not* seeing the absolute truths of our experiences, but we also engage in conflict because we cannot understand or tolerate a different set of stories and perspectives by others. Our ego is convinced that its own stories and resulting perspectives, values, expectations, and belief systems are absolute and represent truths about us, others, and life. Our ego is not willing to entertain conflicting information as being truths because our ego would rather be right than see the truth. Let me repeat this again for emphasis . . . *our egos would rather be right than see the truth.* Let that statement sink in for a minute. Do you see how wanting to be right more than see the truth impacts how we interact with others and the world?

Our ego is filled with fear that if we are not right, what that would mean for and about us. If we are not right, then the ego would be faced with a fear of the unknown, or of not knowing or being in control. The ego is not willing to be vulnerable, let alone be *wrong*. So, the ego would rather fight to be right at the expense of just about anything. When our ego fights to be right, it uses its imbalanced tools to enforce its position that sabotages relationships, as well as our own internal mental and emotional states. The ego chooses a desire to be right over a desire for harmony, peace, love, and compassion, whether it be towards others or ourselves. Remember the two–year–old child who insists on getting what it wants or it will throw a tantrum.

The Polarization of the Ego. Part of the ego's toolbox is to use polarized perspectives of good/bad, right/wrong, us/them, and so on. Therefore, judgment arising from the ego will often incorporate extreme, no-middle-ground thoughts and expressions. When you find yourself using such polarized opposite terms, you know you are functioning from your ego, letting it dictate your thoughts and emotions.

You may object to the idea that use of the polarized words, right/wrong or good/bad, is always coming from the ego. You may believe that there are certain behaviors that are clearly *wrong* or *bad*. Therefore, you may ask, how can these just be egoic statements? The answer is that such terms are characteristic of the ego because they require a polarized value judgment. The value judgment of good/bad or right/wrong allows only a zero-sum game on an absolute polarized scale, like the ends of a see-saw being up or down, without balance. These polarized terms come from a state of judgment that rejects what is as if it *should not be that way.* This kind of rejection and attachment to something different with condemnation will never be found arising from your higher self. In place of such polarized judgments, a better approach is an assessment, or observation, aligned with rational thought, with a more non-emotional alignment or preference, one without a right/wrong or good/bad judgment, condemnation or vilification.

When assessing whether something is aligned with our values, objectives, rules and laws of how we want to live in community, no value judgment of good/bad or right/wrong or vilification is required. Instead, we look at what is aligned with, or not aligned with, what we decide is conducive to a productive, equally beneficial community. This type of alignment assessment may include gradations of alignment and preferences. While judging is usually directed at a person, assessment is directed more at behavior. We can assess a behavior as not being aligned with our objectives without judging the actor to be *bad* or *wrong*. Using assessment instead of judgment allows us to make choices about desired thoughts and behaviors without rejecting or judging the individuals personally as *bad* or *wrong*, and without judgment's nature to put others down so that we raise ourselves up. The assessment of alignment is one of detachment that allows for compassion instead of condemnation of the one who may be out of alignment with their actions. Throughout this book, I will refer to this assessment alignment combined with compassion as *compassionate detachment*, which is the path of balance and healing.

Because the ego sees a need to have separation, the ego perceives in black and white polarizations, such as if you are not entrenched into one end, then you must, therefore, be on the opposite pole. As discussed, the basis of the ego's polarized perspective is fear and the need, therefore, to have extreme separation. The ego does not like diversity of any kind, and, out of its fear, it must have separation from anything and anyone it views as different from it through using labels of opposition. This is the source of the *us* and *them* mantras of the ego.

This belief in the need for separation with such polarized labels is part of the ego's operating manual. When operating from the ego, we typically treat the *them's* by isolating them, avoiding them, and not engaging with them. Our egos fear them, so we resent them and want separation from them. As a result of our desire to separate from the *them's*, as defined by our egoic mind, we become increasingly ignorant of who they truly are. This frees up our egoic thought-stream to continue to create storylines about *them* that can never be contradicted because we never allow ourselves to get close enough to *them* to see anything other than our own storylines. When we see something from a *them*, our ego is always looking for how it can reaffirm its perspective and story about *them* because, as we now know, the ego would rather be *right* than see the truth. This distant relationship our ego has with the *them's* makes it easier to view *them* and the circumstances through our ego's colored lenses with rationalization and justification to affirm its storyline. The only way the ego can be disabused of its belief system about a *them* is to be so closely in contact with a *them* that we cannot deny seeing something that doesn't fit into the ego's narrative. Unless we see this contradictory information regularly that doesn't align with our ego's storyline, the ego will quickly go into rationalization mode with "well, that may be true in this case, but . . ." In many cases with deeply fearful egos, even with regular exposure to contradictory information, those egos will entrench themselves in increasingly aggressive ways into their rationalizations in order to interpret that information as aligned with their beliefs.

Chapter 3

Who We Truly Are

The only way that we can see past our egoic beliefs and values is to realize that there is something else beyond them. In other words, there must be something to us other than our egoic self. There is. I have already been referencing it up to this point—*the higher self.* Throughout this book, I will discuss our true nature using any of the following terms: the higher self, divine self, consciousness, or conscience.[5] Others might call it the Christ consciousness, the Krishna consciousness or Buddha nature. Regardless of your personal religion, spirituality, or philosophy about our nature, we all know and believe that we each have a conscience. In my view, each of these describe the same thing - an internal compass that gives us messages and inspirations about what is or is not aligned with kindness,

---

[5] As mentioned in the Introduction, if your inclination is to use the term, "soul," here to describe who you truly are, that is fine for the purposes of this book. As long as you can distinguish between who you truly are, as distinct from your egoic self, that is the most important thing for this book and its exercises. As indicated in the Introduction, I believe there is a slight distinction between the soul and the higher, true, self; however, that is a subject for another book.

compassion, love, mercy, courage, honesty, and all the other qualities we admire. This internal compass is our innate being. Where that internal compass comes from must be saved for another book, so it is enough for now only to know that it exists as distinct from our ego. Whatever term you use to describe our inner most being can be used to describe who we truly are. However, throughout this book, I will continue to use the term, the "higher self," to describe our inner nature. If you feel more comfortable with any of the other terms, feel free to use that instead.

This higher self is who we truly are. We are not our egos. We are not our thoughts. We are not our emotions. We are not our intellect. We are not even our outward identities such as our gender, ethnicity, nationality, religion, or any other outward identity that pertains to our body, our thoughts, belief systems, or where, or to what family, we are born. Who we truly are is this higher self. This higher self is a consciousness that is the observer of all our thoughts, emotions, behaviors, and experiences. Who we truly are is the consciousness that is *aware of* our ego, and its stories and their ripple effects into our emotions and experiences. If our ego is our operating system, then our higher self is our operator and system user. Our true self is the one who sees and observes everything. Our ego is the thinker of the thoughts that make up the stories, whereas, our true, higher self observes and notices these thoughts. When we have thoughts or emotions that are uncomfortable that our higher self tells us are not in alignment with our best self, that is our higher self acting as the observer of what is going on in our mental and emotional bodies. Our ego is the operating system of having a human body, and it lives in the thought-stream, while our higher self is the observer and operator that lives in the heart. This egoic thought-stream is not to be confused with our intellect, which is our rational brain that is our mental analyzer and calculator. Our intellect—our rational brain—is a tool, which can be used by either our higher self or our ego.

An illustration of how our higher self can use our intellect to solve a problem of an undesirable circumstance by staying balanced in our higher self can be seen in the following example.

> *You are walking on the sidewalk, a little close to the edge near the street, on your way to the subway to get to work. It has been rainy, so there are puddles in the street. A bus drives by, through a puddle, and splashes you with muddy water. Your clothing is now soaked with muddy water. You look down, thinking that this situation is annoying. You release that thought of annoyance before the emotions of irritation, anger, sadness, or resentment can take hold of you too deeply. Instead, you now shift to focus on solving the problem of a muddy outfit when you need to get to work by 10 am for a meeting. You walk back home and put your clothes in cold water to soak them. You call the office to explain your delay, so no one worries, and confirm that they can still depend on you to show up in time for the meeting. You continue to use your intellect to calculate that it will take you 40 minutes to get to work by subway, and only 20 minutes to get to work by cab, so you determine that you will sacrifice the extra cost to conserve time and take a cab, so you can get to work by 10 am for your meeting. You arrive in time for the meeting and have a chance to gather your things in preparation. You feel grateful and pleased you made it to work in time, and you feel ready to go to the meeting. During the meeting, your attitude is one of gratitude, and all goes well, with*

most people responding positively to you and your ideas because you bring a can-do *attitude to the topics. Later in the day, you overhear a couple of colleagues planning a task force on a subject that intersects with your work, and your name comes up, as both colleagues agree that you are a must-add. One colleague mentions that you will contribute much to the discussions, and the other agrees, adding that they know they can rely on you to come up with innovative ideas as a constructive team player.*

The scenario above is an example of experiencing one of life's less than desirable moments while staying centered, allowing the uncomfortable thoughts and emotions to come in and flow out, as if they were just cars passing through on a highway. You use your intellect to solve the problem, while not letting the circumstances move you into a negative egoic consciousness. This example also shows how the ripple effects of the energy of your consciousness affects others in that moment as well as your internal lens for how you approach life. In this example of being in the balanced consciousness of the higher self, we can see that this consciousness state attracts positively aligning life circumstances to you because of how your consciousness affects not only your behavior but also how others respond to you. In other words, what you resonate outwardly is often what you attract and receive back. You create ripple effects that align with your consciousness states.

In contrast to this first example above, let's explore examples of that same scenario above if we reacted from our egoic consciousness in both the aggressive and submissive sides of imbalance to the same circumstance. First, the aggressive imbalance:

After the bus drives by spraying you with the muddy water, you are immediately overwhelmed with negative thoughts such as "Oh, that's just great! How typical! The bus driver wasn't paying attention and was so inconsiderate to those on the sidewalk!! He should have seen this would happen!! I guess life just wants me to be covered in mud! Why don't I just roll around in the mud puddle then?!" You go pick up some mud from the puddle and throw it after the bus, while cussing the bus driver. These thoughts continue to circulate around in your head, including possibly calling the Transit Authority to complain. Your thoughts then bring up other situations in which you believed you were a victim of life, as well as others who interfered with your life circumstances and that you've resented. Mired in your lingering thoughts and growing anger, you go home, rip off your clothes, throw them in the trash, and call the office angrily, telling them you don't know whether you'll make it in time for your meeting now that life has dealt you this terrible experience because of such an idiot bus driver. You think and complain about how life is always so screwed up. You believe and expect people at work to pity and commiserate with you on your bad luck, and that people will just have to deal with you being late. If the alternative of a cab comes up in your mind, you immediately dismiss it because you see no reason to spend the extra money to take a cab when the office won't pay for it. You get to work late, show up to the meeting late, exasperated, annoyed, feeling like an angry, entitled victim who doesn't deserve the rotten experiences that always seem to land in your lap, and you're just sick of it. Your presence changes the entire energy of the room as well as the tone of the meeting. Because of your irritated mindset, you see fault in much that is presented and discussed in the meeting. The meeting ends up with bouts of discord and tension, especially when you are involved in the conversation. You end up having a frustrating day, engaged in several conflicts with others, feeling as if other people just don't get it and are always just screwing up and wasting your time. Later that day, you overhear a couple of colleagues planning a task force on a subject that intersects with your work, and your name comes up. One colleague says "Do we really have to invite her? She's always such a naysayer, finding fault with anything that isn't her idea. Isn't there someone else who we can include from that area that can contribute more constructively instead?" The other colleague agrees, "Yeah, I know, she's so difficult to work with. It's always her way or the highway, and she always knows-it-all."

Now an example of the submissive side of imbalance:

After the bus drives by spraying you with muddy water, you immediately suppress your feelings of annoyance and give out a large sigh, drooping your head and shoulders, saying to yourself, "Oh well, what can I do about this? I'm going to just ignore this because I can't do anything about it now." You think to yourself that you have to get to work soon, and you can't control the circumstances, so you believe that you just have to go as you are. "Probably no one will notice anyway, and if they do, they'll see how I was a victim, just walking along, and BOOM. They'll maybe even feel sorry for me." You get to work feeling more self-conscious by the minute because of all the stares you perceived you received on the subway, and you try to get to the office attracting as little attention as possible. You feel beaten down by the experience, embarrassed, and just worthless around all the people at the office who are wearing nice clothes and looking professional. You are afraid people will think you are a bum because you look like a disaster. You get to the meeting, and you try to attract as little attention as possible. You sit in a corner, keep silent, not contributing to the meeting, looking down at your notes, trying not to catch the eyes of anyone else. You look forward to the time when you can just leave. You feel so embarrassed and unworthy that you can't speak or call attention to yourself. You don't trust yourself or the value of any contribution you might make at this point, and you don't believe anyone else values or trusts you either. The remainder of the day, you allow people to walk and talk over you because you don't think anyone will take you seriously, so you won't speak up, you keep to yourself, you feel alone, and unworthy. Later that day, you overhear a couple of colleagues planning a task force on a subject that intersects with your work, and your name comes up. One colleague says, "Why bother adding her; she doesn't contribute much. We'll just tell her what we decide, and she'll be fine with it." You then believe that your presence, contribution, and value is so insignificant and you can't seem to get ahead, believing that you don't have the skills, personality, or other traits to be or do more. Everyday seems to confirm this in de-meaning ways. You feel more depressed, and just want to go home and be alone because being around others who are succeeding while you feel like such a failure makes you feel even smaller and less worthy.

Do any of these examples sound like something you've experienced or have seen in yourself or others? These scenarios reflect the ripple effects of the energy of your consciousness, and state of being. Your mindset, your thoughts, your behaviors, others' views and treatment of you, and how you attract, repel, or resist the positive things that you want in life all flow from your consciousness state. In sum, your consciousness determines your experiences in life.

It is important to note here that the natural energy ripples of your consciousness to others does not relieve anyone of the responsibility and ownership of their own actions. This may seem contradictory, but it is not because we always have a choice in how we react (egoic) or respond consciously (higher self) to anything and anyone else's behavior. An example that can help illustrate this dynamic is a multi-car accident on the highway. The driver behind you may run into the backend of your car, but whether you hit the car in front of you in a ripple effect reaction will depend upon your state of being balanced and cautiously alert or too aggressive by driving too close to the car in front of you, and whether you have the presence to respond quickly and immediately break hard to stop your catapult into the person in front of you. This is a reason why the traffic laws will hold you responsible for hitting the car in front of you despite the fact that someone hit you from behind and propelled you forward. When you hit another, it is then their responsibility whether they hit the person in front of them, but this does not change the fact that you may start or perpetuate the ripple effect of the energy flowing through the circumstance. If you had been balanced in your state, you could have stopped the flow of that destructive energy. You either perpetuate energy or you diffuse, convert and redirect it. You always have a choice. You are never a bystander.

Distinguishing the Ego from the Higher Self

When we look at personality character traits and qualities, as distinguished from the ego's storylines and beliefs, it can be more accurate to think of the imbalanced expressions of those qualities as turning a volume dial up or down, instead of rejecting or submitting to a story as with the ego's belief systems. In the egoic storylines, we saw the aggressive expression as rejecting a perceived story by aggressively presenting a different story, although usually by attacking. With an individual character quality, the aggressive expression is like turning the volume dial up to an extreme, producing distortion on the sound. With a submissive expression of an egoic storyline, we saw the imbalance produce a retreat into internal submission of the story, absorbing it as an internal identity. With individual traits, the submissive expression is like suppressing or turning the volume dial way down, so that you can't perceive the existence of the sound. The volume in this analogy being the quality or trait. As you look at the character quality of confidence, the aggressive expression is arrogance as an extremely high and distorted turning up of the dial on confidence. The submissive or suppressive expression is insecurity, as a turning down on the dial of confidence to a muted state. The balanced place of confidence, to which we aspire is a place of equilibrium where we have confidence with strong self-assuredness balanced with humility. This place of equanimity is neither aggressive in arrogance nor submissive or suppressive in insecurity.

Each quality of the higher self that we admire, whether it be courage, kindness, compassion, love, patience, diligence, and so on, will have out of balanced expressions on both the aggressive and suppressive sides. Many of the qualities of our higher self are presented in the chart below in both their balanced and imbalanced expressions. Of course, there are varying degrees of the quality dial being either up or down, so the chart below reflects the poles of the character. The pink column in the middle is the ideal balanced quality that comes with the consciousness of our higher self. The columns on either side represent the unbalanced expressions when the ego distorts these qualities.

How the Ego corrupts the Higher Self's Qualities on the Aggressive side	Qualities of the Higher Self	How the Ego corrupts the Higher Self's Qualities on the Suppressive side
Martyrdom	Kindness	Self-centered; Indifference
Oppression	Strength	Weakness
Foolishness	Courage	Fear and Cowardice
Enabling	Love	Passive Resentment
Know-it-all	Wisdom	Ignorance
Phony Giddiness	Joy	Depression and Sadness
False Propheticism	Discernment	Delusion
Passivity and Numbness	Peace	Angst and Stress
Rationalization and Justification	Compassion	Indifference leading to resentment in severe imbalance
Feigning self-deprecation	Humility	Pretentious and Insolent
Workaholic	Purposefulness	Aimless and Unmotivated
Ungrounded with an irrational tendency	Creativity	Uninspired and Unimaginative
Blind Faith	Optimism	Pessimism
Passive	Patience	Impatient

How the Ego corrupts the Higher Self's Qualities on the Aggressive side	Qualities of the Higher Self	How the Ego corrupts the Higher Self's Qualities on the Suppressive side
Self-Sacrifice	Responsibility and Reliability	Irresponsible, Reckless, Unreliable and/or Absent
Obsessive-Compulsive	Diligence	Careless
Harshness	Discipline	Lazy and Unfocused
Rigidity and Blind Adherence to Tradition	Endurance/ Fortitude	Gives up in desperation, Frustration, or Anger, and Fickle
Stands for Nothing/ Malleable	Adaptability	Rigid
Obsequious and Ingratiating	Gratitude	Dismissive

Some of these imbalanced expressions may surprise you. Like a passive aggressive behavior, the behavior can fool us into thinking it is one thing when it is actually a nature of the opposite expression. This is like how the jumping, barking behavior of little dogs is often viewed as cute because of their small, unassuming appearance, but instead their behavior is actually aggressive. The ego will challenge us as we try to embody the above qualities in balanced expressions. Our higher selves may be in the lead, moving us to act in a compassionate or kind manner, but the ego will jump in and try to gain control, and try to talk us out of that balanced behavior arising from the higher self. For instance, the ego will tell us instead that our kindness is just setting us up for victimhood or is naïve. The ego will generate thoughts in our head trying to counter our motivations and inspirations of our higher self over which the ego is not in control. If we are not aware of the tools and tricks of the ego, and how it functions, we can be easily swayed, ultimately getting hijacked by our ego into allowing it to run the show.

Values and Perspectives

Because, as discussed, the ego lives in fear and lack, its objectives are to conquer, control, dominate, and obtain, especially when the ego tends toward its aggressive expression. When the ego tends toward its submissive expression, its objectives will be to avoid, distract, and suppress. Therefore, the ego has superficial values, such as power, beauty, attention, intelligence, status, things, control, and dominance. Even when acting on the submissive side, the ego still seeks superficial values, such as power, control, and dominance; however, it merely uses different tools and expressions to get its objectives. Remember, the ego's storyline is the same in both imbalanced expressions, but how it reacts to that storyline through rejecting or submitting to it and the tools it uses vary. Deep down, the ego is the ego and *its storyline is the storyline.*

Most people understand the superficiality of valuing power, beauty, status, material things, control, dominance, and attention. Therefore, I want to take a moment to address intelligence here. Because our intellect is simply a tool, it is analogous to our appearance. The intellect is not part of the core identity of our higher self. When we say, "I am smart," it is as superficial as saying, "I am attractive." Comparing our intelligence levels to one another is like saying, "my hammer is bigger than your hammer." Neither intelligence nor physical attractiveness is part of our true self identities, and so intelligence is a superficial value of an artificial identity of our physical being. The intellect is a powerful tool, however, that can be used either constructively by the higher self or destructively by the ego. The chart below shows the differences between the ego and the higher self's objectives and values.

The Ego's Values and Goals	The Higher Self s Values and Goals
Safety, separation from others	Happiness and joy with wholeness
Security with resources	Peace with life
Wealth and status	Love and generosity
Comfort	Creativity
Recognition	Fulfillment
Power and position	Growth
Pleasure	Fun
Performance, or the end game	Compassion, or how you live
Immediate gratification	Patience and trust
External strength and status from having and doing (external)	Inner strength derived internally from the higher-self state of being (internal)
Has desires, believes happiness comes from acquiring and possessing (external)	Is satisfied, believes happiness comes from just being and experiencing life from our higher-self state (internal)
Outward appearances (external)	Higher-self inner qualities of love, compassion, and so on (internal)
Pride in winning	Joy of unity in teamwork, creating, and growth
Path of what people think they *should* do or think (external)	Path of disciplined self-mastery for peace and happiness (internal)
Path of default ego and societal values, which is the path of least resistance	Path of strength to follow the higher self through steadiness and discernment, which is the path of mastery and conscious choice

The Ego's Values and Goals	The Higher Self's Values and Goals
Values money and power (obtaining and owning)	Values peace and love (service to others, generosity, growth and creativity)
Values profits and economic value most, so less concerned with the means to profitable ends, allowing humans and the environment to be compromised	Values the lives of humans, animals, and earth most, so balances these interests with economics, protecting against abuses
Values achievements and status, so it creates a world of competition and rewards for "winning"	Values what all people bring and wholeness, so creates a world that prioritizes the larger picture of equality, service, and collaboration through diversity in perspectives and roles
Values thoughts and mental preoccupation with entertainment, so uses technological advancements to serve the ego's attachments and addictions, even at the expense of exploiting others	Values learning and growth, so uses technological advances in service to others, helping others to grow, educate, create
Values opinions and separation through labels and judgments, so uses technology and communication to spread negative opinions and prejudices	Values growth and collaboration, so uses technology and communication to create educational information, and strengthen collaboration, cooperation, and unity
Values its own children and the *us* group, so tries to create separation in the educational systems with special treatments for their *us* group	Recognizes the value in all children as part of the whole, so focuses on creating equal access for all in the educational system
Values its own and the *us* group, so puts its nation above all others and creates systems and groups that prioritize benefits for its own and the other *us* nations	Values all, so creates systems that do not exclude, but instead allow equitable participation and access to resources and decision-making with the goal of creating wholeness in the world as one representation of all of humanity

Objectives and Behaviors

Because the values of our egos are different from our higher selves, the objectives and resulting behaviors will be different as well when we are operating out of our egos versus our higher selves. The ego's objectives and resulting behaviors will flow from its service–to–self values and its belief systems that revolve around fear and lack. Regardless of how much power, control, dominance, and things the ego believes it has achieved or acquired, it can never be satiated. The ego's objectives and desires are like an endless black hole that can never be filled and is constantly in competition for more. Because the ego searches for satisfaction and affirmation from external things, the ego will continue to require validation of itself through more external acquisitions and achievements. It is an endless cycle of struggle and striving with the ego.

In contrast, the objectives and resulting behaviors that flow from our higher selves will be correspondingly different, focused instead on *service–to–others* with trust and compassion, drawing upon its internal strengths. The chart below is a reflection of these differences in how circumstances are viewed through the ego versus the consciousness of the higher self. As you read through this list, at times, you will likely recognize yourself in both columns. That is a normal response, and to be expected because we ebb and flow between the consciousness of the ego and our higher self. The challenge is to be the master of this ebb and flow, so we are not just aware of it (the first step), but can become the master of our own consciousness, by making conscious, knowing choices about how we want to be. Only then can we make the shift once we realize we're in the egoic state that is taking us out of our equilibrium.

Perspectives/Tools of Ego	Perspectives/Tools of the Higher Self
Values being in control more than being loving or having love	Values love and compassion more than anything
Seeks to be right	Seeks the truth
Controls, both rejecting and refusing to allow life as it is	Surrenders to life with love and compassion, prioritizing truth and divine will
Fearful	Courageous
Mistrusts life	Trusts life
Relates from the emotion	Relates to the emotion
Reactive	Reflective, and consciously responsive
Participates in the emotions, stories and thoughts, identifying with them as part of its identity	Observes the emotions, stories and thoughts, understanding and relating to (and not from) them with full awareness, without identifying with them
False Self—ego-consciousness	True self—higher self or divine/Christ consciousness
Service to self	Service to others
Lives in the past and future	Lives in the present
Lives in the thoughts/mind	Lives in the heart
Sees problems	Sees possibilities
Has desires	Is content and grateful
Sees, feels, and believes in failures	Sees lessons and valuable growth
Feels and believes it is alone and is lonely, feeling life is cold and harsh	Knows it is part of a whole, never feels alone or lonely, and is in love with others and life
Sees and feels it is lacking	Sees and feels it is complete
Gives up	Perseveres
Clings and attaches	Lets go and allows

Perspectives/Tools of Ego	Perspectives/Tools of the Higher Self
Tells negative stories	Tells the truth
Is frustrated and impatient	Believes in perfect timing
Sees the negative and all possible negative outcomes with an expectation of negative outcomes that fit its negative narrative	Maintains a positive outlook and feels prepared for any circumstance
Has fixed beliefs based on past experiences and stories	Stays open and adjusts beliefs based on what is discovered in the present
Sees only the stories that are illusory, created by conditioning	Sees truth about reality
Sees life as a struggle	Sees life as an adventure
Loves life when/if _____	Loves life just as it is
Views challenges as frustrating obstacles, believing life is at war with it, trying to defeat it	Welcomes challenges for growth opportunities and takes none of them as personal attacks
Is unwilling to make mistakes and is shamed by them, and must always be right or perfect because it sees mistakes as impacting its identity	Willing to make mistakes and learn from them without taking it personally
Hides and/or condemns things and people that it is uncomfortable with or that are different, separating these into polarizations of good/bad and right/wrong	Willing to investigate, heal, and release limiting beliefs of negativity and untruths about itself, others, and the world, and does not see us/them separations
Allows emotions to become destructive through repeated negative thought-streams and allows emotions to drive choices and behavior	Masters emotions through mastery of thoughts, and either allows thoughts to flow out or uses them as fuel for constructive behaviors and perspectives
Wants to follow the thought-stream that drives the superficial and illusory stories and desires	Willing to follow the heart and surrenders the thought-stream

Experiences

Just as our values, objectives, and behaviors are different when we are operating from our egos versus our higher selves, we experience life differently as well when we are in the egoic consciousness versus being in the consciousness of the higher self. You will likely see yourself in both columns of the following chart below at different times as well. One of the key characteristics of experiencing life in the egoic consciousness is seeing life as a constant struggle, always looking to the future for the moment that life will be better and worth loving. The ego is never happy for long, and therefore little is good enough for it because it always wants something more, or something different altogether. This dissatisfaction that comes from the ego is not just about life, it is also dissatisfied with ourselves and others. While in our egoic consciousness, we are in a constant state of conflict within our own heads, as well externally with others and life itself, both seeing and feeling lack everywhere, while being fearful about our standing in life and with others.

Ego's experience	Higher Self's experience
Suffers in its attachments to its desires for what it doesn't have	Satisfied with what it has (which is not complacency)
Struggles in between achieving its egoic goals	At peace with life whether in challenges or ease of life
Rush of elation and relief upon attaining an egoic goal, which then fades, an emotional roller coaster with high highs and low lows	Even-keeled and consistent joy without roller-coaster emotions because it has no attachments to thoughts or desires
Numb, distracted, without compassion to others in their pain and suffering	Compassionate and present, seeing the truth of others' suffering and struggle

Ego's experience	Higher Self's experience
Takes things personally and defines self through *successes* and *failures*	Knows things in life are not personal, doesn't define self by attaining successes, and views challenges as growth opportunities
Pride in winning, achieving, and acquiring, taking these as part of its identity	Can enjoy egoic successes, but without the attachment or high highs and low lows of the ego's roller coaster because these are not taken personally as implicating our identity
Happiness is dependent upon achieving the egoic goals and upon circumstances	Egoic successes not necessary for happiness because life is filled with contentment, joy, wonder, gratitude, awe, and delight
Actions and objectives are informed by the thought stream	Actions and objectives are inspired by the being of the higher self
Takes job for security	Takes job aligned with the heart
Eats for pleasure and indulgence	Eats for sustenance
Attached to the *should's* and is compulsively driven by or struggles with them	Has no attachment to should's and meets life's flow with balance of service-to-all with boundaries
Associates with people who feed its ego and is part of its perceived *us group*	Associates with those who support its higher self without judgment or need for them to be different
Fights to pursue its service-to-self goals	Allows life to unfold with an intention of service–to–others, following the higher self's inspirations for its goals as life unfolds
Doesn't trust, so is attached to having a plan for everything (which causes suffering when life doesn't work out as planned)	Trusts life and itself so has no attachment to particular outcomes and needs no intricate plan
Attached to having a need to know where it is going	Knows it doesn't know what life has in store, but trusts itself to be able to respond to life, so is not attached to needing to know

Ego's experience	Higher Self's experience
Has fun by engaging in pleasures that feel like indulgences	Takes pleasure with everything, so experiences joy every day
Has service-to-self reasons for doing things	Has service-to-others reasons for engaging in inspired acts with no expectations
Creates and is addicted to stress and copes through imbalanced submissive and aggressive expressions (escapism and indulgences)	Doesn't create stress and is balanced with peace and joy
Attached to and preoccupied by the mind's thoughts and opinions	Has mastery over the mind and its thoughts, remaining free to see truths and inspirations of the higher self
Attached to its beliefs, wanting to be right more than wanting the truth, so keeps a closed mind	Wants the truth more than wanting to be right, so keeps an open mind
Uses intellect to try to control life	Uses intellect to inquire for truth and to release attachments, freeing itself from egoic mind
Doesn't trust life, feels a need to control it, so puts it at war with life, and it is always on guard, readying for battle to try and bend life to its will	Trusts life and feels at one with it, never believing life needs to be or can be controlled or be different than it is
Always has something it wants	Is grateful for what it has, and never feels anything is missing
Safety is most important because believes it isn't safe from life	Knows life is safe and trustworthy, so does not feel fear or have exaggerated need for safety
Reacts based on knee-jerk conditioning	Responds consciously by choice to life in the moment
Focused on the future (and distracted by the past especially negatively)	Focused on the present
Lives in lack and dissatisfaction	Lives in gratitude

Ego's experience	Higher Self's experience
Always pushing and striving, often exhausted	Balanced between action and being, with wisdom to know when to allow circumstances to just be and rest
Never seems to have enough time to do what gives it internal joy	Understands the balance of worldly and personal responsibilities with personal boundaries, so makes time for its personal joy

The *no plan* implied by the higher self does not mean being listless, complacent, or without a direction. Instead, it is a state where we rely more on inspiration, rather than an attachment to a confined plan. Our inspiration occurs with what gives us joy with what life is presenting in the moment, and how we are inspired to move in directions that are aligned with life's flow in the moment in ways that are consistent with that inspiration. Instead of relying on a cemented plan of action, we employ a flexible plan designed to carry out that inspired goal yet remain open to new inspirations that modify the steps for achieving this inspired path as the flow of life and circumstances change. The result is that we are going with the flow of life, while being able to respond to its unexpected challenges. Being in the higher self is like having a sturdy kayak with a sturdy oar that helps us steer effectively and masterfully through the rapids, avoiding boulders and dips in the flow of the rapids as they change unexpectedly. As we increase our mastery of our ego so that we are more often in our higher-self consciousness, we thereby further increase our ability to flow both effectively and efficiently in that sturdy kayak on that river of life.

We can think of our evolution in self-mastery of the ego and living from the consciousness of our higher self like being on different radio frequencies. If we assign the egoic consciousness to the lowest number on the FM radio frequencies of 88 and the higher-self consciousness to the highest frequency of 108, we will be working to attain that frequency of 108 on the dial. We may start at 98, which is halfway there, where we spend half our lives in our egos and the other half in our higher selves. Frankly, that is better than many people who spend their entire lives living far more in their egos at around a figurative 90 on the frequency scale. We will always ebb and flow on the frequency dial, just as you can often tune into a radio station based at 98 anywhere from 97.5 to 98.5. You ebb and flow from a particular point. As you evolve and grow in your awareness and skills at mastering the ego, you move up the frequency scale to a figurative 101. Then you ebb and flow from that new point, as you continue on the path of mastery and living more from your higher self. There are still egoic challenges, but you grow out of many of those that burdened you while you were ebbing and flowing from point 98 on the dial, and you can no longer hear or see those tunes any longer.

The path from our egoic to our higher-self consciousness is not so linear, but this radio frequency is a good example to help you understand what is happening and your own role in it. A great example of the non-linear nature of this process in reality is when we get triggered by deep-rooted conditioning, such as when we are around family after having been away as adults. Who doesn't revert to similar patterns of thoughts, emotions, and behaviors when we're around family? We may revert to having moments at that 98 or lower on that frequency dial during family visits. You might think, "What was that all about? I thought I was past all that drama! I can't believe I fell right back here again!" That sudden reversion to childhood knee-jerk reactions comes from suppressed, unhealed conditions from storylines created in childhood. These reactions are typically visceral ones that just come out of us without any warning or build up. They are automatic, immediate reactions caused by our shadow. These reactions are stored in the long-shut closet doors on old pains, patterns, and irritations that we've shoved away where the shadow lives, breathes, and controls us, despite our best intentions.

Chapter 4

The Shadow[6]

You may have heard of the *shadow*. It may sound scary or dark. You may be reticent about exploring the shadow, afraid that it is something negative or will require you to face all the negative, painful, and *bad* things about yourself. The truth, however, is that the shadow is not nearly as scary as it sounds, or as its reputation suggests. In fact, looking at your shadow is actually liberating. The only way to take away the fear of something is to shine a light on it. By learning about it and exploring the shadow, we shine that light on it, thereby deflating its power and impact. The mountain versus the molehill adage is again

[6] The origination of the concept of the "shadow" is typically attributed to the work of the psychologist, Carl Jung. Many psychologists, New Age and other theorists and authors have taken Jung's original concepts and expanded upon them with and through hundreds of other works. In this book, I do not cite to any specific theory or work of Jung, as I have not read or relied upon any of Jung's specific works from the early to mid- twentieth century. Instead, I have drawn from the basic, general and pervasive knowledge of the *shadow* as commonly used in the present day discourses, having drawn from no work or author in particular.

relevant here. It is the unknown that is always most feared by the ego, so let's shine the light on the shadow and illuminate its sequestered, hidden, unknown status that summons up fear and liberate ourselves from the shadow and its fear.

What is the shadow? The shadow is the unconscious sabotaging agent of the ego (as if the ego needed a cohort for sabotaging thoughts, emotions, and behaviors). The shadow, however, takes sabotage to a new height in our relationships with ourselves and others. The shadow is essentially the thoughts, emotions, and egoic storylines that we suppress because they are too uncomfortable and painful to think about, feel, or acknowledge. Instead of allowing ourselves to think and emote the uncomfortable thoughts and emotions that arise from painful experiences and stories that our egos tell us, we push them down, locking them away in a closet in our mind, trying to avoid dealing with them. However, as we might hope, these uncomfortable thoughts and emotions don't go away. The old cliché, *out of sight, out of mind,* does NOT apply to the ego and its shadow. The closet in which we stow them leads to the shadow that lives in our subconscious[7] mind. These uncomfortable thoughts and emotions take on a life of their own in the shadow in the seclusion of the subconscious mind away from our conscious awareness. They become overblown and powerful in the shadows of our mind. These suppressed

---

[7] There are several psychological theories that distinguish between the unconscious and subconscious mind. This discussion is not intended to engage those theories or other deeper psychological theories about the make-up of the subconscious and unconscious mind. For the purposes of this discourse on the ego and shadow for the mainstream audience, it is enough to identify the shadow as not contained within the conscious mind. Whether we call it the unconscious or subconscious mind is not material to shining a light both on the subconscious mind and its impact in order to heal it and minimize its sabotaging effect.

thoughts, emotions, and storylines of our ego are still active and alive energies growing deeper roots in our subconscious. They come out in knee-jerk reactions to life experiences when we least expect it, and without warning or ability to control. These triggering situations remind us of, as well as resonate with, the energies of our stories.

Because these shadow energies come from our unconscious mind, we have little to no conscious control over them. Instead, they come storming through from our subconscious into our current thoughts, emotions, and behaviors in an instant without us knowing they are coming, and without us having made a conscious choice about whether or how they come to the surface. The shadow reactions can be recognized by the visceral, abhorring, disdainful, condemning, and rejecting thoughts and emotions that accompany our knee-jerk reactions. These viscerally abhorrent and disdaining thoughts and emotions can be directed either internally, externally, or both.

A visceral response is an extreme, uncontrolled or un-tempered set of thoughts, emotions, bodily sensations (usually tension, tightening, shallow breathing or shaking) and knee-jerk reactions that arise immediately in response to something. That response is not just an observation, but rather a deep, overwhelming reaction. For instance, there is a difference between observing that someone makes a hypocritical statement where you might say something like, "Gee, Mary, that seems to be a little hypocritical for you to say, don't you think?" and the visceral response of "ARE YOU KIDDING ME??!! YOU ARE SUCH A HYPOCRITE!! WHO DO YOU THINK YOU ARE TO SAY THAT??!!" The first response is an intellectual observation made with calm assessment and communication, whereas the second response is an extreme, emotionally-charged aggressive shadow reaction based on being triggered in the moment.

What we express outwardly toward others is just an external expression of what we have going on internally. *As within, so without.* We have certain triggers and experiences that produce overly dramatic and exaggerated reactions through our words and deeds. We've all experienced scenarios where we have come away from a situation after having said or done something and thought, "I can't believe I did that...," "I can't believe I said that . . . ," "That's not how I feel," "That's not what I think," or "Why did I do that?" When you have this kind of experience, your shadow has come out and provoked a knee-jerk reaction that seemed to come out of nowhere. This reaction, in fact, came out of the shadow of your egoic mind.

The shadow is made up of these painful stories that our ego told us about who we are or are not, and because we didn't want to think about or acknowledge them, we bury them. These stories are often our own illusory perceptions about ourselves having negative qualities, such as "I'm worthless," "I'm hypocritical," "I'm judgmental," or "I'm mean . . . or unlovable . . . or unwanted . . . or stupid," and so on. These thoughts, like our conscious words, thoughts and emotions still carry energetic frequencies that can attract and resonate with those thought and emotion frequencies of the conscious and physical world, just as we previously learned with Dr. Emoto's study on the energy of words affecting water. Therefore, when the same energy exists in our conscious thoughts, or that we *think* we are perceiving from others, those shadow energies are pulled out like a magnet in extreme reactions.

The degree of vehemence in our reactions is an indication of the degrees of pain and power of our shadow storylines. I'll discuss projection in a later chapter; however, for now, it is enough to realize that when you have these visceral, intense reactions, these thoughts and emotions that are busting out are really your shadow expressing and projecting onto another what you most fear about yourself and that you've hidden away, refusing to acknowledge or handle. The good news is that just like our egoic storylines, the shadow stories are just as false. These stories simply contain some overreaching egoic spins about uncomfortable circumstances that have become both hidden and powerful.

An extreme example of shadow creation is in the case of experiencing abuse as a child, whether physical, emotional, or mental. While significant psychological or psychiatric counseling may be required to heal from these experiences, there is a set of false storylines that get created and absorbed into our psyches from these situations. Those who are subjected to this type of treatment will usually believe a storyline that they are "bad," "stupid," "unwanted," "undeserving," or other derogatory stories that are the result of the abuse. In other words, this is what someone who has been abused may think they deserve, or that they were responsible for the response from the abuser (and this may be what the abuser tells the victim). The result is that the victim's ego will simultaneously both believe and fear this story: "Why else would someone treat me this way," they may ask themselves, as victim's ego will think in its motor mind thought-stream. The ego will then allow this story to become part of both its psyche and identity. The victim's ego will further suppress this painful story about not being deserving or worthy into the shadow as part of its pain. That victim will then later express that shadow story in either an aggressive or submissive pattern if the shadow is not healed.

These shadow secrets that we keep from our conscious minds continue to keep us sick with these false storylines and uncontrolled, sabotaging shadow reactions that jump out of our mouths, minds, and behaviors without our ability to see or choose them. As discussed earlier in the conversation about the ego's conditioning, the ego's stories and identities become addictions. This is also applicable to the shadow side of the ego. We often feel comfortable in our misery because that is what we know, and what our egos think keeps us safe and secure—like the Stockholm Syndrome where victims become attached to their captor oppressor. As with any addiction recovery program, one of the mainstays of addiction recovery is to acknowledge that *your secrets keep you sick.* This is equally true with the ego, with its shadow's secrets and our addiction to the ego's conditioning with its stories and persona archetypes. This addiction makes us feel as if we understand ourselves, others, life, and our place with respect to each other. These addictions do not reflect truths, however, so we've just become addicted to illusions. We fear that we cannot be successful or know our direction without maintaining an understanding of who we and who others are, which is the subject of the ego's stories, whether conscious or stored in the shadow. Without these stories and personas, our ego thinks we are facing the unknown about who we are, who others are, how life is and our place in life. The ego fears not knowing. This is why the ego would rather be *right* than see the truth, be happy, or have love.

When we make an effort to see what we've hidden away in our shadow, we disempower it, and then empower our higher selves to regain the control through conscious choice. Exploring our shadow to see what is there allows us to shine the light on the lies that we've told ourselves and that remain hidden in the shadows. Doing this work takes time, effort, and courage, but is liberating because it is how we heal our pains. As we contemplate going into our shadow, it can seem overwhelming and uncomfortable, as if it is an enormous, dark, scary mountain to climb. Like anything that seems overwhelming at the start, once we begin the process, that mountain soon starts looking and feeling more like a mole hill than the imposing, scary mountain that we initially thought. In the Companion exercises to this book, I will lead you gently through your own shadow so you can heal these false stories, releasing them from being a painful part of your perceived identity.

How the Shadow Shows Up

Just as with the ego more generally, the shadow can show up either in an aggressive manner or a submissive manner. Both the aggressive and submissive expressions of the shadow produce visceral overreactions to circumstances. Just as with the ego generally, the shadow's aggressive expressions are overreactions expressed outwardly towards others, while the submissive expressions are overreactions expressed internally towards ourselves. The ego's overreactions are based upon stories it believed about historical circumstances and experiences that have become a very painful part of its conditioned beliefs and behaviors. The painful thoughts in that story revolve around interpreting ourselves as lacking in worth or ability in some way, having a negative characteristic that become deep-seated, spurring painful beliefs that we would rather not acknowledge. These suffering thoughts and emotions are what trigger the shadow's destructive, sabotaging behavior.

Our ego works hard to suppress these stories and either pretends the opposite (aggressive expression) or succumbs to the stories as part of our identity, acting as if they are true (submissive expression). Both expressions stem from the same painful beliefs. In each case, the ego tries to suppress the negative storyline, whether overtly and aggressively rejecting it or absorbing it as a silent identity. You can view any shadow reaction, whether aggressive or submissive, as oppressive. The aggressive expressions are oppressive to others, and the submissive expressions are oppressive to ourselves. As with the Stockholm Syndrome analogy, the ego is the captor, while the shadow is the enforcer, or oppressor, within that ego captivity.

As mentioned earlier, our objective is to do more than just face our shadow—our goals are understand and heal it. When we heal the shadow, we don't have to experience the suffering of the initial derogatory thoughts and emotions created by our ego. When healing the shadow, we become aware of the lies and misinterpretations of the ego, and we can then change our perspectives from the demeaning, painful stories to love, compassion, and liberation through experiencing the truths of our higher selves. An important note here: none of the discussions that follow are intended to be medical diagnoses or replace diagnosis, counseling and/or treatment by licensed medical professionals.

Aggressive Expressions of the Shadow

The aggressive expressions of the shadow are automatically triggered knee-jerk reactions that vent outwardly towards others.

Extreme Defensiveness. Extreme defensive behavior happens when the ego feels as if it is being attacked. The shadow will jump out in an aggressive defense by returning the attack outwardly on another. This reaction will often surprise others by its aggressiveness because the situation is often misread by the overly sensitive ego. The ego's buried storylines that have been shoved into the shadow become triggered at the slightest of slights the ego perceives. This egoicly-perceived slight energetically resonates with the thoughts and emotions of the uncomfortable storylines that the ego buried within the subconscious shadow. Even a simple question can be perceived by the ego as a slight or a judgment and a questioning of its worthiness. In that moment of perceived slight or judgment, the shadow bursts through the closet door and drives the behavior before the conscious mind sees it coming. In the aggressive expression of extreme defensiveness, the shadow expresses itself in an extreme, aggressive attack in defense, rejecting what the ego and its shadow perceive to be the slight and judgment being lodged against it. To the ego and its shadow, when expressed aggressively, the best defense is an aggressive offense, so it goes on the attack. You have likely experienced this kind of scenario as either the receiver or expresser of this shadow reaction.

How to recognize this. When you find yourself jump immediately to an attack after a question or challenge from another, believing that you were threatened, attacked or demeaned, then you might want to take a closer look at what actually transpired without an attachment to being right. If you lashed out without taking time to hear, consider, or evaluate another's position, comment, or question, you are likely dealing with a shadow reaction. With this shadow reaction, you often experience initial thoughts of being put down, criticized, or victimized, followed quickly by a visceral backlash reaction of quickly rising and heightened emotions of fear of judgment. This fear of judgment then quickly morphs to anger combined with resentment as well as a desire for vengeance or "justice" (in the mind of the ego). Shortly after this initial knee-jerk reaction, your ego will create thoughts about justification and self-righteousness in your attacking others in your defense, standing up for yourself.

You may notice some other thoughts questioning the extreme nature of your response, such as "Where did that come from?" This is your higher self. Unless you want to see the truth more than you want to be *right* your ego will quickly try to drown out those inspired thoughts with more of the self-righteous kind. Feeling justified always feels better than facing areas where we may not have been our best self. Therefore, it is the easy, and initially more comfortable, path to allow the ego and its shadow to drive our thoughts, emotions, and behaviors because these always end with justification. Unfortunately, however, if we allow our ego and shadow to drive, we don't fully appreciate how the ego actually created the suffering and struggle we experience both before and after the righteous anger, justifying thoughts, and sabotage to our relationships. Instead, if we are able to see the truth of a circumstance, we are likely to see that we weren't being judged. In the event that we were being judged, our higher self will recognize that another's judgment is only a reflection of their own internal state, and not us.

Extreme Attachment and the Need to Be Right. I refer to this as wanting to be *right more than you want the truth*. This mindset is the classic egoic consciousness behind the adage of *listening with the intent to respond* (wanting to be *right*) instead of *listening with the intent to understand* (wanting the *truth*). When someone disagrees with you, presenting a different perspective, your ego often finds that offensive, as if it were a personal attack. This is because the ego is self-centric, so sees everything as self-centric. To the ego, everything is personal, about *it*. When your ego believes it has been personally attacked, your shadow becomes triggered, attaching to that internally generated energy of perceiving a personal attack, and then jumps out without your conscious mind having time to think, evaluate, or consider the other person's statement, interrupting that person, beating them down with all of the reasons why they are *wrong* and you are *right*. You have no interest in their thoughts, emotions, or feelings, or in respecting them because the entire interaction is about proving your *rightness*. You lose all connection to that person, feeling no compassion or respect for them. Your ego's identity is wrapped up into proving you are *right*. Your ego's perspective is that if you are not *right,* you must therefore, be *wrong,* and therefore you *lack worthiness*. This scenario can also coincide with the aggressively imbalanced shadow expression of extreme defensiveness.

In your ego's conditioned, and often buried, storylines, not being *right* communicates a lack of worth, and therefore triggers your shadow to come out to defend and protect you by oppressing others into your *rightness* and worthiness. Such a reaction is the ego using the shadow both to reject and push back against its own storyline of lacking worthiness. The fact that we see this so often from so many people in our world today tells us the degree of collective shadow we have in terms of how much we allow the ego to drive our thoughts, emotions, and behaviors. This is just one example of how well the ego does in beating us down these days—both internally and externally to others. We have become a society with a collective belief system in lack, a lack in ourselves, and, therefore, a lack in others, and even in life itself. This condition can allow us to see the need for compassion, rather than judgment, attacks, and confrontation. Such behaviors only mask our internal fears and beliefs of our own unworthiness.

How to recognize this reaction If you constantly interrupt people before they complete their sentences in order to contradict them, or to try to prove them wrong and yourself right, you are attached to a need to be right. This egoic need is what makes us listen only with the intent to respond to show others that they are wrong and we are right. You don't listen with the intent of understanding because if you agreed with them or saw their perspective as having validity, then your ego would have to believe it is *wrong*. This belief of being wrong would be a painful validation of your own lack of worth in terms of your knowledge, perspectives, abilities, or any other aspect of the identity of *you* that your ego has adopted. As a result, when in your egoic consciousness, you would rather be *right* than know the truth because being *right* feels better to the ego. You, therefore, get angry, feeling a need to convince others of your *rightness*. You must have the last word, and can't let others just agree to disagree. To the ego, when there is lack of agreement, there must be something *wrong* with them, with you, or with the world order if they don't agree with you. To the ego, it is a zero-sum game, with winner taking all.

When in your egoic consciousness with this need to be right, you may often find yourself calling others names, or denigrating their views, either in your head or actually out loud, such as "idiot," "stupid," or worse. These words, thoughts, and emotions just jump out without you having time to control or monitor them. You find that you cannot accept any part of another's perspective as having any validity whatsoever; it's all or nothing. They are all *wrong* and you are *right,* and unless they acknowledge that, they are just idiots. Of course, there are both levels and moderations of this behavior where your higher self may try to jump in and help. You may listen to some inspirations from your higher self to acknowledge some of the other's points, to just release and allow for a diversity of opinion. If you struggle with an appreciation for diversity of thought, wanting and needing to be right, enjoy seeing other's perspectives contradicted, then you are in a tug-of-war between your ego and your higher self.

If you look back at situations with the intent to see truth, heal and recognize this kind of behavior in yourself, then you will also want to recognize that this response is your shadow expressing itself aggressively. This reaction is just your ego's need to be right because of an unconscious belief, and fear of a lack in your own self-worth in some way if you are not *right*. However, don't shift to shaming or blaming yourself for this behavior because that just moves you from the aggressive to the submissive sides of imbalance. Remember that you are worthy, not lacking for anything. This is just your ego acting out of fear and a desire to protect unnecessarily. In such an aggressive expression, the ego believes it needs to protect itself by presenting to the world that you do in fact have worth, which is the opposite storyline of what it actually believes. For the ego, this projection is so important that it will engage in such aggressive behavior to prove to itself and others that it is worthy (or superior), even if it means you have to be dominating and beat people into submitting to your view.

Venting. You find that you just can't contain your irritation, anger, frustration, resentment, and self-righteousness towards another, and you explode in a burst of anger, irritation, and/or attack another. This could include a tirade of remarks or physical violence, such as slamming and throwing things, or a burst of frustration that produces a screaming explosion or sobbing cry.

Each of these reactive behaviors involve sudden bursts of emotions such as anger, irritation, and frustration by using egoic tools of blaming, shaming, and/or judging people or circumstances outside of yourself. These reactions also coincide with poor coping skills in handling uncomfortable or undesirable situations that highlight the shadow's sudden appearance. These poor coping skills provide more power to the shadow because the shadow will remain unchecked, without boundaries, respect, or tolerance for others, or for things outside of your ego's conditioning, control, and expectations. These reactions can also accompany, or even be an escalation of, other aggressive expressions of the shadow, such as an extreme defensiveness that goes on the attack in an extended tirade.

How to recognize this reaction If you find that you often resort to violent outbursts involving throwing, slamming, or physical outbursts, you are usually engaged in shadow behavior. This can also include screaming, shouting, or intensely raising your voice where you aren't looking for a return engagement but are rather just venting. Instead of seeking engaged communication, you are verbally and energetically attacking another. Losing one's temper is a shadow reaction, especially when it is a sudden outburst. This could also include the passive aggressive expressions of doing physical harm to yourself such as cutting, hitting your hand against a wall, throwing yourself into harm's way, or even engaging in some eating disorders, if, and especially when, they are used as a manipulative tool to try to inflict guilt or shame on another. Eating disorders will usually be a submissive expression using aggressive tools and oppressive techniques against ourselves of denying us food and sustenance with the submissive belief that we are unworthy.

When people view others who often lose their temper as "She's just emotional," or "He's just passionate," or "She's a hot head," these thoughts and statements are doing a grave disservice to that person, for several reasons. First, these statements carry energies that reinforce the false narrative that these reactions equate to identities of the individual. When we tie these reactions to traits of the individual's identity, this purports to validate and rationalize those behaviors while attacking the person because of these perceived inherent traits. This simultaneous identity creation and condemnation plays right into the hands of the ego's storylines and shadow forces because it continues to self-validate and thus become self-fulfilling experiences.

Second, these rationalizations do nothing but impede that person's ability to transcend and transform these behaviors and heal the thoughts and stories that created these emotions and aggressive behaviors. Healing these thoughts, stories, emotions and behaviors occurs through reframing the circumstances that gave rise to the false beliefs and storylines[8], while changing our perspectives on those circumstances to those of the higher self, not the juvenile, narrow-minded, and fearful ego. Once some of this reframing and truth-bearing can take place, it can be easier to learn better coping skills for the ego's tricks and tendencies.

[8] There is a psychological concept referred to as *cognitive reframing* that appears similar to the reframing concepts discussed in this book. More information on this psychological theory can be found in general here: https://en.wikipedia.org/wiki/Cognitive_reframing. These psychological concepts were not researched or relied upon for the writing of this book. As best I can tell upon a cursory review, there is a distinction between this formal psychological theory and that espoused in this book in the way that the past circumstances are reviewed and how reframing of past circumstances are approached.

Blaming. Blaming is a form of venting that doesn't always rise to the level of physical venting. Blaming is an aggressive expression of the shadow using projection tools (which are discussed in greater detail in the chapter on projection).

Submissive Expressions of the Shadow

The submissive expression tends to create a deeper, more powerful shadow because it often involves further and deeper suppression of the uncomfortable egoic storyline. While both imbalanced expressions create the shadow through suppressing uncomfortable thoughts and emotions, the submissive expression often forces it further into the recesses of the psyche in order to avoid the pain it is acknowledging and submitting to as truth. When the shadow expresses itself through a submissive expression, it reinforces that shadow storyline in a conscious expression. This reinforcement of the shadow, through the submissive expression's further suppression of those acknowledged, absorbed, and uncomfortable false beliefs, results in further suppression to dull the increased pain. The shadow, as one of the ego's enforcers, is particularly oppressive in the submissive expression, using ourselves as the targets. Such submissive expressions of the shadow include the following behaviors:

Shutdown. Shutting down occurs when the present circumstances mimic a long-standing egoic story that energetically resonates with and brings back a flood of painful thoughts and emotions with which the psyche cannot, or refuses to, deal. The reason that these circumstances are so painful is because you both believe and submit to the ego's story about some unfavorable trait or unworthiness about yourself. The shadow will thus dictate a complete shutdown of the thoughts and emotions that spring forward from believing this negative story in a knee-jerk reaction, and you then suddenly turn off like a light switch. Because poor coping skills often coincide with the shadow expressions, the person expressing the shadow in this fashion will completely shut down, not being able to communicate in any way about the present circumstances, or even to the individual(s) involved in that situation.

Instead, the person shutting down will refuse to engage in any way with anyone with respect to the circumstance. This shutdown will often extend across topics with others involved in that painful circumstance, and can result in a complete shutdown until the ego can recover and compartmentalize that circumstance, suppress it, and move past it, as if it didn't happen. Until some level of healing, distance, and some truth-based understanding has occurred, the person may not be able to communicate about those circumstances, even at a later date. This shutdown mode is likely to continue into the future with respect to those circumstances because the pain of believing the shadow's story is too great to think about, and that person has insufficient coping skills to work through the pain and discomfort, or to see the circumstances in any other light other than their own egoic storyline.

How to recognize this reaction. When you shut out all forms of communication from and with others, which can include conversation about anything, even beyond the circumstance triggering you into an extreme discomfort, you are engaging in the submissive shutdown form of the shadow. This expression will likely involve more suppression and deeper shadow creation. This is different from, and potentially more dangerous to your psyche than only seeking a distraction for disengagement or withdrawal discussed below. With this shutdown behavior, your psyche cannot handle acknowledging on any level the thoughts and emotions that are arising within your mental and emotional bodies.

In such a reaction, unlike withdrawal, your mind must completely shut down to all thoughts and acknowledgement about the circumstances, and your emotional body becomes like a cement wall, usually with no emotion, whether positive or negative. You force yourself into an empty shell in that moment by suppressing all thoughts and emotions about that circumstance in an attempt to become numb. To continue functioning, you suppress all related thoughts and emotions, completely ignoring the situation, as if it never happened. This may also require that you not engage on any real level with the individuals involved in that circumstance for some time. If you are forced to relate to those individuals because they are coworkers or family members, then you will become robotic in your interactions, completely closed off to them, while numbing yourself.

This shutdown state is potentially very dangerous from both emotional and mental health standpoints because you don't allow those thoughts and emotions to flow through and move on out of your mental and emotional bodies. Instead, you keep them buried deep inside where they fester, infecting your inner thoughts and emotional health with deep-rooted resentments, anger, and sadness, while further creating deep wells of shadow and darkness. The long-term effect of this can be one of two extremes: first, those deep dark wells can become deeper and thus take longer to climb out of each time they happen; or, second, you become increasingly numb, verging on, or even possibly taking on sociopathic tendencies.

Seek a Distraction and Disengage. This submissive expression occurs when you see, feel, and hear the thoughts and emotions that arise in reaction to an uncomfortable circumstance that you believe is real, but you want to immediately deflect, so you can avoid facing it. You don't shut down as described above, but instead you want to pretend the circumstance doesn't exist by focusing on something else. This expression can happen both in the shadow's immediate reaction to a circumstance and as a cumulative effect after a period of time that has involved extended exposure to, and belief in, the ego's negative stories or other stresses. This can also be a result of simply needing a break from stressful experiences, thoughts, or emotions that weren't processed with effective coping skills. Whether it is a shadow knee-jerk reactive expression or a cumulative poor coping skill reaction, you behave like an ostrich sticking its head in the sand to avoid the discomfort. This shadow reaction of disengagement could present itself in the form of moving immediately to a distraction, such as food, binge-watching shows, drugs, smoking, drinking, and so on. These go-to crutches soon become addictions used as coping mechanisms for difficult circumstances that our egoic storylines and shadow reactions create. Because we believe those storylines, we must disengage and distract to avoid the discomfort. In addition to physical addictions, these go-to coping mechanisms can also become psychological ones.

How to recognize this reaction. This expression of disengage and distraction of the shadow can be recognized as the distractions that often appear as the go-to crutches, or coping mechanisms, that we turn to when we feel uncomfortable and want to lift ourselves up. Where this expression can be a little more subtle is when we simply shift our focus from the uncomfortable situation to another task, conversation, topic or project. This can also include simple procrastination or disengaging from certain people by focusing on other relationships. These redirecting behaviors often will be rationalized and justified with egoic storylines that allow us to feel justified for putting off or disengaging from the thing that reminds us of uncomfortable thoughts and emotions.

Overvaluing Being Positive. A very common submissive expression of the shadow today, particularly in certain spiritual, New Age, and other similar communities, is an overvaluing of the positive, while demonizing anything that is not rosy and optimistic. This expression is often referred to as *spiritual bypassing* and is the ego's judgment using its polarized good/bad, right/wrong labels. As a result, this expression is often passive aggressive, with the belief being submissive, and the behavior being aggressive. When the shadow shows up here, there is an immediate aversion to any uncomfortable thoughts or emotions around sadness or anger or any other negative emotions. These beliefs are typically born from ourselves having been judged, and so we now harbor a fear of being judged again, along with the emotions of anger and/or sadness that accompany this belief that lurks in the shadow and that shows up in the present experiences. As a result of sensing any of these perceived negative thoughts or emotions flowing through, the shadow will immediately react with thoughts of that being *wrong*. The ego will then continue to push down those thoughts and emotions as being *bad*, forcing a series of feigned positive thoughts that ignore the natural response to uncomfortable circumstances, without allowing an acknowledgement, presence, and pass-through of balanced, natural anger or sadness thoughts and emotional energies.

This knee-jerk judgment often accompanies contrived positive emotional outward expressions, which continue to create a deeper, wider shadow by suppressing as *bad* the momentary, natural discomfort with certain life circumstances, creating a negative shadow story that vilifies a natural, healthy experience when it is processed with the higher self's balance. This refusal to allow those naturally responsive sad or angry thoughts and emotions to be present and move on through with reconciliation and exploration of lessons to be learned, and/or harnessing for positive and constructive expression, results in walling them off, suppressing them, and shoving them into our shadow psyche. However, with a balanced mindset, we do not allow those thoughts to linger. Instead, we allow them to move on through without replaying them over and over in our minds or creating overreaching stories about them, or venting them in dysfunctional ways.

Overvaluing the positive can turn into a purely aggressive expression as well when it is used as a judgment of others who exhibit signs of anger or sadness. When we believe that the emotions of anger or sadness are *bad,* and we see another exhibit those emotions, often we will express that shadow aggressively as well by judging, shaming, or blaming that person for having those emotions. This will often coincide with a judgment of how immature or unevolved that person with anger or sadness is, and how *advanced* and superior we are for not having anger or sadness emotions. However, there are no *bad* emotions, just emotional energies used in dysfunctional and imbalanced ways.

How to recognize this reaction. If you find that you experience great concern about having any thoughts or emotions that you judge as less than positive and glowing, you will want to look more closely at being overly positive. There can be a fine line between being concerned if you experience unbalanced anger and sadness and being concerned that you experience *any* sadness or anger on *any* level. The concern that represents an unbalanced suppressive expression will be more extreme than simply having an observation that you may be thinking some thoughts that don't serve you. The shadow reaction includes fear, shame, and a lack of worthiness in your maturity, spirituality, or other quality because you have these thoughts or emotions. Just as with all shadow reactions, the extreme over-valuing of the positive is a both a visceral, extreme revulsion and rejection of thoughts and emotions that are that are judged by the ego to be *bad*. The ego, then, immediately suppresses those thought and emotions, forcing instead a reaction of contrived positivity, without allowing yourself to feel or to deal with any of the thoughts or emotions judged to be *bad*. You instead immediately suppress those less–than–rosy thoughts and emotions without exploration or reconciliation, chastising yourself for having them, while fabricating positive thoughts, often with overly people-pleasing, submissive behaviors.

Just as how someone with this shadow reaction judges him- or herself, they will judge others with the same vehemence, and this is when this shadow expression turns aggressive. When it comes to seeing these less–than–positive thoughts and emotions in others, you will experience an immediate visceral reaction of both judging and rejecting others' thoughts, emotions, or behavior that you believe are coming from a place of sadness or anger and that you deem to be *bad*. You jump to judgmental conclusions about where that person is or is not in their spiritual and emotional maturity, and you think thoughts about their immaturity compared with your superiority over them in terms of how much more advanced you are. This results in treating others with the same condescension and disdain that you judge as deserving of unacceptable *bad* thoughts and emotions. Having a shadow that reacts this way includes having your and others' identities tied to whether you and others do or do not have such thoughts and emotions that are deemed as anything less than positive.

As I will discuss later in the chapter on anger, when we express the shadow through its submissive mechanisms by suppressing anger, it often accompanies a weakness in our boundaries, and we will find that we allow others to cross our boundaries too easily and too often. This will engender more anger that we then suppress as well, adding to the heap of suppressed anger we already have until it becomes explosive and aggressive, or results in a complete shutdown in a further sabotaging submissive expression.

Withdrawal. This submissive reaction from the shadow is different from the shutdown reaction discussed above in both a matter of degree and intention. With shutdown, there is a more extreme suppression that results in a lack of acknowledgement and an inability, or refusal to, continue an interaction in any fashion. Withdrawal can be both a shadow reaction when it is severe with an immediate and extreme visceral reaction, as well as a standard ego tool that comes with less extreme reactions that tend to be the ego's coping mechanism. The shadow use of withdrawal comes with a hidden, suppressed extreme fear or re-vulsion that won't allow you to be direct or otherwise engaged.

How to recognize this reaction. When withdrawal shows up, whether as an egoic tool or a shadow reaction, it will often include behavior and statements that refuse to acknowledge the uncomfortable thoughts and emotions with statements such as, "I'm fine; it's fine," just so you can move past the un-comfortable thoughts and emotions, and not have to deal with them or the people involved in that moment. This includes not apologizing when you know you've hurt another. Because of your withdrawal, you refuse to acknowledge their hurt in the situation. So you do not apologize for your own behavior because you cannot apologize for something you refuse to acknowledge. In this reaction mode, you lose connection not only with the circumstances, but with the people involved in the uncomfortable situation. Therefore, you lose connection with your own thoughts and emotions that are uncomfortable that you shove deeper into your own shadow closet, as well as disconnect from others, and how they are thinking and feeling.

You may think this submissive withdrawal reaction is really helping to solve or resolve conflict; however, the reality is that you do harm to both yourself and your relationships with others because you will appear to others to be as both numb and lacking in concern or compassion for them, and their thoughts and emotions. The truth is that you are exhibiting those uncompassionate behaviors to others because you are numb and lacking compassion for yourself with your own thoughts and emotions. You cannot give what you do not own or acknowledge within you. This withdrawal behavior can also be part of a passive-aggressive behavior discussed below.

The passive-aggressive use of withdrawal. This is an expression that uses a submissive tool to create an aggressive impact on, or towards, another. This is the opposite interplay of passive-aggressive reactions, such as self-cutting and some eating disorders that have an aggressive tool for a submissive, consciously-absorbed shadow belief. Withdrawal, too, can just be part of an expression of aggression in a passive-aggressive behavior. When your visceral reaction is more of an aggressive anger, resentment, or disrespect, and instead of expressing that as an outward venting, you may use withdrawal simply to ignore a person or a scenario with an aggressive intention of doing harm, or imparting a subtle (or sometimes not so subtle) disrespect through your withdrawal.

How to recognize this reaction. If you have a severe aversion to conflict, or if you have certain behaviors you interpret to be so inappropriate or *wrong* that you cannot or refuse to acknowledge or deal with them, then you likely have this type of shadow in your psyche that comes out, often unexpectedly. When your withdrawal is a normal part of your egoic reactions, which you see and have observed in yourself, this may not be a shadow response, but rather simply a go-to tool of your ego. When the reaction is intense, visceral, extreme, and sudden, that is a shadow response usually driven by judgment and intense emotions, such as fear or anger accompanied by underlying stories about fear, lack, and unworthiness.

Other Signs of the Shadow.

In addition to the types of extreme, visceral, and over–the–top reactions described in the previous section, there are more subtle signs that may also help you identify when your shadow is being triggered, driving your behavior. If you find yourself saying or thinking "I always pick the same guy/girl," or "I'm always running late," or "I always seem to be swamped," or "I always wait until the last minute to . . . ," you are identifying some shadow behaviors. Not until you look at what your ego has shoved away in the shadow's closet that are based on its fears, judgments, and half-truths will those sabotaging coping mechanisms and the psychological pains be truly healed.

Your shadow is also likely making an appearance if you think, or if others say to you, "You always say that," or "You always react that way," in responding to similar situations with anger, stress, fear, or other destructive thoughts, emotions, or behavior. A common example that most of us experience is when we are around family. We often find that we revert to old patterns of behavior, thinking, and emotional destructiveness around family. This makes sense when you remember that your ego's stories underlying your shadow started when you were younger, likely from family interactions. Being away from family does not necessarily change your ego's stories about who they are, or who you are in relation to them. As people go through life, many do evolve past old patterns when away from the family dynamics that created and triggered them. However, when we are around our family members, we often and easily revert back to old patterns and triggering.

You also may not allow others to show up any differently than what your ego labeled them as years ago. As a result, you often see them through that same colored lens you created as a child, and thus you expect to see similar behaviors from them. Naturally, then, you will judge everything they do through that colored lens. Your ego wants to be right more than it wants the truth, so it will interpret others' behavior to reflect validation of its stories at every opportunity. This may cause even more sabotaging damage to relationships, as others may feel unjustifiably accused or judged. The triggering, and the resulting projections and ego triggering, can be an endless cycle when people have pre-set expectations and don't allow others to show up as who they really are. Unless, or until, someone in the cycle recognizes the ego's tricks and tools, and stops giving power and credence to them, personal relationships continue to come under the sabotaging influence of our egos.

Let's look at another example that uses one of my own shadow stories as a base. In this example, imagine you were the firstborn to a very young, ambitious couple of very modest means a mere ten months after they were married. Life in this young family was initially challenging with limited salaries, small apartments, and many ambitions by both parents to make their mark and improve their position in life. Their pregnancy with you was not welcomed at that time, although they did eventually want children. What you did not know until later in your childhood, was that each of your parents grew up with very dysfunctional family dynamics that failed to give them good role models for relating constructively to others, particularly as between parents and children and as between men and women.

As you grew up, your parents were not affectionate, rarely speaking the word, love, to, or around, you. They were constantly preoccupied with money, working jobs, and dealing with the stresses of trying to increase their socioeconomic status. When they did pay attention to you outside of birthdays and holidays, it was not to play with or spend time with you, but rather to take you to some sort of lesson or sporting practice, to take you on a lamented (for them), but deemed necessary, shopping trip to get needed clothing when they were rushed and irritable, or just to tell you what you were doing *wrong* and where you needed to improve in some way. From time to time, you heard some encouraging words. You knew your parents loved and supported you, theoretically, and that they wanted to have children; however, you were never really sure where you fit into their hearts, or whether you were just viewed as more of an obligation than anything else.

As a young girl, one of your parents mentioned that, had they not gotten pregnant with you, their lives would have been much different. That same parent also mentioned that your other parent had really wanted a boy. The message absorbed by you as a child was that you were not really wanted by your parents, they lamented you being the girl that you were born as, that your parents were *stuck* with you, and they just accepted their bad luck having you. You always felt that when your brother was born several years later, he had been joyously anticipated and welcomed, and there was a completely different feeling and treatment of him than what you had received. Despite the improved economic status and the planned (versus your unplanned) pregnancy and other life circumstances, something just felt as if this different treatment by your parents was also a little personal. This was, at least in part, your child-like ego taking circumstances and your parents' perspectives personally. So, you, therefore, saw circumstances with that lens.

As a result, there are several examples that stick out in your mind about how both parents treated your brother differently than you on a regular basis, whether it was attending events involving him that they did not for you, or planning events for, as well as spending more time with, him than they did with or for you. You may have recognized that time and circumstances changed within the family over time, which contributed to the many differences you observed, but there were things you believed were not time or circumstance related. As a result of these various circumstances and how you experienced them, you grew up believing that, while you knew your parents technically loved you as their child, you believed that you really weren't wanted, at least not at that time, or as who you were. Instead, you believed and *felt* you were always the less preferred child.

What did that thinking do to your storyline about who you believed yourself to be, who your family members are, or how life is? You grew up feeling you weren't truly wanted, that you were just tolerated because you were a responsibility, and you were less preferred by those who were supposed to love, nurture, and support you. This created the uncomfortable storyline of being unwanted, always seeing others as being preferred over you, feeling less desirable because you were female, thus creating a sense of lacking self-worth, and feeling slighted in favor of others. These uncomfortable storylines get shoved to varying degrees into the shadow, and the more conscious storyline of being the unwanted and second choice because of who you are, both as a gender and as a person, become an active part of your conditioning. As a result, the lens that you put into your eye is about being *second best*, whether it comes to family, friends, sports, romantic relationships, and so on. Therefore, you end up reading into every interaction you have with people that the reason you weren't invited to the party, or that you didn't get a call back, or someone doesn't seem to take initiative in spending time with you, is because they prefer others over you.

Whatever the circumstances are, you believe undesirable things occur because you aren't as good or as desirable as others. You may still have a good dose of confidence and rational thinking that this isn't the case, thinking that if people don't see your value, that is their loss, and so on. Your higher self will play tug-o-war with your ego and will also drive your beliefs, feelings, and behaviors at times as well. However, the deep shadow storyline you fear still exists in the darker corners of your mind. In your reactions and responses to triggering circumstances, there is often a mix of reliance on your higher self's truth in that confidence with a good dose of the aggressive form of the shadow coming out with a reaction of, "You're the one with the problem." The submissive form of the shadow reaction may also appear where you feel unwanted and dejected, and thus simply withdraw.

The truth is that often we create our own experiences and self-fulfilling prophecies. Because we feel we're likely to be a second choice or unwanted, we will ourselves initially withdraw, and not engage in a circumstance or a relationship, which can cause others to believe we are the ones not interested, viewing us as disinterested or aloof. We don't always see that there are many other valid reasons for others' behavior that do not involve them viewing us as less desirable or unwanted. Instead, when we are in our egoic consciousness, we see only the ego's storyline.

Now, let's apply the example above of that person conditioned to feel second best to a hypothetical family situation at holiday time twenty years later. Imagine you have spent years having good relationships, learning from those experiences, believing that you have grown and moved past all the dysfunctional family dynamics and old uncomfortable thoughts, emotions, and feelings of the past. One afternoon, when the family is together in the same room, a parent asks your sibling by name "Hey, Johnny, what do you want for dinner tonight? I have this chicken dish, or we can grill some tuna?" You are also in the room, but your parent didn't ask you or involve you in the conversation at all, as if you were not present. How do you respond? Here are the possible likely responses:

- *Shadow aggressive response*: In a triggered, incensed outrage at being treated as both insignificant and unvalued for the umpteenth time, you say, "Gee, thanks for asking me, too. That's okay; don't worry about me. I know I don't matter anyway to you, but I'm just as important, and don't deserve to be ignored," and you storm out of the room. Because you expect to see your parents exhibiting a preference for your sibling, that is your interpretation of the circumstances, so that is how you experience the situation. You don't see any other possibility.

- *Shadow submissive response*: You get up, and just leave the room since those two are having the conversation, and it isn't worth even trying to interject since it is clear they don't care about you or your preferences, anyway. You just withdraw, accepting the parental preference for your sibling will always be there, and divert your attention to a book, or just getting away from being reminded of your constant second-choice treatment, believing you will always be viewed as less than worthy in this family. Thereafter, your interactions are muted through your withdrawal, and you don't really engage, keeping up a wall between you and your family, looking forward to the time that you leave.

- *Healed response*: You are genuinely interested in what your sibling says, and you have no problem in adding your perspective as if you believe you belong in the conversation since you are also going to be eating the dinner. You don't take anything personally, and you don't see yourself as being left out, or otherwise not as important. You see the possibility that you will get your first choice on another night, so you view the circumstance with gratitude that your parent is taking preference suggestions for dinners.

- *Possible truth of the situation*: You find out that your sibling is leaving early the next day, so that is why your parent asked him for his preferred meal, so as to give him his choice since you will be able to have your choice the following night.

- *Possible truth of the situation:* It could be that your parents, in fact, do prefer your sibling. However, their dysfunction doesn't have to affect your healing and knowledge that their thoughts, emotions, and behaviors speak to their own egoic consciousness states and mindsets, and not who you are. You therefore don't let their dysfunction and lack of lovingness or of seeing who you truly are, or your value, to be a reflection of your identity and your worth. You understand how they think and behave is a reflection of their consciousness states, not of yours, so you don't take it personally, and you don't create an identity for yourself based on their behavior.

Distinguishing the Shadow from its Creator—the Ego.

The difference between a garden variety egoic reaction and a shadow reaction is the degree of animosity and the immediacy of the shadow's knee-jerk reaction, which has a more extreme visceral response that seems to suddenly come from nowhere. The egoic stories and tools are more visible and out in the open to us—we just don't always see their dysfunction. We may even see the ego's destructive, negative objectives, values, and tools as our drivers, but we don't label them as coming from the ego, and we often justify them through our ego's rationalization tools. Examples include the valuing of money, power, status, things, appearances, "winning," as well as being *better* than another at something. The ego will strive for these things, while fearing not getting them, or thinking that we are *less than* if we do not.

Whereas, with the shadow, its stories, objectives, and triggers are nearly, if not completely, hidden from us. Our shadow is made up of the ego's discarded and buried negative thoughts that the ego created about ourselves. These negative and extremely painful thoughts and stories about ourselves often pop into our heads for an instant before we jump into the unexpected shadow reactions, and the ego then pushes them down again using its tools of rationalization and justification. We rarely get more than a split-second glimpse of our shadow thoughts and stories before they are pushed down again by the ego, away from our conscious sight of them. Examples of this include the deeper unacknowledged reasons why we detest particular qualities in others when we think we see them, such as hypocrisy, judgmentalism, and prejudice.

When our distaste for these qualities in others is an extreme visceral reaction of shame, judgment, near hatred, and ill-will towards another, those reactions are hiding our shadow story about ourselves. We think we don't like these traits (and the people who we think exhibit them), but the reality is there is something in our suppressed egoic story about ourselves that threatens our ego's desire to have a more positive view of ourselves. We have hidden from ourselves our ego's made-up stories about its own perceived flaws. The irony of the ego is that it will drive us to use those very same behaviors in protecting itself, so we will display them ourselves from time-to-time in covering up our ego's own beliefs in our unworthiness. These egoic efforts turn into aggressive expressions in projecting them onto others and projecting the opposite storyline about us when challenged. It is a vicious cycle of dysfunction that hides our true self at each turn. Projection, which is discussed in greater detail in the next chapter, is integral in this cycle.

The line can be thin between (i) a healthy allowing of the initial thoughts about discomfort, annoyance, anger, sadness to flow through us, along with the resulting emotions engendered from those thoughts and (ii) allowing those uncomfortable thoughts and emotions to linger, so the uncomfortable circumstances sabotage and disempower us. Just as the line can be thin between (i) a healthy working-through those thoughts with their corresponding emotions in order to find the optimism in the lessons and hope that arises from that reconciliation and (ii) an unhealthy repressed anger or sadness combined with a contrived optimism.

Self-fulfilling Prophecies.

When we establish these ego-invested stories, we create self-fulfilling prophesies because those ego-created beliefs become the lenses through which we view our experiences. Our ego sees circumstances in ways that validate its stories. As a result, they become how we experience our circumstances because our egos expect to be *right* about their stories, labels, and beliefs about who we are, who others are, and how life is. As a result, we see what we expect to see because the ego can only see through its own illusory, self-created lenses. Our experiences then become nothing more than projections of our own egoic mind with its labels, storylines, and beliefs that we expect to see played out as truths. In short, our conditioning produces our experiences. *As within, so without.* This is a truth of the egoic human experience. It is only when we release the labels and egoic storylines that we can allow life to unfold without expectations or labels, and only then can we see the truth about life, about others, and about ourselves.

It is only when we are in the moment without judgment or expectation that we experience what is real and truthful because only then can we allow life, others and ourselves to be just what, and who, they are in that moment. Because the ego's need to be right will produce perspectives on our experiences that support its expectations and beliefs, seeing and experiencing life from our egoic consciousness will always make us susceptible to living from a veil of illusions. Remember, our egos want to be right more than they want the truth, or even love. Therefore, we must let our higher self, and not our ego, drive our consciousness in order to see truth and experience reality. Otherwise, we see only what the ego wants and expects to see. The ego creates a colored lens that we put in our eyes. If you've put a yellow lens in your eyes, you will never see the sky as blue—it will always appear green. You can never see the truth of a circumstance when looking through the ego's lenses. The ego doesn't know that it sees a tinted experience that does not represent truth because it cannot see itself or the edges of its lenses. It is only our higher self—the observer—who can see the ego, its tools, and lenses, and therefore make choices that are not just a default, self-fulfilling operation of the ego.

If we've suffered abuse, and we have bought into the ego's (or others') stories that we are unworthy, stupid, clumsy, or whatever stories the ego spun from those circumstances, we will continue to expect ourselves to be unworthy, so will not allow ourselves to believe that we are worthy of compliments, awards, advances, promotions, love, and so on. As a result, if we have adopted a submissive expression, we will not expect to be treated with respect or value in any of our relationships, whether personal or professional. We won't allow ourselves to show up as valuable, smart, worthy, or lovable because we have bought into our ego's false storylines by continuing to give them attention, allowing them to define us with that identity. If we have adopted an aggressive expression, we will take on the identity of entitlement using the aggressive tools, whereby we believe we are always the most worthy recipient of all such attention, awards, acknowledgment, and so on, and will be incensed when we are not the awarded recipient. That aggressive expression of entitlement will sabotage our behaviors and relationships, making it less likely others will view us as deserving of such awards.

Not allowing ourselves, others, or even life to show up as who, and what, each truly is sabotages our relationships with ourselves internally, with others externally, and our trust and love of life in general. Consider this real-life circumstance that comes from one of the women who was in the first offering of the curriculum I created in 2018 that is the basis for this book. Halfway through the program, she shared with the class one of her experiences at her job that week. There was a man who she had previously labeled with several derogatory characterizations and personas that included such labels as "jerk," "bully," "arrogant," "rude," and other identity labels. As a result of her buying into her ego's storylines about who this person was, she had been putting up a barrier to him, trying to avoid having any interaction or communication with him. After going through the first half of the program, she recognized that she was not allowing him to show up any differently than those labels her ego had given him.

Therefore, one day she decided to suspend her belief in those identities and allow him to just be who we was going to be in that moment with no expectations. She experienced a completely different interaction with him as a result of suspending her labels for him in that moment. Instead, she experienced an extended, productive, and pleasant conversation with him like she never recalled having before that moment. She was amazed that he had shown up completely differently than how she had labeled him and what she expected from him. She then recognized that she allowed him to show up differently in that moment—as who he truly was. She allowed him to surprise her and her ego because she suspended her ego's need to be right. Instead, she operated out the compassion of her higher self with a desire for the truth more than her ego's desire to be right about him. She allowed her higher self to be in control. As a result, she was just present in both allowance and acceptance with what was, and she had an enjoyable experience and a productive collaborative interaction that changed her business relationship and her perspectives of him and herself.

Imagine how our world would change if we all did that . . .

Our Gifts in the Shadow.

We know now that when our ego tells us a story that paints parts of us as dark, bad, wrong, and so on, it creates a painful storyline for us that also engenders painful, uncomfortable emotions. Because we don't want the darkness that our ego tells us we have, we try to hide it, stamp it out, suppress it, punish ourselves for it, and shove it in the shadow's deeply recessed closet of our unconscious psyche. Our ego does this so not only do others not see it, but we don't have to acknowledge it, either. However, along with what we think are our deepest darkness and pains, we can also shove away everything associated with a talent or skill that our ego tells us we don't have, along with an egoic storyline about an uncomfortable experience. When we shove away what we believe is our unworthiness, we also shove away part of our gifts, creativity, and authentic self, along with what we falsely think is our darkness. When we do this, we are shoving into the shadow's closet part of our power. Like any oppressor, or dictator, the ego takes shreds of truth and distorts them to such a degree that it can be difficult to identify where the lies and exaggerations have been created, especially since the ego may have started with its perceived truth of an uncomfortable, painful experience.

Let's look at a couple of examples. One thing about which many people have a fear of and belief in, is that they are not good at public speaking or performing in front of others. Many of these storylines in our heads have come from having some uncomfortable experience speaking, or being in front of others. For example, you may have frozen up, stuttered, felt intense fear and discomfort, or have even been ridiculed or criticized by others in those circumstances. You may even have more than one experience in that regard. Whether you've had one, or multiple, uncomfortable experiences, your ego tells you that you are not good at that activity. You believe your ego, and so you have allowed your ego to create this storyline as part of your identity. As a result, you never will allow yourself to show up as someone who can speak or be in front of a crowd because your ego has created an identity for yourself that "I am not a good public speaker."

This deep-rooted belief in who you are, or are not, can now create self-fulfilling results based on what your ego expects to see and experience. Because you expect to feel fear, nervousness, or stuttering, and expect to be ridiculed and judged by others (because that is what your ego did to you, even more than what may have been done to you by others), your thoughts of fear swirl around your head, eliciting the corresponding emotions. The energies of these fearful, anxious thoughts and emotions create nervous, jittery physical responses in anticipation of the expectation of these fears coming true. The physical responses to these thought and emotional energies create the stuttering, pause, lack of continuity, and so on in your speech, further validating for your ego its belief that you are not good at that activity. Your ego's false beliefs about you become self-fulfilling prophecies. The famous story of Prince Albert and his transition to King George VI, as reflected in the film, *The King's Speech,* reflects this causal connection. (How the physical body is both an indicator and reflector of your consciousness state is discussed in a later Chapter).

This is not to say that it won't take some amount of effort and courage to work through some of these initial uncomfortable scenarios, but to label yourself permanently as someone who doesn't have that skill is placing a false storyline on you as an identity, and perpetuating an incorrect, overreaching conclusion as being fact for all time. The truth is that you simply had a couple of uncomfortable experiences prior to having an opportunity to work through your fears about speaking in front of others. By allowing your ego to place the "I'm not a good public speaker" label on you, you have shoved in the closet all the skills and talents that could accompany being in front of a group of people. You could have been born and blessed with a unique message or way of presenting a topic, but because you have shoved public speaking in a closet, you have also shoved in the closet along with it this gift of communication and relating to or inspiring a group of people in a unique way.

Just as the shadow is identified by a visceral negative response, when we have a visceral positive reaction that, too, is the shadow. When we have the reaction of really admiring qualities in others, such as another's kindness, wisdom, courage, and so on, we, too, have those qualities, but our ego has spun a storyline that we do not have that quality. Our belief in the ego's stories prevents us from either showing up as having that quality, or simply not recognizing that quality in us. To reiterate, the shadow is not when we simply notice and admire with dispassionate observations. The shadow is present also when we have a deep, gut-wrenching wish or desire to embody qualities that we believe we don't have.

Let me give you another personal example from my own life about how this shadow gift works. To understand my shadow gifts, you must understand my ego's shadow fears and lies. To summarize an earlier reference to this shadow story presented earlier, from a very early age, I was told that my birth was not wanted at the time (given that I was born ten months after the marriage of my very young, economically struggling parents). Additionally, I was told that a boy was preferred over my birth as a girl. As a result, my ego created and suppressed into my shadow the story of my being unwanted and second best because I was a girl. My shadow story of being unworthy produced an aggressive shadow expression of entitlement, which I discussed earlier in the example of the highway driver conflict as compared to my friend's expression of gratitude. This egoic story had additional expressions in various scenarios that combined with other childhood circumstances, such as moving frequently, which prevented me from being able to experience and establish lasting personal relationships, which further added to my occasional submissive expressions of withdrawal. As with everyone, the ego and shadow elements compete with our higher selves for dominance in our consciousness, alternating back and forth.

These egoic storylines and shadow elements drove me to alternate between excessive drives to achieve and complacent, "I don't care," withdrawals. Professionally, achievement became integrally tied to the identity my ego adopted. During the height of my early years in a profession where I was often both the youngest and only woman on senior management teams, I was conscious about making sure I was "strong," "intelligent," "effective," and "rational" in my professional leadership roles. Back in those early days, there were many collective expectations and opinions about women in business being weaker or *less than* men in various respects, and most every woman in professional life at that time had to fight that expectation and projection onto them. Given my long-standing shadow story about not being wanted or worthy, in part because of my female gender, I had aggressively rejected that storyline and naturally adopted the persona of the workaholic, no-nonsense, rational, tough, and unemotional manager that focused only on the quality and effectiveness of work as well as being equally worthy as any man. I believed that was how I needed to identify and show myself to prove my worthiness and reject my own ego's buried shadow fear of unworthiness, along with the projected expectations about women that were placed on me. (Some of these expectations may have been my own ego-driven stories combined with the truth of the predominant male perception projected onto most women in the workplace at that time). These ego and shadow stories, combined with my higher self qualities of courage, confidence, and sense of equitable treatment, for which I was, and remain, an ardent warrior, could create noble intentions without always having fully balanced expressions.

As a result of my own ego and shadow storylines (in addition to my natural no-nonsense, direct personality), people either really liked me, or really did not like me, and there was little in between. The initial thoughts I often had for brief moments was that I wanted to be liked and valued, but those thoughts would quickly get pushed aside by my ego's manufactured identity and ideal that I wasn't there to be people's friends; I was there to see that things got done—and done well. I knew I had a reputation for being a little on the tough side, without a lot of personal relationship development or schmoozing with the people with whom I worked and supervised, and I was OKAY with that. My ego told me that was how I needed to be in order to be viewed as having been appropriately hired for a role where I was the youngest, and often the only, woman in leadership with a high-level of responsibility. I was frequently praised for my effectiveness and mover and shaker qualities in my performance and work output. This was my objective. My egoic ideal was to be and show this persona to the world, even if there were people who did not always like me.

My natural higher-self sense of wanting to do the best for an organization, with justice and strength in improving conditions, protecting the oppressed against bullies and unfairness, would often combine with my conditioned aloofness and the impersonal persona I adopted, particularly in the workplace and aggressive expressions of rejecting the shadow fear of lacking strength and worthiness storylines. Some of these aggressive egoic expressions that combined with my higher self included mirroring back through my own behaviors to bullies and oppressors their projected bullying energy in how I stood up to them. Sometimes it could be challenging to identify to what degree my behavior was being motivated by the ego or the higher self. One of the ego's tricks is to slide in and try to hijack your higher-self objectives by using its tools of control in the process. The ego can adjust its objectives in order to maintain control with an approach of *if you can't beat them, lead them.*

Given that backdrop, I was once in a conversation with a family member about our respective gifts, based on a personality evaluation we were exploring. When I took this evaluation, I was surprised by the results and showed it to this family member. She confirmed without hesitation that she thought my most prevalent gifts from the list in this evaluation were "grace" and "mercy," which matched my test results. I about fell out of my chair. Those gifts weren't even in the top five that I saw in myself. I asked this family member for some examples because I wasn't seeing those qualities in myself, and she provided several. I didn't see those examples, however, as indicative of "mercy" or "grace," not because they weren't such examples, but because I saw my behavior in those situations as "just what people do." I had an exaggerated view—an almost saintly view—of what behavior looked like in order to be "merciful" or "full of grace." I had this idolized, extremely elevated view of these qualities to which I didn't see myself ascending. Instead, I believed my ego and shadow story of "that's just not who I am; that's for other people who are far softer, kinder, and more compassionate." In other words, those were gifts for others who are far *better* than and more worthy then I viewed myself, in many respects.

Along with my deep-seated egoic fear of lack of worthiness in myself, I had shoved into my shadow these qualities of grace and mercy that I didn't allow myself to see in myself because my ego had convinced me that this just wasn't who I was, and was contrary to the identity my ego had decided I needed to adopt of being "tough," "strong," and "aggressive." These qualities of grace and mercy did not align with the identity and ideal my ego had created for me. I had put those qualities on such an exaggeratedly high pedestal, I placed them out of my reach, especially with the identity my ego had adopted. Instead, I saw only the aggressive expression of my egoic self of this tough-minded manager that I thought I had to be in order to earn respect and worth, especially given my age and gender. Some of this shadow effect was also a reflection of the collective shadow that was created for many professional women in male-dominated professions in the 1970s, 80s, and 90s. I was on the tail end of that market dynamic as well (I'm not saying that this doesn't still exist, but it was on an entirely different level back then).[9]

Allowing my shadow to drive my egoic identity at times didn't mean that I didn't also experience myself from the consciousness of my higher self much of the time as well with confidence and trust in my abilities and qualities. Like everyone, my consciousness oscillated back and forth between my higher-self knowledge of who I truly was and am as a capable, intelligent, objective, and compassionate professional with my shadow story of a fear of unworthiness. This is true of everyone. We are not operating only out of our egoic state all of the time. We always have glimpses of, and time spent in, our higher selves as well. This is another example of that ebb and flow on the radio dial I mentioned earlier. The key is to minimize the ego state, while maximizing the higher-self state.

---

[9] Much could be said on this topic of women in the workplace then and now, but must be saved for a different book.

Chapter 5

Projection

Projection may be the most prevalent and one of the most aggressive expressions of the shadow. Projection is when we project onto others what we ourselves harbor in our inner world, or more specifically, in our shadow. It is when we think we see in others what we are most afraid of or reject in ourselves.[10] The ego wants to hide what it thinks is its own shortcomings by rejecting and pushing them into the shadow closet. When expressed aggressively, the shadow rejects those storylines and project them onto others to represent others as the ones with that problem instead. Envisioning the childhood game of Hot Potato is an apt analogy for the shadow's projection. We see projection when people vehemently accuse others using extreme disdain and accusations of hypocrisy, judgment, entitlement, and other undesirable conduct. We've been discussing effects of projection

---

[10] For those literature buffs and Shakespeare fans like myself, Shakespeare described this shadow effect in his play, *Hamlet*, as "[t]he lady doth protest too much, methinks."

throughout many of the shadow's aggressive expressions in the previous sections.

How to recognize shadow projection.

The shadow expression of projection can be seen when we have a sudden, visceral response, as discussed with the shadow more generally; however, in this case, the projection is directed at someone else or their behavior, accompanied by unflattering accusations. We can easily identify when someone is being hypocritical as an objective observer without it being a shadow reaction, so understanding a shadow projection as distinct from an objective assessment is important. When it is not a shadow reaction, we do not feel it personally, we do not feel extreme anger or resentment, and we retain a rational and relatively calm demeanor in our observation. When we are operating out of our shadow, we accuse (instead of just observe) someone else of exhibiting an undesirable quality, and we feel an immediate visceral anger, disgust, indignation, or resentment with an over-the-top reaction that may include raised voices, hand gestures, and/or other outburst. With projection, this exaggerated reaction is emotional, judgmental, and condemning of another. This is an outward expression of aggressive energy in both thought and emotion, resulting in our own aggressive behavior towards another. When this is coming from our ego's shadow, we react as if another's action is a personal affront, despite the fact that another's conduct has little to do with us personally.

The reason that our ego takes this other person's perceived quality so personally is that our ego has rejected this quality in itself and has instead shoved what it believes was a storyline involving that quality and its tendency in us into the shadow.

The shadow then gets triggered when the ego perceives that quality in another, and ironically, it uses that behavior as a tool to aggressively reject its own storyline. In another self-protective mechanism, the shadow jumps out to accuse another of its own aggressive expressions. The ego projects what it wants people to see—that this undesirable quality is in others, not in us. What we accuse others of in this vehement, disdainful, angry, and extreme resentful state is the shadow tool that we often use, but fear of being in us. Like the film strip we have playing in our own heads, the shadow behavior comes out and gets projected onto the screen in front of us when it is triggered, and we think we're seeing something that is outside of us instead of the projection of our own film strip storyline. *As within, so without.* The irony is that these undesirable behaviors or traits we think we see in others are often just our ego's own imbalanced expressions that it uses to hide its painful stories in the shadow. The ego is full of these self-fulfilling creations of misery for which it then uses even more misery to try and solve what it believes is the misery problem, which is self-created. The imbalanced ego is an endless cycle of self-created, self-perpetuating struggle and suffering.

As noted, the ego sees everything through its tinted lens. We must remember when dealing with the shadow that the ego's stories are not truths. Therefore, we don't need to fear these projections. While we may not have always acted kindly from our higher self, the ego's stories about who we are, and are not, are not truths we have to fear. We must, however, pay attention to the stories we're allowing the ego to propagate in our minds, how our ego and shadow express, and the tools of behavior we use. When our shadow jumps out, or when we are using the ego's tools of judgment, blaming, and so on, that tells us that we are in our egoic consciousness in that moment.

We want to break away from these illusions of the ego and discover the truths, which can only come from being situated in the consciousness of our higher self.

Let's look at some more examples. Often, we tend to use the ego's aggressive judgment tools when we have a repressed egoic storyline about our being unworthy and judged. As a result of that egoic belief and fear, which is shoved into the shadow from the pain of that story as well as fear, we may respond to this repressed story aggressively by rejecting it, and instead projecting the opposite, which is superiority. In expressing our superiority, our egos judge others as inferior. When that shadow-suppressed story is triggered through a scenario where we are, or where we *believe* we are, or someone we consider to be in the *us* category is being judged, our shadows will often jump out, reacting with an extreme, aggressive outward judgmental behavior that could involve yelling or other aggressive shadow behavior. As a result, we vehemently react to and project onto others what we have in our shadow selves that we don't like and fear—judgmentalism. This judgmentalism in our own story comes from us first being judged, and then judging ourselves, which is then what we have to give to others—both judgment and a lack of compassion.

This internal judgmentalism often stems from being judged as a youth where we created a storyline that we are unworthy and deserve judgment. We can then express that storyline either aggressively by rejecting it, or submissively by submitting to it. The example above reflects the aggressive expression. If we express this shadow story submissively, we will submit to this unworthiness as deserving of judgment. Because both expressions are hiding the same story of inferiority, that of being worthy of judgment, we expect to see judgment from others at every turn. This story that, "I am unworthy," and "I should be judged as unworthy," is ironically a story that our egos have created, shoved into our shadow's closet, fears, and energetically reacts to viscerally as a shadow reaction. In both expressions, we will internally judge ourselves harshly; however, the aggressive expression will likely project onto another in some way in rejection of this storyline.

As a result of this shadow story on judgment, the ego will have created a conditioned lens in seeing judgment, and interpreting any inquiry, or even a look directed towards us as a judgment or accusation. While there is no denying that some people will project their own use of judgment through the form of a question, those of us with judgment in our shadow and ego tool kit (which is true of most people on some level) will see judgment being levied against us often in many innocent or genuinely inquisitive gestures from others who are just seeking to understand, and not judge. I'm sure you have been taken aback by an aggressive defensiveness or accusations you've received from another when you asked what you thought was a simple question. You may have also reacted aggressively towards another as well to a simple question. Afterwards you may have thought, "I didn't mean to get that angry, it just came over me." Your ego will quickly rationalize your behavior, however, as justified based on your ego's spin, which is just another projection and aggressive expression of judgment of others. The ego immediately starts spinning stories in self-righteousness justification and rationalization, often using the tools it accuses others of using.

Let's take an egoic aggressive tool of bullying as an example. We may be triggered at any hint of bullying we perceive in others. The thoughts that immediately jump into our mind likely center around the perception of the bully as oppressive, wanting to control others, putting others down to raise up himself and even possibly believing the bully is a sociopath, without empathy or concern for others. Our shadows' strong reactions to this perceived bullying quality does not mean that we are ourselves a sociopath, or an uncaring, oppressive bully. There are many different expressions of bullying, and the version that we may have a tendency to use in our own expression could be very different from the version that may trigger us. In many cases, this shadow behavior will be a pattern that replicates itself from perpetrator to victim, who then becomes a perpetrator that victimizes another who becomes another perpetrator, and so on down the line, based on learned behaviors, egoic tools responding to its shadow stories and other similar conditioning. Each may have their own unique expression of the behavior. Here is how this could play out with different expressions:

- You were bullied when you were young by a parent, other adult, or school peers who you perceived to be more powerful than you. "Bullying," could include being pushed around physically, mentally, or emotionally, being treated dismissively and oppressively in a condescending or demeaning manner as being lesser or weaker than others, being forced to do things while being ridiculed or demeaned, having things taken or threatened to be taken from you that you valued or viewed as important to your survival, or similar behaviors.

- This bullying treatment was painful and made you feel small, insignificant, without value, and fearful of what this bully could do to you, affecting how you felt about yourself after being bullied.

- As a result of the treatment you received, you viewed yourself as powerless, weak, and easily controlled or oppressed by others.

- You believed that the bully was mean, without compassion, abusive, uncaring, aggressive, rude, and untrustworthy with qualities that you do not value, do not want to have in yourself, do not want to have in others around you, *should* be feared, and should not be a quality in anyone in a position of power, control, or influence.

- As you age and gain more perspective on your past, as well as how much you feared and resented such treatment, you find that you have turned your fear into anger, resentment, aggressive defensiveness, and aggressive rebuffing of any perceived attempt to control or dominate you. You react quickly and aggressively to scenes where you perceive either yourself or others being dominated, controlled, or coerced. You engage in dramatic condemning and rejecting of what you view as bullying attempts. These reactions are not just standing up for yourself and others, they are over-the-top, extreme reactions where you want to exact vengeance or extreme punishment on whom you view as the bully.

- When others who you accuse of being bullies or trying to control and dominate try to explain their intentions or perspectives, you immediately cut them off, don't let them finish their sentences, and are so irritated, incensed, and intolerant of any such behavior, you will not allow them to have a word, or to use a minute of your time, to try to justify their behavior. You often express extreme anger, judgment and resentment, while vilifying them.

- You are aggressively vocal in calling them out as bullies, getting in their face, yelling that you will not accept, and not allow others to endure, that treatment, and won't hear any excuses.

Do you see how such reactiveness to bullying here, whether actual or perceived, is bullying in its own nature as a response? It could be that someone who is perceived as bullying is not, in fact, being as overtly bullying as perceived. Because of an aggressive expression to reject the painful shadow story of being weak, easily controlled, and unworthy, an overly sensitive ego and shadow may see pressure or controlling and bullying behavior in many circumstances through the ego's conditioned lens. This does not mean that the person perceived as being a bully is not, in fact, being controlling or oppressive, but it may not be to the level or with the intentions that most associate with bullies. We often associate a bully's qualities as being mean, selfish, domineering, intensely oppressive, and without compassion, or even sociopathic. Yet, that is how we may treat them in return.

By not allowing them to explain themselves, cutting them off, and calling them names, we exhibit a type of reactive bullying behavior to what we perceive as bullying behavior. This reflects the Newton's Cradle of energy relationship—*for every action, there is an equal and opposite reaction.* However, the energy to which we respond could be our own internally generated thought and emotional energies based on the ego's perception, whether in truth or illusion. Whether the initiating energy was our own internal energy or that of another, we end up using bullying behavior and tactics in reaction to what our egos perceive as bullying behavior. Whether the others' behavior is actually bullying behavior, or is a misinterpretation based on how we perceived the scenario from our own colored lenses about bullying behavior, is irrelevant. What we do and say is a reflection of our own internal state, and not of another's behavior. We do not have to bully a bully. Our reaction is our responsibility, and another's behavior is never a justification for our own dysfunctional behavior.

The above example is an illustration of an aggressively out of balance reaction to bullying using anger, fear, and resentment emotions with venting, blaming behavior, creating our own form of aggressive bullying behavior. In contrast, an illustration of expressing the submissively imbalanced reaction could produce an exaggerated withholding or withdrawing into a state of fear and submission, believing the bully's story that you are weak, and that you must submit to their demands in order to survive. This would likely produce a state of stress, submission, and fear. A mix of an aggressive, and submissive expression could produce a passive aggressive reaction, which could feed off the anger, fear, and resentment of the purely aggressive expression into a different form of bullying in trying to control, manipulate, or otherwise oppress another into doing what you wanted them to do by using submissive behavioral tools of withdrawal, appeasement, or cajoling.

The balanced, higher-self approach to handling the scenario above, given the history outlined there, would be to hear out another's perspective, while listening with the intent to understand instead of with the intent to judge, react, or respond. Your higher self realizes that if you perceive their intentions to be controlling or domineering, you meet them with calm resolve, seeing them with compassion, knowing that *hurt people hurt people*, and that how people behave is a reflection and projection of their own internal state. Refusing to be someone's victim does not require turning the tables on them by being their oppressor, either. The notion of *giving someone a taste of their own medicine* is an egoic projection behavior. There is no justice in that. It is only a perpetuation of the same dysfunctional, imbalanced egoic consciousness energy, just as reflected in the Newton's Cradle.

The visceral reaction of the shadow response results from the ego taking another's behavior personally, as well as the egoic desire to hide an undesirable story, and, when expressed aggressively, project the image it wants to adopt in its place. The aggressive ego becomes so involved and attached to its reaction, its storyline, and its desired egoic identity image that it is as if another's behavior is somehow infringing on its own identity. You may read this, and say, "I've never thought that my identity was at stake from someone else's behavior." I'd like to suggest that instead you may not be appreciating the connection of your own shadow's extreme reaction and the ego's self-centered perspective on everything. You may not consciously believe that your own identity is at stake when you vehemently react to another's perceived judgmentalism or hypocrisy, but if thoughts creep into your head such as, "I'm not like that," or "I'm glad I'm not like that person who is so judgmental/hypocritical," then your ego is reacting because it does, in fact, believe the integrity of its own identity is implicated. This is not a conscious thought the ego will typically float through your thought stream, but it is what underlies its need to defend itself. The aggressive ego must reassure itself of who it is, and who it is not, when it is faced with its own shadow and the triggers that bring out the aggressive shadow's extreme, defensive reactions.

The point here is not to issue blame or judgment of the ego or its shadow for being *bad* or *wrong*. The point instead is to recognize this shadow response, so you can become conscious of it. Awareness is the first step in healing and retaking your power. These egoic and shadow behaviors are standard operating procedures for being human with an ego. Everyone has both an ego and a shadow because everyone has had uncomfortable experiences as a youth, along with an unsophisticated egoic mind. The goal, therefore, is for you to use this book as an operating manual for the ego, so that you can understand how to become a master of the ego and its shadow, instead of allowing the ego and shadow to run the show. Only when we see and understand our shadow triggers, behaviors, and fears can we heal them and engage in conscious choices about our thoughts, emotions, and behaviors.

Taking responsibility for our own projections

My experience of irritation and anger from my projected entitlement onto the highway driver who cut me off, versus my friend's reaction of gratitude to the same scenario, is a perfect example of how we must take responsibility for our own projections. I had never considered the possibility that I could have been the one with overly-entitled expectations with thoughts of ownership of a public road. Because our thoughts and reactions are a reflection of who we are in that moment, and never anyone or anything else outside us, I was forced to do a U-turn on that finger-pointing I was doing. This is just one more example of how others can be unkind, inconsiderate, and so on, but how we respond or react is a reflection of ourselves, and is, therefore, our own responsibility.

How we respond, feel, think, or react is *never caused by another*. Our reactions are always caused by our own thoughts, expectations, and emotions. The difference in my usual reaction of irritation and anger versus my friend's response of gratitude was not the difference between more egregious lane changing offenders following me around versus her offenders. The difference in our reactions was my egoic mindset of entitlement stacked with expectations, which was easily irritated and offended, versus her higher-self mindset of gratitude for having avoided an accident with everyone coming out of the circumstance safely.

In contrast, having viewed the lane I drive in as *my* lane, identifying myself with ownership of that lane with expectations that everyone needs to stay out of my way and allow me the space that I want, so I can drive as fast and as far as I want, was my ego generating thoughts of entitlement. I was projecting onto the other driver the label of being entitled without knowing anything about him, or what drove him to do what he did on the highway. I was projecting my uncomfortable shadow story of unworthiness in an aggressively imbalanced reaction of entitlement onto the other driver. This was my own ego creating my experience of irritation, not the other driver. When we see or experience road rage, with its immediate and extreme reaction of anger and entitlement, we are seeing a shadow projection of entitlement, trying to reject false egoic storylines and beliefs in lack and unworthiness that have been shoved away. What we have in our heads, whether consciously or unconsciously, is what we see externally. If we have the internal mindset of our higher self, we will not be attached to a storyline, and can see truths, but if our internal state is our egoic consciousness, we will be attached to an egoic storyline that will be our internal and externally projected filmstrip. We can only see the filmstrip that is available to us. *As within, so without.* Therefore, we must take responsibility for our own experiences because how we experience any situation will always be a reflection of our own inner state.

The shadow stories are clamoring to get out because we refuse to acknowledge them, and these aggressive expressions are the way they come out to breathe. The shadow sabotages our relationships externally with others, as well as internally with ourselves. When someone is beating up others verbally with judgment, it is because that person is beating up him- or herself internally with self-judgment on a regular basis. That is what they have to give to others. With this knowledge, it can be easier to show compassion for those who need it the most because of what they are doing to themselves inside their own heads, as well as to others.

This is when we are called by our higher selves to show compassion. None of these ego- and shadow-produced thoughts, emotions, and behaviors give us space for conscious choice. Because we aren't making conscious choices in how we are reacting (ego) or responding (higher self) to our life's circumstances when we are in our egoic state of being, it is the ego's thoughts and shadow's knee-jerk reactions that are shaping our experiences of our lives. This egoic conditioning shapes *how* we experience those circumstances. This is how two people can experience the same circumstances very differently.

When in our egoic consciousness, we end up going through life suffering with anger, irritation, sadness, and hatred based on lies and half-truths, at best from expectations of our egoic conditioning that prevents us, others, and life from showing up any other way. We've not only put our brains in a box, but now we've put our entire identity and life experiences in a box, and it is usually not a box filled with rainbows and ice cream. We create our own suffering experiences through the self-fulfilling prophecies of our own egoic storylines. This book is about breaking that cycle to illuminate the ego's illusions, so we can break out of its captivity and the oppression of its shadow. We want to be who we truly are, allow others to be who they truly are, and see life how it truly is.

We will all have to face painful circumstances in life, like boulders and level-5 rapids in the river flow that we want to steer around and through with skill as we travel through the river of life. These challenges are normal, but the suffering from those painful or uncomfortable challenges is not necessary. We create suffering when we buy into the ego's made-up stories that are based on fear and lack. I want to repeat this again for emphasis . . . *pain is normal; suffering is not.* Believing the ego's stories about fear and lack around those painful circumstances is like seeing those boulders in the river and knowingly crashing into them because we think that must be what we are supposed to do since they are in our path. Just as we want to learn the skills to be able to maneuver around the boulders and through the rapids on the river, we want to master the ego to avoid the unnecessary suffering of the ego's perspectives, stories, reactions, and sabotaging behavioral tools.

Chapter 6

Why Addressing the Shadow is Important

Wanting our decisions about our beliefs and behaviors to be conscious choices.

Because our shadow is an unconscious or subconscious set of beliefs reflecting our ego's greatest and most uncomfortable fears about ourselves, its expression will rarely, if ever, be a conscious choice. Nevertheless, the shadow will nearly always be sabotaging. As a result, we have a part of us, which, if un-addressed, produces sabotaging results that we neither choose nor can control when we don't see or understand it. Not un-derstanding the shadow is like riding backwards on a speeding train as the train approaches a split in the tracks, and we can't see the existence the fork in the road to choose the safe track and avoid those leading to a dead-end cliff. Because we create our own experiences of our circumstances based on our own perspectives, expectations, and consciousness state, we have the power to choose how we experience our life circumstances, but only when we can choose from which consciousness we live out those circumstances. Unless we address our shadow, we will, by default, be allowing our ego and shadow to choose our experiences for us, and they will rarely be positive. Whether we want to deal with our ego and its shadow comes down to a very simple question. Do we want to be motivated by joy and gratitude, or by fear and lack? The higher self is motivated by, and produces, experiences of joy and gratitude, whereas the ego and its shadow is motivated by, and produces, experiences of fear and lack.

If we aren't consciously aware of these default positions taken by our egos and our shadows, we aren't allowing ourselves to make conscious choices. When our true selves—our higher selves—aren't making conscious choices, we are in the back-seat while something else—our egos and shadows—is making choices for us with which we must live. Where our egos and shadows take us will never be a pleasant place. Therefore, we want to get our egos and shadows out of the driver seat. In order to get them out of the driver seat, we must be conscious of and understand when they are, in fact, in the driver seat, or trying to get into the driver seat. The only way to achieve this understanding and awareness about which part of us is driving, is to face our egos, to dig into that closet of the shadow, to understand them as well as how to recognize their presence, and have the tools to master our ego and shadow in order to leave space for our higher self to be our driver.

The good news is that once we start inquiring into our ego and shadow storylines and their tricks and tools, the ego and its shadow begin to have less power over us, and we often find gifts that we didn't previously acknowledge. The ego, and its shadow in particular, thrive in the darkness of secrecy and subversion. Bringing them into the light deflates their power, and they begin shrinking in size and intimidation, from the mountain that they first seemed to be to just molehills. With repeated practice of observation and conscious choices, the ego and its shadow stories can revert to mere dust particles in the air that we can wave away, as we live in joyful truths, instead of in the struggling egoic lies. Thus, we can heal and reframe our thoughts and stories about who we think we are, who others are, and how life is through shining our inquiring light on them that uncovers the joyful truths.

The more we investigate these egoic stories and shadow triggers to see what belies them, the more truths we see. With observation and awareness, we equip ourselves to make conscious choices about both our behavior and belief systems that drive our choices in values, objectives, and how we experience our lives. When we stop seeing ourselves as unworthy, we stop expecting to be treated as unworthy on the submissive side, and we stop being disappointed and angry because of others not fulfilling our expectations of entitlement on the aggressive side. When we can do this, we stop seeing everyone else's actions as having meaning about us, such as implying a belief in our lack of worth. As a result, we start seeing truths of our own circumstances as well as of how others' thoughts and behaviors are not personal to us. This is when we can allow others to show up as who they are instead of how our egos have labeled and expect them to be. We begin to see the truth of others' behaviors as a reflection of what is going on inside them, and not about us.

When we can detach from and de-identify with others' behaviors, our experiences of those moments can be filled more with joy and compassion. Anything that isn't joyful just passes through us like cars passing on a highway - just moving through. We acknowledge and absorb lessons from the uncomfortable experiences, which can then create more gratitude. Any un-kindness we experience just moves through us without parking and lingering in our thoughts, preventing the extended stay of extreme or painful emotions because we no longer identify with the ego's interpretations and characterizations of others or their behavior. We minimize our pain because we no longer give the ego's interpretations attention or meaning. Here is where our experiences cease being clouded with the egoic sto-rylines of negativity towards ourselves and others. Whether we allow those egoic storylines to stay and hold power over us through our attention and focus, or whether we allow them to flow through us without parking in our thought-stream, truly becomes a choice now because we see them for what they are—misinterpretations by our ego. We see that the ego falsely takes things personally because, to the ego, everything is about *it*.

Our shadow is the home base for our most uncomfortable thoughts and emotions, so is the root of our triggers that pro-duce our sabotaging behavior. In order to minimize, or even eliminate, our knee-jerk reactive triggers, we must open our shadow's closet and pull all those belief systems out into the light. When we do this, we learn more about what the trig-gers are that set us off that we've been blaming on others, and cause us suffering. Without this awareness and conscious con-trol, not only do we sabotage our relationship with others, but others also are able to manipulate us and elicit thoughts, emo-tions, and behaviors from us that are neither within our con-scious mind of choice nor our control. Through our shadow triggering, others' behavior becomes the tail that wags our dog because of our reactivity. In order to be in control and not be reduced to whimsical, reactive behavior orchestrated by others in collaboration with our egos and shadows, whether inten-tionally or unintentionally, we must gain control over our own thoughts, emotions, and behaviors. This means illuminating our shadow psyche to better understand ourselves.

The shadow shapes our views at the deepest levels.

The shadow is not only the source of our deepest fears about ourselves, it is also what we secretly believe about ourselves in the darkest, gloomiest, judgmental and negative storylines about who we are. All these shadow stories are misrepresentations, misunderstandings, and overreaching falsehoods, but we will continue to believe them until we look at them, see how they arose, and reframe the circumstances that gave rise to them. Until then, these shadow stories will continue to subconsciously drive our beliefs and experiences. The shadow is where most of our wounds reside. The spiritual wounded child lives here, and it is a depressing place if we believe the ego's false stories. The only way to heal these wounds is to bring the shadow into the light, so we can see that the storylines creating and burying our wounded child are lies. In doing this shadow work, we must remember that, while our circumstances were real, the storylines our ego created about what those circumstances meant are not truths. Let me state this again because it is critical: *Your circumstances are real, but your stories are not.* It is our consciousness, and the degree to which we allow the ego's stories to drive us, that determines *how we experience* those circumstances, whether in pain versus gratitude and joy, or in acceptance versus resistance. *Therefore, our experiences – as distinguished from our circumstances - are a product of our own consciousness state.*

When we are in an egoic consciousness, allowing the ego's motor mind to run amuck with its extensive detail on what everything means, our experiences will be negative much of the time, and, as a result, we will suffer with anxiety, fear, anger, and lack of worthiness beliefs. Experiences are mostly negative when we're in our egoic mind because it spins stories that revolve around itself based on fear, lack, and separation. Therefore, every uncomfortable circumstance will be taken personally, usually in a negative light. The ego will interpret everything as saying something about us, who we are, or how we are viewed by others, often with a negative egoic storyline that then gets interpreted and internalized as part of our identity. When we are in our higher-self consciousness, we recognize that our circumstances and others' thoughts and behavior have little to do with us. When in our higher-self consciousness, we recognize that others' thoughts and behaviors are only a reflection of the inner state of that person. So, when we are in our higher-self consciousness, what another person does or says is seen for what it is, and thoughts about it don't park in our minds where we continue to look at them, review them over and over, making up stories and conclusions about what others' behaviors say about us.

Our state of consciousness and thought energies can bring to us and attract undesirable circumstances. Like the different circumstances described in the f muddy water spray example in a previous chapter, our different consciousness states ripple differently, creating different impacts, based on how we think about, handle, and experience those circumstances. How others react to us is still a reflection of themselves, but our energy still has ripple effects. We saw in the three examples of balanced and imbalanced states in the muddy water example that others reacted to us differently. Regardless of whether we are experiencing a natural, energetic response from another to us of our own state, or a projection and reflection of another's egoic or shadow state of mind onto us in their behavior, we still have the energetic impact on, and opportunity to choose, our experience of that situation. If we are in our egoic consciousness, we will be more likely to trigger another's egoic behavior, and it will be more likely to escalate into a more destructive situation. Conversely, if we are in our balanced higher-self state, we will be able to deflect another's egoic behavior, and would be more likely to draw out another's higher self to allow for a more constructive situation. Only when we want the truth more than wanting to be right will that discernment and choice be clear about how to handle challenging circumstances in alignment with our higher self.

When you are operating out of your higher-self consciousness, you may see that a previous unkindness you may have shown to another requires both an acknowledgment and apology on your part. An egoic consciousness mindset will never apologize, as the ego always finds a justification and rationalization for its thoughts and behavior. Regardless of who is the actor versus the receiver of a behavior, egos can trigger egos in others, while our higher selves can trigger higher selves in others. At a minimum, if you are in your higher-self consciousness, you can deflate another's ego so the circumstances do not escalate further. Remember the energetic relationship of the Newton's Cradle balls. The scientific physics and energetic truth of the Newton's Cradle is reflected in each of our personal energies that resonate from our consciousness states as they come into contact with others. When thinking of how that energy impacts others, think also of Dr. Emoto's studies showing the impact of our thought energies expressed through words.

Hopefully, you can see now that your state of consciousness determines how you experience a circumstance. Whether your experience is positive, negative, or simply neutral without taking it personally or internalizing it will be determined by your own consciousness state in that moment. If we have not put a leash on our shadow by shining a light on it in order to gain an understanding of it, we will experience circumstances in life far more negatively than what is in fact the truth of the circumstance. This means that we will experience unnecessary suffering. It is possible to experience joy, compassion, and gratitude in even the most undesirable circumstances when we are in the consciousness of our higher self. As previously mentioned, when we are in our egoic consciousness state of mind, undesirable circumstances will produce miserable experiences. This is why life for someone who understands their shadow, and who can remain in the consciousness of their higher self will be joyful, grateful, and trusting, regardless of their life circumstances more often. It is also why life for someone in their egoic mindset without insight into their shadow will often experience life as miserable and untrustworthy, regardless of the circumstance.

Facing our shadow allows us to be our best and truest self.

The illumination of our shadow allows us to be the person we were born to be. Because parts of our gifts nearly always end up in the shadow's closet, along with the ego's most painful storylines, we must go into the shadow to retrieve these gifts. When doing so, this accomplishes several favorable things. First, it allows us to separate the truths and facts from the ego's spin and lies. Second, seeing the untruths also allows us to see that the circumstances of another's unkind behavior towards us was not a reflection of who we were, or are, as a person. Third, we can then instead see that others' behavior was simply a circumstance where another was in pain and acted out of their own egoic mindset and shadow; we just happened to be present to receive the brunt of their expression of their own pains.

Let's look at another real-life example from one of my students. A young boy is playing with his siblings in the house, and they are throwing pillows and playing a little rough. The older boy, the third child of four in the family, throws a pillow, which misses his younger brother, and instead hits his mother in the head. As a single mother with four children, she is stressed about finances, she is tired from working twelve or more hours a day cleaning, doing laundry and other laborious jobs, so she reacts angrily, venting to her older boy, "I wish you had never been born!" That older boy, as a middle child, had often felt overlooked by his mother because he was not a girl with a mother/daughter connection, nor was he the baby of the family, whom he interpreted as being doted on by his mother and older sisters. As a child, with a child's mental and emotional sophistication, he interpreted this harsh, unloving statement by his mother as meaning that he was unloved, un-wanted, and unworthy of love and appreciation, especially within the family. At that age, he could not see his mother's frustrated outburst as being driven by her own fears, as well as her own dysfunctional parental and male relationship ex-periences in her own storylines. He has internally carried this feeling of rejection all his life, making him driven to prove his worth in an expression of extreme workaholism in his drive for success and acknowledgment.

As he looked further into his shadow, however, this cir-cumstance and experience is brought to the surface for further scrutiny and inquiry as a deep pain that still haunts him. Ini-tially, it was difficult for him because it brought up the same thoughts and emotions of his being both unloved and un-worthy of love that he felt as a child when his mother told him that she wished he had never been born. When he takes a step back as an adult, however, in order to look at that circumstance in the context of the larger picture in a detached (non-personal), but not suppressive, view of the circumstances, he can see what the truths of that situation were without taking them personally.

Here is what he could see as **truths** of the circumstance:

- His mother was tired from her long, laborious work over many days, weeks, and years.
- His mother was stressed about being able to adequately care for her four children, having no education and little resources.
- His mother was generally unhappy with having been abandoned by her ex-husband and left with an overwhelming responsibility of raising and caring for four children with little help.
- He unintentionally hit his mother in the head with a pillow, which she did not enjoy or appreciate.
- His mother became angry at being hit with the pillow and vented, being driven by her tired and fearful frustrations.
- His mother had a difficult childhood without good parental role models, having been abandoned by her own parents.
- His mother had a very dysfunctional relationship with both her ex-husband and other men in her life.
- She was unkind in her response to him and in blaming him instead of both the boys.
- His mother always made sacrifices to ensure he was taken care of at the same level as his siblings.

- He could also see what was NOT true in this situation—the lies:
- He was, and is, unworthy of love.
- He was, and is, less than, or lacking in worth for any reason.
- He was, and is, a bad or undesirable person.
- It was a mistake for him to be born.
- He had, and has, no value, or no worthy contribution to this world.
- His mother did not love him.

What **may** be **half-truths:**
- His mother may have favored his younger brother as the baby of the family, which, if so, was a reflection of the state of mind of his mother, and not a statement of his value.
- He may not have had the same closeness with his mother as his siblings, but that was a reflection of the relationship between others, and it was not a statement of his value or goodness as a person.
- In that moment, he was not behaving in a way that was helpful to his mother, and she did not appreciate that.

When we separate the facts of the circumstances from the ego's stories and interpretations of those circumstances, it becomes easier to see where we can be our own worst enemies in making ourselves miserable, sad, angry, and so on, by allowing our egos to spin storylines that just aren't true. By giving these stories attention, they linger, getting replayed over and over in our egoic minds – the thought stream. With those stories lingering, these thoughts engender painful emotions that align with the energy of our thoughts. The addition of the emotions to our thoughts into our energetic bodies make the stories seem even more real. These egoic stories, now bolstered by thoughts and corresponding emotions, become belief systems. As previously discussed those belief systems become our conditioning.

As also previously discussed, these painful stories get shoved into the shadow's closet because we don't want to feel these pains arising from both the thoughts and emotions of an egoic story. These conditioned thoughts and emotions from this storyline unconsciously stay a part of us as a deep-rooted fear and belief about who we are. You can see from this example that his belief system of lacking worthiness, when expressed aggressively to reject that story, created his need for acknowledgment and heightened levels of *success* to prove his value. His deep-rooted fear of his own unworthiness came from his belief in his ego's lies about his circumstances, and who he was. When he looked at his fear of unworthiness generally, this was the first story that came to his mind. Thereafter, he saw that he would look at circumstances in his life through that lens of fearing that others did not view him as being worthy, valuable, or appreciated. This drove him to his workaholic nature, with an overly active desire for acknowledgment. This fear could, at times, also manifest through an aggressive egoic expression of exaggerated puffery in his desire to think of and project himself to be viewed by others with as high of esteem as possible. As a result, he would at times project braggadocios behavior.

When we can look objectively and rationally at the facts of our circumstances, without being attached to a personal meaning, we can more easily see the manufactured storylines that were spun by our ego. Through a compassionate detachment view, we can see that a significant number of leaps in judgement and negative assumptions made by his ego do not necessarily follow from those circumstances. Our egos make rash judgments and see others' behavior as being about us. We must delve into our shadows to relieve ourselves from these dark, untrue beliefs with which our ego has burdened us. We need to be released from these storied yokes around our necks that drag us down, preventing us from being who we truly are and were meant to be—our best, and highest selves. Going into our shadow gives us the opportunity to be our best human self. The shadow actually gives us gifts when we pull out some of our hidden qualities stored there, liberating us from the lies we told ourselves about our greatest pains.

Allows others to show up as who they truly are and allows for compassion.

Because our shadows have a negative view about who others are, and how life is, in addition to who we are, illuminating the shadow and healing the pains we've shoved there allows others to be viewed in a different light as well as ourselves. In the example above about the mother and son, when the son goes into his own shadow, seeing those circumstances from his higher self without the ego's characterizations, he can more easily see that his mother was not a cold, uncaring mother-zilla to him like a Cinder-fella. Neither is he unlovable or unworthy in any way. Instead, he can now see how tough it must have been for a single mother of four, having been abandoned by her ex-husband (as well as her own stories from being abandoned by her own parents), with limited skills and education, working herself to exhaustion, constantly tired and stressed to try and give four children the life she wanted them to have, and never had herself. He could now see how easy it would be to be irritated and frustrated by roughhousing that was not helpful to her with all she was trying to do to provide for the family with her limited resources.

By going into his shadow and investigating his pain, he was able to heal his own false belief systems and strengthen his respect and gratitude for his mother with what she was going through. He began to heal himself with a more enlightened perspective on others in his stories and on his own sabotaging behavior of being a tireless workaholic, needing acknowledgment, and afraid to see himself being slighted and unloved. He could see that his belief in being unloved and viewed as a lesser priority by his mother caused him to distance himself from her, furthering both his and her pains, as she likely took his distance as validation of her own storyline that he was ungrateful for what she did and sacrificed for them, along with her own story of unworthiness of having been abandoned by both her parents and her ex-husband. His mother's usual submissive expressions of her ego and shadow would produce further withdrawal, and the cycle just continued. Once he could see this, he could choose to break that cycle and start a new spiral upwards with compassion instead of perpetuating the downward spiral of pain, blame, resentment, and fear by them both. The unfortunate part of this story was that his mother had already passed, so he was not able to mend his relationship with her. However, he could begin to reverse and stem the sabotage of his relationships with others and put an end to this perpetuating cycle.

It is important to insert a few words about expectations here. We should not expect that these deep-rooted pains will be immediately and permanently healed on all levels, never to return, after the first time of seeing through them. Many of these deep-rooted pains shoved into the shadow are likely still to surface on a smaller scale as uncomfortable thoughts and emotions surface in response to certain triggers. This was evidenced in the example discussed earlier regarding the female believing she was a less preferred child still getting triggered back into old shadow patterns when around family. Many of these deep-seated pains must be healed in layers. With knowledge and understanding of them, we can see them, observe what is happening, and with that observation, heal them at each layer. Each layer of healing produces a deeper recognition of our shadow, along with a deflation in the pain and impact of those stories. With this observation and understanding, we have greater control over our thoughts, emotions, and behaviors, and then we can choose whether we allow those thoughts and emotions to linger with us or just allow them to be passing cars on the highway of our mind. In other words, our thoughts and beliefs, as well as our resulting emotions, can now can become more conscious choices. We can now see how we are the source of, and responsible for, our own thoughts, emotions, behaviors, and experiences, and that no one makes us sad, angry, or anything else. We can begin to see instead how we solicit these emotions ourselves from our own thoughts and expectations, or lack thereof.

Over time, if we continue to give the egoic stories less and less attention, by continuing to bring our attention back to the rational, unattached, and impersonal view of our circumstances of our observer state of the higher self versus the ego's spin, these egoic thoughts and expectations are likely to eventually disappear into the past as old fairy tales that no longer serve us. Through our higher-self awareness, we experience greater and greater healing on a deeper, more sustainable level. This is what clears the way for us to elicit more and greater joy, happiness, gratitude, abundance, compassion, and love in our lives instead of the opposite. Remember, what we have inside us is the only pool from which we can draw to give to others, and what we give to others we often receive from others, whether from our own lenses because that is what we see, or from the Newton's Cradle of energetic exchange. These are physical, scientific, spiritual, and energetic laws we've learned from Newton's Cradle, Dr. Emoto's energetic water crystal studies and every philosophical, religious, and spiritual teaching from around the world. *As within, so without. What you sow, so shall ye reap*[11].

As we change our stories, we change our belief systems. As we change our belief systems, we change our conditioning and the lenses in our eyes that cloud our views of who we are, who others are, and how life is. When we change our lenses, we change our experiences of our circumstances. When we change our experiences of our circumstances, we cease to feel offended, angry, and sad in response to life's challenges or others' behavior towards us. When we can remain in our higher selves, and not resort to knee-jerk egoic and shadow responses of anger, sadness, resentment, judgment, and other egoic tools and emotional distortions, we lower the triggering we do of others' egos and shadows. When others are in their egos, feeling threatened by us in our higher selves, staying in our higher selves, and not allowing ourselves to be triggered by their egoic behavior, keeps situations manageable for a higher outcome. When we stay in our higher selves, we can trigger others' higher selves instead of perpetuating egoic in-teractions.

[11] Restatement of the Bible, Galatians 6:7

If you question this ripple effect, think of experiences when you have been pulled into a joyous or animus mood yourself by being around others in that same mood. You have also likely noticed times when you've pulled others into one or the other mindsets as well. When another in the room is happy, gleeful, and sees positive perspectives with joy and gratitude, it is easier to be pulled into a smile. Conversely, if someone is negative, in a bad mood, brooding, attacking others, or otherwise exhibiting a negative egoic state, it is easier to get pulled into your own negativity of judgment, irritation, anger, and so on. What is important to also remember here, however, is that you being pulled into an egoic state is not the fault of someone else because of their behavior. If you are grounded in your higher self, there is nothing another can do to pull you out of your higher state. You retain authorship, ownership, and responsibility for your thoughts, emotions, and behaviors at all times in all circumstances, as do others. There are no exceptions to this rule of accountability and responsibility. You can always choose how you respond to another's abusive behavior, as can they, which can produce productive energies and outcomes, instead of escalated chaos, exchanging anger for anger.

This is energetic relationship is a perfect illustration of the common saying that *hurt people, hurt people* and *healed people, heal people.* It reflects the energetic relationship of the Newton's Cradle. Our own energetic thought and emotional state in any given moment will have ripple effects, and we are either contributing to the egoic consciousness of others or to their higher-self consciousness. *Ripple effects are powerful.* If we don't have awareness of the deepest, darkest crevices of our psyches, we cannot effectively make a choice as to which consciousness we want to perpetuate, and to which one we want to contribute.

Changing our relationship to our thoughts and emotions.

Because each person's behavior is their own responsibility, regardless of what another does, no one makes you sad or happy or angry. Therefore, you bring on those emotions yourself through your own thoughts and expectations. As a result, it should be clear that we must change the nature of our relationship to our thoughts and emotions in order to have greater control over ourselves, our emotions, behaviors, and experiences. By going into our shadow, we will be changing the nature of our relationship to our thoughts, which produce our emotions, behavior, and how we experience life. When we change our relationship to our thoughts and emotions to a more balanced and healthy relationship from our higher self, we allow the thoughts that are part of the egoic storylines to just rise and fall with the moment, passing through our motor mind like cars passing through on a highway. Instead of believing and relating *from* the storylines, like we're a passenger in that car, we just observe them, relating *to* them at an arms-length distance, watching them drive by. When we are relating *to* our thoughts and emotions, instead of experiencing them as part of who we are, we can observe them and see that they are not us. That makes facing these thoughts and emotions easier without the same degree of pain or suffering. When we are in a healthy observer state, we keep our thoughts and emotions at an arms-length distance without withdrawing, suppressing, or absorbing them. When we can see our thoughts and emotions at arm's length, we can become more knowledgeable about them, we can more easily see that they do not represent truths, and we don't identify ourselves, others, or life generally with them. Then, we don't let these thoughts park in our minds by giving them repeated attention as if they represent truths.

By controlling to what thoughts we give our attention, we thereby streamline the emotions that arise within us. Having this self-management and mastery over our thoughts ripples into having better emotional hygiene and mastery, which creates more constructive behaviors and more positive experiences about our life circumstances.

Releasing these egoic thoughts before they linger long enough to elicit corresponding emotions is the path to self-mastery. If the egoic thoughts linger a little too long, or if we attach ourselves to particular expectations or outcomes, we could create uncomfortable experiences for ourselves by not catching the initial thoughts in time before the corresponding emotions start flowing into us. If we can observe and identify to what thoughts uncomfortable emotions are attached, and see our attachment to those thoughts, we can just breathe through those emotions, releasing our attachment to them, allowing the emotions to rise and fall with the moment. We can then begin to understand how to relate to both our thoughts and emotions through observation, instead of relating from them by identifying with them as just how life is or as having any truth associated with them. The longer we allow the egoic thoughts and emotions to linger by giving our attention to them, whether through attachments to expectations, outcomes, or the stories, the more difficult it will be to release them and the belief systems they perpetuate. Therefore, the more painful the experiences will be.

At this juncture, it is important to mention some counseling treatments that have been used that, in my opinion, are harmful related to this discussion. There have been (and in some circles, there still are) some counseling protocols that direct people to *act out* those feelings or *feel the feelings*. In my opinion, this is just the opposite pole as suppressing them, which is just another imbalanced egoic expression. *Acting out* is venting the emotions, which is just an aggressive expression of imbalance, whereas the suppression of them is the submissive expression that deepens and widens the shadow that this *acting out* is intended to prevent. This theory of counseling just trades one version of imbalance for another in its polar opposite. In contrast, a balanced expression and behavior is neither to act them out nor suppress them. Acting out and *feeling the feelings* is just asking the person to roll around in those thoughts and emotions, which only heightens them, and then vent them into a pillow in an aggressive expression. This is not healthy, in my opinion, because it is just another egoic expression that can create attachment and identification with those emotions and thoughts. In my opinion, the healthy way is to process these emotions in a way that _sees_ what they are, from what thoughts they arose, and what underlies those thoughts – what attachments and expectations created those thoughts. This is the awareness and release that heals them. We must understand and heal the thoughts in order to heal the emotions. Venting is not healing. Without real healing, the same thoughts and thought patterns, with their same triggers, will continue to flow into our thought streams, provoking the same emotions and egoic reactions over and over, creating the same suffering over and over in a continuous cycle of suffering and venting. There is nothing healthy or healing about that kind of cycle or treatment.

When we move into the observer state that is the higher self, we can see what is actually happening, and we can naturally take some of the wind out of the intensity of those thoughts and emotions, allowing them to process and move out of us. We will feel the energy of these thoughts and emotions as we allow them to roll through, but the intensity of them will be muted and not as much in the forefront because they no longer have control over us. When we see the thoughts connected to the emotions, we can see truths more clearly, and see where we—and not others—were the source of our emotions. This becomes a growth and learning opportunity to prevent similar sabotaging emotions in the future. Our higher self is in control when we move into the observer state, and our higher self can use any emotional energy as fuel for a productive behavior, or just allow it to move on through with our acknowledgment, but without attachment or rolling around in the emotion and its generating thoughts. You will see that there is nothing to reject, and instead you will be able to work through those thoughts and emotions with compassionate detachment.

Many of you may be familiar with the saying, *ten percent of life is what happens to you, and 90% is how you respond to it.* If you aren't addressing your shadow, 90% of your life can be pretty miserable if you are in an egoic or shadow reactive mode much of the time. This ego and shadow work of changing our relationship to our thoughts and emotions will enable us to affect that 90% of our life through how we experience our circumstances. What storylines we are, or are not, buying into and what consciousness we are in when we face our life's circumstances determines how we experience those circumstances. Life has often been likened to the flow of a river, and sometimes you are in beautiful pools of serene calm stillness, while other times you are running down level-5 rapids. When you're in the level-5 rapids, you want a sturdy canoe with a sturdy oar to withstand the pull of the undercurrents, to steer around the boulders and push through the dips. Undergoing this ego and shadow work and changing the nature of your relationship to your thoughts and emotions is giving you the observation, coping, and healing skills to give you that strong, sturdy canoe and oar, while moving through those rapids of the flow of life.

When you have this understanding, and you can make that choice, your relationship to your thoughts and emotions will be one of mastery instead of victimhood. When you change your relationship to your thoughts and emotions, you change your attitude. When you change your attitude, you change your perspective. When you change your perspective, you change your experience. When you change your experience, you change your life. This is when you become the hero and master of your own life, and you realize that you are flowing down that river in a sturdy canoe, with a sturdy oar, and with great skill. With this work and understanding, those rapids are just small bumps that might even be a little fun and exhilarating when you know how to navigate them. Without this understanding, you are instead like a flimsy box being strewn about on the flow of life, hitting boulders, getting caught up in the whirlpools of the dips, and feeling bruised, cut and miserable about this flow of life. How sturdy is your canoe and oar as you go through life's river flow?

Seeing our self-imposed limitations.

There are many popular sayings that motivate and bring people into a different frame of mind, such as the "glass half full" versus the "glass half empty," or "think outside the box." The reality is, however, that the glass and the box are both still just confined limitations. So, whether we are in the half-full glass or outside of the box, both the glass and box metaphors still limit our perspectives. Instead of relating our thoughts and behaviors to a fixed placement of a glass or a box, we want to see the truth that those glasses and boxes are just figments of our egoic storylines. The glass and the box are, themselves, limitations and illusions that keep us attached to dragging around our stories and conditioning like a ball at the end of a chain.

To illustrate this concept, I would like to bring up an image that many of you have seen in the film, *The Matrix.* The irony is not lost on me that I am using a make-believe movie scenario to illustrate what I believe to be a truth about our illusions. I do, however, think this movie scene will help people see more effectively what I mean with respect to the glass and the box. Early in the movie hero's awakening to the illusory life of the Matrix, the hero, Nero, goes to see a wise, all-knowing oracle for advice and validation of him being "the one" who will save the humans. While he is in the waiting room, he is in the midst of many gifted children. He focuses on one child who is seemingly bending a metal spoon with his mind. So, Nero tries to do so, too. He focuses and focuses, trying with all his mental might to move that metal spoon head with his mind, but it barely moves. The child makes the spoon head bend as if it were liquid pouring over. The gifted child says to Nero, "*Do not try and bend the spoon, that's impossible. Instead, only try to realize the truth . . . there is no spoon. Then you'll see that it is not the spoon that bends, it is only yourself.*" From that point forward, Nero does things no one else believes are possible because he is no longer tied, as they are, to certain rules and stories they think define life, as well as what is, and is not, possible.

I'm not suggesting that we ignore what science tells us are physical laws of gravity by jumping out of windows or trying to fly through the air like Nero does in the movie. Instead, I want to make the point that our conditioning of how we think life is, what we think we can do or not, and who we are, or are not, are ego constructs that are just as illusory as that spoon in the *Matrix.* We want to untether ourselves from those constructs. *There is no box. There is no glass.* Therefore, we want to stop relating ourselves to whether we are in, outside, half-full, or half-empty in it. These tethers are what keep us small and limited. We are not in a box or in a glass—unless we choose to put ourselves there. Get rid of the boxes and glasses, and just BE in your life with no limitations on who you are and what you can do. *Untether yourself. Only then can you be who you were meant to be and who you truly are.* This is how we take back our power and our light as masters and BEcome our own heroes of our lives.

This concept of untethering yourself is what is behind another saying you may have heard to *drop the story.* Often this is said in the context of allowing yourself to *feel the feelings*, and drop the storyline that the ego spins. I believe this saying is incomplete and skips a couple of very critical steps. First, you can't heal by focusing only on the emotions because it is our thoughts that elicit our emotions. Therefore, by focusing just on the emotions, you will be just treating the symptom instead of the cause. If we have only dropped the story without inquiring into the cause, we are just suppressing the thoughts, thereby creating more shadow, not healing. If we have actually dropped our storyline through healing, we won't have the same emotions. This does not mean that we won't feel sadness, anger, or any emotion again, but with healing, we allow those uncomfortable emotions to rise and fall with natural life occurrences in the moment, and not because of another's behavior that violates our storyline expectations.

The other important element to this concept that must not be overlooked is the *how* to drop the story. As mentioned earlier, you can't just ignore, bury, shame, or otherwise just drop it like a hot potato and have that be a healthy behavior. You can't just *drop your story* without doing the work of inquiry and healing. The bulk of this book is about understanding what your story is, how to see it, how it affects you, its triggers that bring it to the surface in sabotaging ways, how to investigate it, and then how to heal it so that it no longer controls you, limits you, and blinds you from the truth of who you are, who others are, and how life is. This process helps to heal you, so you can be who you truly are in the reality of life as it truly exists. You will see that you've put a colored lens in your eyes, you will see that it has tinted the sky an unnatural color, you will know how to take out that artificial lens, and then you see the sky as blue. Through this book's process you will soon start seeing the edges of your colored lenses, you will begin to know how that colored lens got there, how to take it out, how to avoid putting that lens back into your eyes, and how to see truths.

Doing our own shadow and ego work
is how we change the world.

As previously mentioned Ghandi coined the phrase, *Be the change you want to see in the world.* The meaning behind this saying is more profound than what you might realize at first. As we discussed, we have the power to trigger others' egos and shadows or their higher selves, based on our own state of being and projecting energy. As we've established, our behavior is determined by our thoughts and emotions and how much conscious control we exert over those. Therefore, we change the world, not by pointing fingers at others in judgment that *they* must change, but rather by *changing ourselves* by BEing in our higher selves, so we trigger the higher selves in others, instead of our egos triggering their egos. *Changing the world is a ripple effect result of changing ourselves.*

The effects of transmuting and healing our
shadow and reframing our experiences.

By illuminating our shadows, healing, transmuting, and reframing our egoic stories buried there, the impact can be life changing. What follows are some of the most impactful results:

- Your perspective shifts from the misery of the ego, with its belief in lack and fear, to the higher self, with its trust in life and itself with joy and gratitude.

- Your perspective changes from the ego's storylines and illusions, with its made-up conclusions and expectations, to truths.

- You stop locking yourself or others into a narrow box of expectations and labels.

- You become happier, loving life more.

- You become connected to the qualities of the higher self that enable you to cope with the challenges of life that inevitably come and are designed to give you lessons for growth, so you can be your best and highest self. It is only after being challenged that we become stronger through growth.

- You regain the power to choose what perspectives and experiences to have and how to see life. You have the choice to see life from your higher self and truth and not from the ego's fear, lack and illusions.

- You regain the power to choose what thoughts to believe without the ego's control, manipulation, and fears.

Over time, you will be able to sense and recognize more your true self, and live more in your true and highest-self consciousness as your interface to the world, instead of remaining buried under the egoic self. You will see that you *do* have the ability to create or deflate your emotions – and that only you have this ability. As previously mentioned, *you are in control of your emotions at all times, and you have the power to choose them* through the thoughts that you allow to linger in your thought stream. If you are not consciously in control of these thoughts through your higher self, your ego will default to being in charge of them, and they will run amuck, getting triggered through the acts of others, causing havoc and suffering, and subjecting your joy or suffering to the whims of others' behaviors. Starting down this path of mastery is incredibly empowering. This is the path to taking back your power. Once you realize that other people can affect you only if you allow them, there is nothing to fear about yourself, others, or life. You have the power to choose whether you want to be motivated by fear and lack, or by joy, love, compassion, courage, and all of the other qualities of the higher self.

To explore more the difference between how you respond to challenges while in your egoic self, in contrast to being in your higher self, think of something that recently made you sad or angry and all of the thoughts and emotions that arose from that situation, please access the *Audio Companion for Section I, Exercise 1—The Difference Between the Egoic Reaction and the Higher Self Response.*

SECTION II

IDENTIFYING YOUR EGO, ITS SHADOW, TRIGGERS, AND EXPRESSIONS

In this Section II, I will discuss the various ways in which you can identify when your ego and its shadow will reveal themselves and you can identify them. It will be important to understand and note that the ego and shadow expressions are inherently imbalanced expressions, and will show up on either the aggressive or submissive side. Some of this may surprise you, particularly with respect to submissive expressions.

Chapter 7

Pulling Out Your Shadow from the Darkness Into the Light

It takes courage for most people to face their greatest fears. People often think about their greatest fears being an external manifestation – fear of not being loved, fear of failure, fear of poverty, fear of losing a job, fear of death, and so on. The reality is that all these external fears really stem from fears held by the internal egoic self about itself and its place in life with respect to others. These external fears all stem from the fears that the ego has about who we think we are, who others think we are, and how well we'll be able to survive any circumstance. These are all fears based on a lack of both loving and trusting oneself, others, and life. All of these fears come from the egoic storylines that are too painful to acknowledge in thoughts or feel in emotions, so they get shoved into the shadow. In other words, our greatest fears lie in our own shadows. This is the reason why when people think of or hear about the shadow, it is scary to many. While they may not understand what the shadow really is, they immediately react with fear, rejection, and reticence about facing the shadow. This is the ego's reaction. After all, it is the ego that shoved these fears into the closet, thereby creating the shadow. Therefore, by definition, the ego fears facing its own shadow creation. The ego is *deathly* afraid of its own shadow.

As a result, it takes courage to challenge the ego, to go against its urgings to look away from the shadow, and instead to stare directly into the face of the shadow – where the ego's greatest fears reside. The first thing is to pat yourself on the back for getting this far along in this book and following the urgings of your higher self over the objections of your ego. The good news is, as mentioned in the first section, the shadow is full of lies and half-truths, at best. Therefore, the shadow work will be a joyous revelation when you see that the darkest, gloomiest storylines of the ego that were shoved into the shadow are not truths. You are not what your ego and shadow say you are. Seeing the truth is freedom. This freedom is not just from the ego's box of who it says you are and are not – it is freedom from the ego's fears.

This freedom from the ego's fears and lies, whether in our conscious awareness or stored in the shadow, allows you to experience joy, gratitude, courage, and strength as well as all the other qualities that are instilled in your higher self. Be prepared, however, to be observant of the ego's distracting flags and alternative stories that it will throw at you during your walk through healing the shadow. In order to stay focused on uncovering all the lies, healing the fears, and reframing the beliefs of lack, your intentions must stay firm. Saying to yourself (out loud if you can) the following affirmation can help you maintain the intention to find the truth more than wanting to follow the ego's default need to be *right*. As you say the following affirmation to yourself either silently or out loud, be certain to affirm, with the deepest of intentions, every word below. Repeat this affirmation to yourself or out loud three times. (You will also find this affirmation in the Companion Workbook as Section II, Exercise 1.)

- *I intend and affirm that I AM – and will continue to BE – open, alert, honest, willing and courageous to see the underlying stories, limitations and sabotaging beliefs and behaviors of my ego and its shadow that are overshadowing my higher self and hiding my lessons, growth, higher qualities, fractions of my true self, and my innate power.*
- *I intend and affirm that I SHALL take back my power, integrate my full self in a balanced way, accept the lessons, heal the fractures, transcend the limitations, extend my growth, and step into my full and highest self.*

Please access the Companion Workbook, Section II, Exercise 2. Before reading any further, now is the time to complete Section II, Exercise 2 in the Companion Workbook. Answer all four questions and their subparts before continuing to read below.

The questions in the Workbook for this Section II, Exercise 2 are designed to shine the light on your shadow in several ways. First, these questions bring forth what most irritates you, asking additional questions about those qualities, people, and circumstances. These questions will reveal your beliefs and reactions about these triggers. This process forces you to lay out and look at what your ego hides, masks, and projects out onto others, which it has shoved into the closet that has become your shadow, cloaking it in a costume of illusions and projections. What follows is a review of some of the questions in this exercise and their implications.

The qualities you condemn in others

These are the qualities that, when you think you see them in others, it provokes the deepest sense of rejection, judgment, and condemnation from you. These are the qualities to which you have the most vehement objections, reactions, and triggers, provoking immediate thoughts or feelings of disgust or disdain. This is your visceral reaction I discussed in the first section.

These abhorred qualities that you think you see in others are triggers to your shadow. Look deeply at your reactions to these qualities. Look to see what emotions or thoughts you have about yourself for just an instant before you criticize or condemn others or become defensive. There will always be something you think or feel for a split second about yourself as you face the qualities that you abhor the most in others. Do you fear that you might also have these qualities in you? Do you have shame that you might have exhibited them at any point in the past? Do you hold fear, resentment, or anger for having been exposed to, or harmed by, these qualities by others, and what this could mean for your status or advancement, or what this could say about who you are? Identify what thoughts, emotions, and reactions you have when you believe you are faced with these qualities from others. Be sure to look at what you think and emote, or even feel, about yourself separately from what you think, emote, or feel about others you perceive are exhibiting those qualities in that moment.

The thoughts you think, the emotions you emote, and the feelings you feel for an instant about yourself before jumping to the judgment and condemnation of others will be uncomfortable. Don't turn away from them. The only way to discover the lies that your ego has set up in your psyche is to face these uncomfortable thoughts, emotions, and feelings and look at them. Remember that what these thoughts and emotions are expressing are not who you are, even if you may have slipped into exhibiting these qualities on some level at times, so don't identify with them—just see them. This observation technique of seeing them, as if they are sitting across the table from you, has an immediate effect of deflating their power and meaning when you relate *to* them and not *from* them.

When you relate to others *from* thoughts and emotions, you are integrating with those, making them part of your being and identity, as well as your subsequent thoughts and behaviors will then arise from those mental and emotional states. However, you don't want to integrate, or absorb, them as part of you, nor do you want to push them down and ignore them. Instead, you want the balanced position of an arms-length observation, as neither identified with you nor shoved away. While those thoughts and emotions are not you, or who you are, you did, however, elicit them, inviting them to run in your thoughts. It is important to not see these emotions as bad, as the enemy, or even as truth-sayers. Just observe them at arms-length. You can even mentally or verbally say to them, "*I see you.*" It is even more valuable to give them a name . . . fear, shame, anger, and so on. Call them out and name them as what they are, so you can better identify them. These emotions are, in fact, separate energies from you. You just invited them to enter your emotional energetic space. The thoughts behind them are egoic thoughts, just passing through on the information highway of your thought-stream. Both the thoughts and aligning emotions are just energies flowing through you like electrical currents flowing through a conductor when you turn on the corresponding switches.

As you try to identify the thoughts and emotions underlying your shadow and projection behaviors, think of a specific example that you've personally experienced lately, and go through the analysis of the thoughts you think about others and yourself to see the resulting emotions running through you. See yourself in this situation as an objective observer without any attachment to a characterization or outcome. Your intentions to see the truth more than you want to be right will be critical here. This activity is like moving your focus from a tree back to seeing the forest as well as how the tree is situated within the forest. This is the view you want to have as you move through this process of looking at your shadow and its triggers. Remember that there is nothing wrong with or bad about you, regardless of the outcome or truth of the situation. Now, you should be able to see that tree of your shadow and egoic thoughts, emotions, beliefs, triggers, and projections within the forest as one that you planted. That tree is clearly not you, but you planted the seed, you nurtured it to grow, and so it grew with your attention and effort; however, it is still separate from you. Nevertheless, the fact that you planted that tree can never turn that tree into you. You may even see how this tree is growing. What do your initial inspirations tell you about how healthy this tree is?

Since your emotions flow from your thoughts, you must look at what thoughts you are giving attention to through your continued replay in your thought-stream that become beliefs. As you look at these thoughts and corresponding emotions, feeling their effect on your body, you do not want to blame, shame, or ignore these emotions. Instead, you want to acknowledge that you nurtured them with your thoughts, so they just flowed where your attention went. You may be familiar with the saying *energy flows where attention goes*. This saying is a representation of how the relationship between thoughts and emotions work. As you get better at moving into the observer state, you begin to be less integrated with, and attached to, your emotions, without dismissing or ignoring them. Instead, you can observe them flowing into and through you without relinquishing your control to them, allowing them to take over your body and mind. Instead of demonizing or suppressing the emotions, thank them for responding to your attention. You treat the ego and its shadow as you would the good intentions of a two–year–old child, with loving compassion, however, without indulgence for its misguided perspective.

Please complete the questions in the *Companion Workbook* for *Section II, Exercise 2*. After you have written down your answers, please access the *Companion Audio* for *Section II, Exercise 3* to move through the guided exercises regarding your answers that you can record in the *Companion Workbook Section II, Exercise 3*. What follows below are important points to explore with respect to each of the questions in Section II, Exercise 2 that will be explored further in the Companion Audio.

- Note the physical bodily sensations you feel as you think about the thoughts leading to your uncomfortable emotion, and then observe and remember them. Write them down. Consider the physical sensations you feel in your:
    - ✓ Forehead (is your brow furrowed or relaxed)?
    - ✓ Jaw (is your jaw clenched or tight)?
    - ✓ Neck (do you feel any tightening of your muscles)?
    - ✓ Shoulders (do you feel any tension)?
    - ✓ Chest (do you feel any tightening)?
    - ✓ Breathing (is your breathing shallow, short, full, or long)?

✓ Gut (do you feel a caving in, a tension, an expansion, a hollowing, comfort, and so on)?

✓ Lower back (do you feel tension, tightening, or relaxing)?

- Ask yourself the following questions as you are in the observer mode. It is important that you ask these questions and do this exercise in the observer state after having identified and observed the physical sensations the thoughts have created in you. You must be in the state of having taken a step back, looking at the forest of yourself as an observer with the thoughts and emotions that are the subject of this exercise as only a tree within the forest of you.

  ✓ *Why did your ego feel a need to protect you or have a fear that created this storyline and emotion?*

  ✓ *What is the truth of the situation?*

- The answer to these questions above are what the ego feared most and are the reason for this part of the shadow's existence, as well as what fed and sustained it in the subconscious shadow. Once you see this egoic fear and the thoughts, beliefs, and emotions, the shadow loses its power, as well as its secrecy. You can now see the falseness of the story that gave rise to this part of your shadow, which has the effect of deflating this element of your shadow.

  ✓ *What are the positive constructive lessons and progress that you can take forward from this exercise into managing future experiences of these trigger scenarios?*

✓   *How do you constructively make peace with, accept,*
     allow to pass, or resolve this emotion and story?

Based on the steps through which you are guided in the Companion Audio and Workbook, you can now go back and reframe the circumstances that initially caused you pain. You can revisit those circumstances as an informed, enlightened adult, re-experiencing those circumstances in this new light. You will now see the circumstances very differently, where the facts are just a behavior from yourself and others in that moment, and that others' behaviors have little to do with you. This reframing of the circumstances further changes how you see the experience by eliminating and healing the egoic storylines and the beliefs that arose from it.

One of the important parts of these exercises is noting how the body is an indicator of what consciousness you are in at any given moment. You likely identified uncomfortable physical sensations when you allowed uncomfortable thoughts and emotions into your field of attention. Our physical bodies are reflectors of what energies we are emitting, receiving, and generating. Therefore, our bodies' physical sensations are going to be aligned with whatever consciousness we are in at that moment.

The discussion in this book is great for helping you intellectually to understand the origin of your beliefs, perspectives, emotions, and behaviors; however, nothing can substitute for the experiential nature that the Companion Workbook and Audio will give you. It is only with the experiences of the physical sensations combined with the mental observation and inquiry that can you recognize these states, as well as how they express themselves in you personally, not just in theory. You will notice distinct physical sensations when in each of these states as well as with each of the ego's imbalanced expressions versus the higher self in balance. The Companion Workbook and Audio will also help you as you work through these exercises, so you can experience these concepts and teachings which lead you to your own healing.

The Projection Behind Us and Them Labels.

The characteristic we attribute to *them* that we judge and condemn is the quality we don't like or fear the most that we have in ourselves. This us/them labeling is just another projection mind trick our shadows play

As you did with the first exercise you completed in this Section II of identifying the quality you abhor and condemn the most in others, now take a look at the following additional scenarios which provide more opportunities for you to identify your shadow projections:

- *The person in your family or circle of friends whom you judge the most.* This could also be the person who judged you the most as a child, or within certain environments. Just as they may have shown you the least tolerance and compassion, you now show them the least tolerance and compassion. This could have started as an egoic mirroring behavior, but now it comes from the shadow in your psyche because you will only see that person and whatever they do through that egoic colored lens with its shadow tools and behaviors. When it is a true mirroring behavior in that moment, it also reflects another example of the Newton's Cradle, *to every action there is always an opposite and equal reaction*[12], or giving what you

---

[12] This is the formal statement of Newton's Third Law of Motion. The Newton's Cradle is an illustration of all three of Newton's Laws of Motion, all

receive. Remember, however, this mirroring and the physical energy laws cannot be used as justifications or rationalizations for operating out of our egos in our reactions. Not only do these behaviors sets us up for a continuous cycle of giving and receiving what we receive and then give in return, which escalates to the sabotage of our mindsets and relationships, but these types of behaviors also often result in us taking on these behavioral identities through our absorption of their energies and stories. When you were judged as a child, you became very judgmental of yourself, and then you show judgment to others, thereafter. As previously discussed, you cannot give what you don't have, but you will give what you do have in your own consciousness. It is everyone's responsibility to heal their pains, to break these cycles in their own lives. Otherwise, we just continue to perpetuate the downward spiral of our collective consciousness in terms of how we treat one another. Our own consciousness ripples into how we treat others, the environment, our institutions, and everything in our world. This is both how and why dysfunction becomes family storylines as well as a collective community consciousness.

- *The friend of a friend who gets on your nerves the most.* This could bring forth a jealous, possessive egoic state as well.

- *The public figure for whom you have the greatest disdain or disgust.* If you have an extreme disgust or disdain for a public figure who lies, or you believe is hypocritical

---

of which reflect the laws of energy in motion. For a general overview, see here: https://en.wikipedia.org/wiki/Newton%27s_laws_of_motion

or has some other behavior or quality you judge as
bad, you may have a more extreme reaction than what
others have towards this person. In such a case, you
want to check yourself to see clear through to the
truth and what and why you may be projecting and/
or having a shadow trigger. The shadow reaction could
either be to protect yourself or to convey the impression you want others to have. Understandably, most
everyone dislikes others who lie or who are hypocritical; however, their reaction might be more of an eye
rolling and a perpetual distrust of that person, whereas
your reaction may be more extreme, aggressively expressed. Check yourself and your reactions and be
in your higher self as you look at these areas to see
where you may have an energetic resonance going on
that you're trying to hide from yourself and project.
You must always choose to want the truth more than
you want to be right, if you want healing and an end
to suffering. Remember, any projection on your part
does not mean there is no dysfunctional behavior in
the other person. The visceral reaction, however, is
telling you there is also a shadow triggering in you. It
is another ego perspective to see yourself and others as
either all good or all bad, but seeing another's imbalance and dysfunction doesn't mean that you are per-
fectly balanced, seeing the full truth of the situation,
and vice versa, so don't let your ego trap you into its
polarizations or rationalizations.

- *The person in a nearby public space to whom you have a
  visceral reaction.* Whether it is their eating habits, their
  physical size, or other quality or trait, you become
  transfixed with disgust or annoyance.

Look behind your visceral disdains to see what lies underneath in your own closet psyche. The intent is to see what you are doing to yourself, and what stories you have hidden away that are creating psychological, energetic sabotage for you in your internal relationship with yourself as well as your external relationships with others. The idea is to clean up the closets and sweep under the rugs of our own psyches, so we clean out the dirt that has built up for so many years and has weighed us down. Most of this psychological dirt represent untruths.

Let's take an example of the lying public figure: You are more than just annoyed and distrustful of people who are caught lying. You have this overwhelming disgust, disdain and judgment such as *"WHO DO THEY THINK THEY ARE??!! THEY CAN'T DO THAT!! WHAT IS WRONG WITH THEM??!! WHAT A JERK!!!"* These may be the things you say in an aggressive, over-the-top disgust. You may feel completely justified in having this extreme reaction, since lying is clearly wrong and the expectation is that people should always be truthful. If others are not truthful, they must have something to hide. Where is this extreme thought and emotion coming from in you, when others may just shrug their shoulders and say, "Yeah, I know, that person lies, I can't trust them, but what can you do? We know that we can't rely on what they say, and we will do what we can to see they do not get into an important position where their trustworthiness is important." You even may have an extreme reaction to those who don't share your extreme reaction, such as not understanding or tolerating how others can have such a modest reaction to such behavior. You will want to check the following behaviors or tendencies in yourself to see if any of these also stir a reaction from you:

- You felt betrayed when you were younger by someone close to you who was not honest with you on multiple occasions or about something important.

- You may have had significant challenges with being truthful when you were an adolescent, fearing judgment or punishment from others.

- You find that you have the perspective that trust is both earned and easily broken.

- When something goes wrong, your first instinct is that someone did something underhanded, did something wrong, or lied (including didn't tell you the whole story).

- When something goes wrong, after looking to see what others might have done wrong, and finding nothing you can point to, you fear you might have done something wrong, and thus you start to think about how you can find a rationale or justification, or how you might cover it up, hoping no one will notice the problem, that they won't notice your role in it, or you can fix it before others find out.

- When something goes wrong in your plans, you think about how you can tell others about it, so you make it look OKAY, or that it isn't bad, or that it isn't your fault. You are willing to tell half-truths and manipulate the facts in order to avoid responsibility, which you (your ego) interpret would be accepting blame and soliciting harsh judgment from others.

- When you change your mind or want to break plans with another, you think of things you can say that won't make you look bad or make them mad or feel bad, again being willing to tell half-truths and manipulate the facts to avoid responsibility, which your ego views as accepting blame, setting you up for judgment or repercussions of some kind.

- The thought of something being your fault, or having gone wrong, or not being what was expected makes your gut and jaw tense up, and you have a fear that you messed up, that others will judge you for it, that you will get in trouble, or that something will not go as desired, and you will be blamed and judged.

If the lying public figure in the example above produces an extreme disgust reaction in you, it is very likely that at least one or more of the scenarios above also hit you in the gut and made you uncomfortable when you read it. Again, this is not about shame or blame, it is about seeing what is behind it. Therefore, what is behind this shadow reaction? In all the scenarios above, it is fear. It is fear for survival and of being judged as unworthy. These are some of the most common fears that we all have in varying degrees, so they are nothing to be ashamed about. Instead, these fears are a source of suffering, so we just want to heal them, not blame them. If the lying public figure is a visceral reaction for you, you likely also have a tendency not to trust others, as well as to create stories to cover up uncomfortable situations with less than the full truth. This tendency is not because you are a bad person, but rather because your ego has a fear of judgment; it believes that survival will be difficult if people find out about what your ego believes is your own lack of worthiness or failure which will produce blame and judgment.

The truth of the circumstances is that you may have been betrayed by others lying to you or judging you harshly, so therefore you feel you need to hide imperfections. Your ego and shadow now may express aggressively to reject these judgments and project a different image that may require lying.

However, remember that these past circumstances were reflections of who others were in that moment, and not of you. As with all situations, the actor's actions are a reflection of the actor, not of anything externally, just as your actions now are a reflection of your state, and not of another's behavior.

Betrayal by another is nothing you need to take on personally. Did it cause you pain? Most likely it did; however, that pain can be more easily released when you realize that this betrayal was not a reflection of you, but rather the internal state of that person. You may still be hurt by another's betrayal, even if you don't take their behavior personally. There are some lessons in this experience, but if we take those lessons to the extreme by creating a storyline that you can't trust anyone, that is an egoic storyline of fear and mistrust that isn't a lesson, but instead a vast, overreaching, polarized, and false conclusion based on isolated circumstances. It is the same logic behind the ego saying that you are simply not worthy or valuable because one person made a choice that prioritized their egoic fears and pains over showing love towards you. Both are incorrect storylines from those circumstances. Our egos are always trying to protect us, but, unfortunately, they do so with dysfunctional thoughts that produce unproductive emotions and sabotaging behaviors. When we allow the betrayal by one person to affect our view of all others, we perpetuate and deepen the dysfunction and the colored nature of the lenses our ego put on through which we view other people as well as other circumstances thereafter. This doesn't mean we don't take a lesson from these painful experiences. For instance, it could be a lesson on asking questions, learning how to get past painful experiences, how we react, or on something else that is constructive for our growth.

The other situations listed above that likely caused a bit of a stir in you are ways you have absorbed this fear of others' judgment, as you fear for your own survival if the ego's perceived lack of its own worthiness, or wrongness, is discovered by others. This fear is both irrational and exaggerated. This fear makes the ego feel it must lie, misrepresent, hide, and cover up in order to protect you from what the ego believes would be threatening repercussions that it has falsely envisioned. In the ego's distortions, it expects a mountain of pain from others' judgment that could impact your ability to obtain something the ego values such as attention, position, affection, power, respect, and so, if the truth were discovered. In most circumstances, taking responsibility for the truth will not cause you loss of love, loss of life, loss of worth, or any other extreme repercussion. The ego's fears are almost always making mountains out of what is just a molehill. If you think about it, you can likely recall several situations in which you had fears about dealing with something, but when you finally did deal with it, it was not nearly as troubling as the ego was expecting. Afterwards you probably said to yourself, "Oh great, that wasn't bad at all." Just as the ego manipulates stories to falsely represent far-reaching truths from one moment in time, it grossly exaggerates and makes up extreme conclusions that are usually not as likely as the ego's distorted storylines fear. The ego's fears are exaggerated, unrealistic, and unlikely scenarios, based on lies and half-truths. I discuss fears later in another chapter, but for now, you should be able to see that some of your most intense, viscerally condemning thoughts have roots in your own shadow.

When our shadow hides a story about what it feels is our own weakness, and fears our not being good enough, we see everyone around us as not good enough, either. *As within, so without.* We condemn them with a projection of our own fear onto them as a false truth for them, like tossing our fearful story as a hot potato into their lap to be their problem. Projection masks how we feel about ourselves by pushing it onto others. This secrecy and denial by the ego and its shadow is powerful because of its surreptitious nature that we don't see. It is an egoic addiction that our ego tells us is normal, justified, a truth about just who we are, who others are, and how life is. Our ego conditions us to this sabotaging addiction. Just as any addiction recovery program will include an acknowledgment that your secrets keep you sick, this is equally true of our addiction to our ego's conditioning and attachment to its stories. The ego needs to be right about its storylines and fears because the ego's identity is tied to them. If those fears and stories are wrong, the ego fears having no known identity. The ego fears the unknown, especially with respect to its own identity. This is like the addiction to our persona archetypes with which we label ourselves and others discussed earlier in Section I of this book.

Below is a chart with some common shadow behaviors as well as some of the most common underlying egoic stories behind those behaviors that were shoved into and lurk within our unconscious shadow psyche.

Shadow Behavior	Shadow Storyline
Superiority, or arrogance, over others	An aggressive expression that hides, attempting to reject the ego's story about a lack in your own self-worth. Your shadow hides a belief and fear that you are a failure, or that others would judge and reject you if they really knew who you are. The more arrogant the expression (versus a moderate superiority), the more anger and resentment is infused into the judgment of others as well as a sadness in the belief and fear of one's own lack self-worth hiding deeper within the shadow.

Shadow Behavior	Shadow Storyline
Lashing out with a sense of injustice, or unfairness, about what happens to you—a belief that you don't deserve this	An aggressive expression that attempts to reject and hide the belief that you are a bad person, or you're always to blame for bad things happening. You were likely often judged and blamed as a youth.
Extreme irritation—another person or a situation is greatly irritating you	An aggressive expression that attempts to reject the underlying belief in your own lack of alignment and fitting in with your environment and social structure, thus reflecting a lack of worthiness and being valued. There is a strong sense of *us* and *them* underlying your expression, where you want to separate the out them, so you be part of us. As a result, you have no tolerance or patience for anything that is not viewed as like you or as an *us*. You may also be responding to someone who you fear could replace you in that *us* group. This is an outward projection of your shadow belief that you have shoved away and rejected about not accepting yourself because of how you believe others have not accepted you.
Extreme Defensiveness—using withdrawal and refusal to listen to a person when being attacked (extreme defensiveness as an aggressive attacking as discussed in a previous chapter)	Usually a submissive expression, where you are absorbing what your ego perceives as attacks, and in order to avoid the pain of those perceived attacks, you must suppress the pain and withdraw to avoid feeling it. Because your shadow believes you deserve to be attacked, these perceived attacks may not represent actual attacks by others but are just perceptions (with an element of projection). You disguise and try to suppress the feeling that you are to blame or are unworthy, but your ego submits to this shadow belief, and you frequently internally attack yourself for a variety of things.

Shadow Behavior	Shadow Storyline
Blame—I didn't do anything wrong; it's your fault	An aggressive expression of defensiveness that rejects the storyline of being blamed, and not good enough, harboring self-shame. This aggressive expression becomes a projection of blame that you fear about yourself in your shadow storyline onto another.
Idolizing others	A passive–aggressive expression that includes elements of both aggression and submission to an egoic and shadow storyline. • It is an aggressive expression that you are projecting onto another, rejecting your own goodness. These qualities got attached to and buried with a negative storyline, dragged into the shadow along with a fear and belief in a self-weakness or fault. • Submits to the false shadow story that you are weak, unworthy, imperfect, inferior, and don't have the qualities that you admire or idolize in others, which you have rejected in yourself through your aggressive expression of projection. • The quality you idolize in others is a gift you have shoved into your shadow and would love to see in yourself, but your egoic storylines have told you that you do not have this quality. Your ego shoved this quality into the shadow, along with a painful experience, and so it doesn't allow you to think of yourself, or otherwise show up with, this quality. When you have this over-the-top, visceral idolization of others, the quality that you admire is embodied in you, but it is lost in your shadow, and you have to go into the shadow to retrieve it.

Shadow Behavior	Shadow Storyline
Prejudice—view others as one of *them*	An aggressive expression that attempts to reject and disguise your own shadow belief in inferiority, unworthiness, and rejection. This hides an internal struggle of constantly judging yourself (*as within, so without*). This shadow belief is projected aggressively outward onto another in terms of both the judgment issued to them and the belief in their unworthiness, as you reject your unworthiness.
Jealousy—you're angry and fearful about the possibility of betrayal by another or fear that another is better than you.	An aggressive expression that rejects and fears your own disguised shadow belief of inadequacy and unworthiness. This shadow story creates an egoic need for attention and validation to counter this shadow story, which tends to move your own thoughts to betray others in order to fulfill that insatiable need for attention, affection, and validation to counter that belief in lack that your ego shoved into your shadow. This tendency (or unacted thoughts and desires) to betray others for your own validation and attention is then projected onto another in your jealousy.
Paranoia—others are out to harm you, to make you look bad or take advantage of you; you see the conspiracy no one else sees.	Aggressive expression that disguises a deep-seated belief in your own unworthiness and untrustworthiness. This shadow belief in untrustworthiness and unworthiness of yourself is aggressively projected onto others, creating distrust of others and life, which produces anxiety and possibly OCD tendencies.

Shadow Behavior	Shadow Storyline
Keeping secrets	This is typically a submissive expression of the shadow whose fear is more in the conscious mind about the details of what your secrets say about you, or how you fear others might respond to you. You fear others will judge you and/or withhold love, affection, respect, and so on, from you. The ego will engage in one or more of the following behaviors in its attempt to keep the secrets tucked away in its shadow that it doesn't want to acknowledge. • Denial (this could end up being an aggressive expression, depending how vehement the denial is and whether a return blaming behavior is exhibited in your denial.) • Intentional and deliberate deception. This could include making up other false stories to cover up, which extends the dysfunction of the ego and could disguise, or ultimately produce, pathological behavior where the ego simply makes up a story that it prefers over the truth as a general crutch, tool, or go-to behavior. • Refusal to open up to others in an attempt to hide or keep close to the best aspects of your thoughts, desires, objectives, feelings, and other things that make up your life, thoughts, emotions, and beliefs about who you are. • Sharing of information is equated to a fearful vulnerability based on dysfunctional beliefs and conditioning.

Shadow Behavior	Shadow Storyline
Harboring guilt and/or shame	This is a submissive expression of the shadow where you have submitted to the egoic storyline about something that you think is wrong or bad about you. Therefore, you think that you are bad and unworthy of love, affection, respect, consideration, equal treatment, and so on. There is a deep-seated belief in your own unworthiness as a result of a story that your ego spun about certain circumstances. Your ego has judged you to be bad, which gets shoved deep into your shadow. You have absorbed this storyline as a subconscious identity that provokes an embarrassment or a guilty or shameful feeling about yourself, especially when similar situations present themselves, thus triggering your subconscious shadow beliefs and emotions about yourself.

Recognizing Projection and Pulling it Back.

Because projection is such an immediate knee-jerk reaction that is intense, and often deeply felt within the egoic consciousness, it can be very challenging to recognize it as the ego when it presents itself, and even more challenging to stop it before it is expressed. As with trying to manage and master our emotions, being observant and hyperaware of our thoughts is the key to deflating the expression of intense, unproductive emotions, as well as to stemming the damage they can inflict on both ourselves and others. There are opportunities to halt the shadow's progression, but after each missed opportunity the challenge at the next stage will become more difficult because the force behind the shadow will get greater, more ingrained, as it progresses through each stage—like a snow ball rolling down the hill absorbing more snow. However, this book's techniques provide you with tools to increase your ability to deal with these challenges.

Chapter 8

Countering the Shadow with Compassion

You may or may not know anything about the past conditioning of anyone else with whom you interact, but you can, however, rely on the likelihood that if someone is unkind to others, they are also unkind to themselves in their own thoughts, fearing that they may themselves embody a lack and/or weakness. You don't need to know the details of their stories or their historical facts to see that the reasons people are unkind to others is out of their own fear. The reasons people are unkind or judgmental is because they were treated with unkindness and judgment in their earlier years that created their egoic storylines and shadows. It is a cycle of judgment and fear.

You don't want to make assumptions or leap to conclusions about the details of others' background or intentions, however. That is going too far—you don't know, and can't know, those details. A balanced mindset is simply to view them with compassion because their own pain is reflected through egoic and shadow behaviors and unkindness based on the principle of *as within, so without.* You also do not need to put someone in a box in order to understand who *you* are. You are not defined by others or their behavior. Similarly, others are not defined by who you are, or are not, or by your thoughts, behavior, or even who you think others are. Because we never truly know the experiences and pains of others, we just must remember that how they treat others is not a reflection of you or anyone or anything on the outside. How everyone behaves is a reflection of what is going on with that person on the inside. Therefore, how you've been treated by others, was never about you. Similarly, how you treat others is not about them, either.

The fact that others' treatment of you isn't about you can be freeing. When you apply that to the specific circumstances of what occurred in your life that caused you pain, you start seeing the distinction between the facts of the behavior from the egoic commentary about what that behavior *meant* about who you are, or are not, and who they are, and are not. *The ego's commentary and interpretations of the facts of any circumstance is often an illusory storyline.* So much of popular enlightenment culture today is about trying to find the meaning of things. Whenever we try to find a meaning to others' behavior beyond observable facts of what was done or said, that is often just the ego looking for a storyline to justify, rationalize, compartmentalize, and label things, so the ego has comfort in thinking that it can know and understand as much as possible. The ego feels it needs to know, to be right, and to understand in order to feel comfort that it is in control. That is an egoic drive that will always trip us up by creating false storylines just to make the ego feel it is in control by understanding its environment fully. Resist that urge. That level of knowledge about others is not important, and it is not the marker of whether you are, in fact, in control of your life, or whether you can see the truths of life.

It is important at this point to help you appreciate the distinction between the ego's characterizing commentary of presumed meaning of a particular circumstance from the *as within, so without* universal law. The former we cannot rely upon as fact, but the latter we can. You may ask what the difference is between drawing a conclusion that someone who treats others unkindly is a mean-spirited person who can't be trusted, and drawing a conclusion that someone who treats others unkindly is being unkind to themselves in their own thoughts and beliefs. Why is the former an overreaching egoic characterization that cannot be considered a truth and the latter a universal truth?

First, let's look at a few physical laws that operate in our world. If you throw an object into the air, that object will return to the ground. Why? Because of the physical law of gravity that underlies our physical existence. If you stick your hand in an open flame, it will burn your flesh. The longer you keep your hand in the flame, the more severe the burn. There is a physical causal relationship between the two acts that are defined by the nature of those objects as well as how their physical attributes interact. The interaction result does not change depending upon what color, shape, or weight of the object thrown up in the air or upon what color, age, or gender of the hand that we place in the fire.

Just as these physical cause-effect responses are based upon the physical attributes of the very nature of these objects, the cause-effect relationship of *as within, so without* is a natural law of the human psyche. There are varying degrees in the effects; however, the underlying relationship of *as within, so without* will be the same. Being repeatedly treated with unkindness by important life figures will cause an underlying fear about oneself and others in a deep-rooted belief of not being worthy in some way. An impressionable youth being judged or treated unkindly by someone they trust and rely upon creates an impression in that youth that makes them fear that they deserved that treatment or are what others tell them they are in unworthiness. Different youth will absorb this judgment and unkindness in varying degrees and reactions as well as varying resulting behavior expressions (aggressive, submissive, or balanced) depending on their own mindset and basic personality, but they are not likely to escape unscathed. This is akin to different hands being burned to varying degrees when placed in a flame based on how close to the flame they are placed, and how long.

The degree to which anyone will create this deep-rooted egoic belief in their own lack can vary based upon the degree of treatment received, the constitution of their own ego, and how awake and active their higher self is to counter the ego's stories. Some individuals will absorb this storyline at the deepest levels, dramatically impacting their perceived identity. Others will inherently believe more in themselves, while still harboring some degree of egoic fear of unworthiness. You can see this variability as how far a nail will go into a wooden board, depending upon on the thickness of the nail, the thickness of wooden board, how big or heavy the hammer is, and how much force is used with that hammer. Regardless of these variables, there will be a mark on that board and that nail, just like how a hand in a flame will produce some level of burning because of the physical cause-effect relationship of the acts on those objects.

Since it is human nature to want to be loved and valued, the ego will react to unkind treatment in a balanced, aggressive, or submissive manner. Given the lack of sophistication and learned coping skills of children, the likelihood is very low that the child will recognize such treatment as not being personal to them, so they are unlikely to withstand that treatment with a balanced reaction. This leaves either an aggressive or submissive reaction as the usual natural result of such treatment on a child. If the grown child reacts with an aggressive expression, they will try to reject this unworthiness fear and belief by trying to prove to themselves and show others their worthiness. That judged person will have in their head, whether consciously or unconsciously in the shadow, some amount of fear and belief that they may not be worthy in some way. Therefore, that belief in unworthiness is what they will often have in their own consciousness to give others. This will result in unkind judgment to both self and others.

One of the several ways to aggressively express this fear and belief of unworthiness is through judging others in unkind ways, so they feel above others by putting others down to reject their own storyline of unworthiness. That illustrates three aspects of an egoic dynamic: (1) the ego only believes in polarized positions, so they can't see how they can be worthy unless they are better than another; (2) they give what they receive; and (3) they try aggressively to reject that story by instead trying to show their worth in the only way the ego knows how—raising themselves up at the expense of others— by "winning." These are the ripple effects of being judged as a child and are as natural and automatic in egoic reaction as getting our skin burned when we put our hand in a flame.

Conversely, let's look at characterizations that may be true in some cases, but not in others, and how we can make overreaching conclusions based on limited circumstances. A very simple example might be the weather, and how it appears on the same date in multiple years. One year, in your city, it snows on the date of April 1 after a week of being cold. The next year it also snows on April 1, even though the previous day was warmer. After a couple of similar experiences, you now seem to recall that it often snowed on April 1. Now that date sticks in your mind as a day of crazy snow weather. Therefore, you draw the conclusion that it snows on April 1 in your city. Your egoic mind creates the conditioned conclusion that it always snows on April 1, regardless of what the weather did the few days before that date. Now, you've been conditioned to believe that April 1 represents a cold, snowy, wintery day.

Thereafter, when the last week of March rolls around, you expect to see a cold, snowy day on the first day of April. Since you have characterized that day as cold, snowy, and likely to disrupt any plans you might make, you avoid making any that involve being outside or traveling. This is a characterization that you have made about the nature of that day, thinking it will always be that way because of some number of experiences. Instead of seeing those snow occurrences as simply something that occurred based on other non-related weather patterns, you see these snowy occurrences as an inherent characteristic of that date in your area.

Even though there are examples of a day, person, or experience being different than our expectations, your ego may push memories of a different occurrence out of your mind when it has decided upon a conclusion it wants to be true. Our egos draw overreaching conclusions based on a few occurrences that now drive how we respond to that day, person, or circumstance, not allowing them to show up as anything different from our ego's expectation. While we know that we can check the scientific weather report for predicting the weather in the short-run, this does not change the example of how we often see circumstantial occurrences as characteristic of inherent, larger truths. I use this weather example to show how easy it is for our ego that wants to believe it knows and has things under its control to make leaps in judgments of *fact*, which we can clearly see are not actual truths by their nature.

This is akin to the characterization of labeling someone as being unkind by their very nature who was unkind in one or more circumstances, and now that is what you always expect to see. Unkindness is not someone's nature; however, there are factors that can cause someone to adopt unkind expressions, such as certain weather patterns can produce cold, snowy results in multiple circumstances. Should those weather patterns or internal states of being change, we could see different effects in the weather, just as we could see different behaviors from a person.

When you attempt to define someone by their nature, especially when it is not aligned with the higher self qualities, you will almost always be looking at that person through the ego's lens of overreaching characterizations. If, instead, you look at others' acts and words as indicative of their state of being in that moment, which is not about defining their nature, but rather trying to see the causal connection of their own egoic approach to their experiences in their behavior, you may be looking more at a truth. I just caution you against attempting to identify the details of their experiences unless you were there to observe them. For example, to think "his mother must have regularly hit him" is still a guess of the details of that person's experiences, and is coming from your ego's creative storytelling with its need to know and believe that it can know the details and *truths*. Thinking that "he was likely treated with some degree of unkindness" is more of the truth of the situation because it recognizes causal relationships that are laws of our egoic human psyche, but does not insert any detail as fact that you do not, and cannot, know. You cannot know the details of another's experience, and you cannot accurately characterize the nature of someone unless you are characterizing a general set of characteristics that are part of everyone's higher self. Our higher self is who we truly are and is defined by the qualities of the higher self which are listed in Section I of this book. We are not, and cannot be, defined by the ego or its negative, dysfunctional expressions. We are not our ego; it is rather only our default programming that can be balanced when we heal and are able to see through the ego's illusions. However, as previously mentioned, we must have our higher self in the driver seat of our consciousness to do this.

Chapter 9

Your Personal Egoic Stories and Conditioning

Now that we have covered the majority of the egoic topics more generally, and the most sabotaging of your personal shadow expressions, it is time to dive into your broader personal egoic expressions. In this section you will be doing a lot of work on your own personal storylines with which you have been suffering. This is where your egoic self and your higher self will come face–to–face at the deepest, most integrated levels of how you have operated and viewed life to date. This process is nothing to fear but is rather something to look forward to in its liberation. Your ego, however, may not be thrilled about being told it was not seeing truths in its perspectives and stories about who you are, who others are, and how life is. It would be valuable to return to the very first Exercise 1 in Section II, and restate that intention several times before proceeding in this Section. Through your work in this Section, you will un-cover many of the most harmful illusions under which you've been operating, along with your worst sabotaging beliefs and behaviors. It will be liberating!

The Exercises in Section II, Exercise 2 highlighted your shadow triggers, and this chapter will highlight your various egoic conditioning and storylines, some of which may have surfaced in addressing your shadow triggers in Exercise 2 of Section II. Please turn to Section II, Exercise 4 in the *Companion Workbook* and answer letters, a through c, of the first 17 questions. This may take an hour or more to complete, and that is okay. Take the time to do this. Please do not go back, ponder, or rethink your answers. Each answer should be the first thing that comes to your mind. You may ask what you will do with these answers. You will be using your answers in future exercises. You may find that your answers to some of these questions stare you in the face on many days. In most all the questions, it is likely that you will feel uncomfortable as you read the questions and answer them. There is good reason for this, so push forward with the intention of Section II, Exercise 1 of intending to see the truth, and push through this discomfort with your courage and strength. You will be rewarded greatly for this work through liberation from the pain and discomfort of these stories by seeing the truths. These questions will help you get it all out on the table for you to see and inspect. This is the only way to heal the pain and suffering of the ego's stories. Remember, as always, awareness heals and can deflate the fears and other emotions that arise when you think of these things. The truth truly will set you free.

The questions in this Section II, Exercise 4 are pulling out your ego's most painful stories that you've told yourself and believed about yourself, others, and life. Some of these stories may be shoved into your shadow, producing sabotaging behaviors, in addition to the sabotaging and painful thoughts and beliefs. These questions will help you identify your fears, shames, blames, beliefs in lack about yourself and life, distrusts, resentments and many other negative aspects of your belief systems. We're going to get at the origin of them in this Section, see what is behind them, where they came from, and root them out as best we can with truths, so that they are no longer weeds growing in your mental garden. This awareness of truth will heal. You may still feel some degree of pain as you open these wounds and inspect them, but it is the lies that produces the suffering, sabotage, and misery. The truth heals.

One thing I will repeat over and over in this Section is that our source of suffering and misery comes from our attachment to our own expectations. In many cases, our own expectations are derived from the expectations that others had of us, which we then adopted for ourselves. This is nothing more than others' shadow and egoic projections that they projected onto us, and which we then took on as our own and integrated into our own storyline film strip. When we are young, impressionable or have a submissive egoic tendency, we buy into others' projections onto us, and then we absorb them as our own. This is one of the ways in which family and societal dysfunction gets perpetuated through each subsequent generation. These ideals of who and what we are *supposed* to be, based on the ego's illusions of *should's*, get projected onto us. We then project them onto others. When we, or others, don't live up to those ideals, we elicit emotions of shame and guilt from our own thoughts of *failed* performance in relation to our own expectations by using the ego's go-to tool of judgment.

The ego's ideals of who we are supposed to be, or who we want to be, will nearly always involve false images of ourselves, stemming from our own egoic sense of needing to be better than others in some way. This is the ego's typical need for separation and to out-race others to the limited resources of respect, rewards, affirmation, affection, and so on. As we know now, the ego does not believe in win/win. It believes in only win/lose, and if you are raised up, that must mean another has been lowered because another is not receiving the same rewards, affirmation, or recognition that you are receiving. Therefore, another is viewed as less or has less. The opposite will be perceived by the ego that, if another receives the rewards and affirmation, you must be, therefore, *lowered*. The ego is on a constant seesaw. The ego's distorted perspective of zero-sum game is based on illusions and fears. Our left hand is not less than our right foot because the hand does not get to walk on the earth, and our right foot is not less than our left hand because the hand gets to wave in the air as the body walks. The ego does not see the same value in different roles because the ego cannot see the whole—it cannot see the forest. The ego sees only itself and how everything relates to and around it, creating its ideals and images in a self-centric vacuum. In seeing through the illusions of the ego's expectations and ideals, we will be looking at the forest and the truths of the whole. As we look at truths and the whole, we recognize that there are different trees of different heights and different stages of growth. A two–year–old sapling is not less than a twenty–year–old tree, nor is a maple better or worse than an oak—they are just different, possibly at different stages of natural growth, and have different roles within the forest.

Through these exercises, we will be looking at your expectations, as well as both why and how they are based on illusions and false ideals of the ego. This requires that we go into the roots of these expectations and ideals, digging into our past experiences. It is our past experiences from which the ego created these false ideals that are at the roots of our illusions and false beliefs. We must dig out the roots of these thought and belief weeds that we continue to water, fertilize, and give them life by bringing them into our present-day thoughts every day. The present-day expectations that we created from these past experiences are part of our conditioning that we created in our past and continue to replant in our present. We cannot just bury or sprinkle rose scent on them. We must stare them in the face, see on what they are based, and see how our interpretations of those past experiences are false foundations. Only then can we release those thought in a healing way that removes them from our sabotaging thoughts, beliefs, and behaviors by rebuilding a new foundation based on truths.

It is now time to dig into the roots of your egoic storylines. Please access the *Companion Audio for Section II, Exercise 5*. In this Audio, you will be asked to take a question from Section II, Exercise 4 to focus on as you complete this Exercise 5. It would be helpful for you to go through this Audio for each of the questions you answered in Section II, Exercise 4. This would be the most effective way to deal with each of the storylines that each of the questions in Exercise 1 reflects. Each of the storylines represented by these questions includes a belief about yourself, in addition to a belief about others or life. Part of your identity to which you cling will be included in a storyline about others and life. If, for example, you believe that others or life cannot be trusted, embedded within that belief is also the belief that you are not trustworthy yourself (*as within, so without*), as well as worry about being a victim of, and vulnerable to, others' untrustworthiness. As a result, your ego will believe it must be wary of relying on others, and therefore, you must fend for and protect yourself. This sets you up for the belief that you must be a lone ranger, never being able to rely on others, producing controlling tendencies in your own behavior. The aggressively imbalanced egoic expression will reject the story that you are a victim, so then you reject the assistance or involvement of others, as well as possibly projecting onto them a judgment that their efforts are not good enough. If you express submissively, you will likely believe and behave as if you are the victim who is regularly victimized by others' actions or inactions, fearful of trusting others. All of the storylines emanating from these questions reflect untruths and illusions built on the overreaching, false assumptions of the ego and reflect the resulting conditioned lenses your ego has put into your eyes.

Your ego has created the *you* identity via its interpretations, ideals, stories, and belief systems of its thought-stream, many of which will be revealed in your answers in Section II, Exercise 4. They reflect the ego's colored lens. Until you can see that these thoughts and beliefs are just the ego's colored lenses, they will continue to shape your ongoing experiences and beliefs. These storied lenses will continue to direct your thoughts, perspectives, and behaviors because your ego will direct you to continue to see all circumstances through those same lenses. This is how they become self-perpetuating and self-fulfilling. Our own egos—our illusory selves—continue to create the film strip that gets projected onto our screen of viewed experiences repeatedly.

When you can see these stories as just that—illusory stories of your ego—you can then make an informed choice. As the observer of your own stories and lenses, you can choose whether you accept or reject those stories. This is when you can start to lay down those stories, take the colored lenses out of your eyes, and start to see truths of your circumstances instead of the characterizations, labels, misinterpretations, assumptions, leaps of judgments, and illusions that the ego interprets in fear and lack that it then needs to validate so that it can be *right*.

As you work through this Section II, Exercise 5, for each question in Exercise 4, you will be guided to the truths of the original circumstances from which the ego created your storylines. You can record them in the Companion Workbook for Exercise 5 of Section II. As you unwind these egoic storylines and conditioning, you will want to see those circumstances for what they actually were. To do this, you will have to look at those circumstances with a new perspective of compassionate detachment. The detachment here is not suppression or avoidance, but rather reflects the release of the attachments of the ego where everything must revolve around it, along with the ego's attachment to a particular outcome or to a particular story so that it can be *right*. The compassion in a compassionate detachment perspective is where our heart and our higher self are in the lead, viewing the circumstances, seeing what was really occurring in that moment with the hurts of others in the circumstances. When we are looking at circumstances with compassionate detachment, we remember that others' actions aren't personal to us, knowing that *hurt people, hurt people*.

Once you have been able to see some of the truths and illusions from your Section II, Exercise 4 storylines, you will want to become more aware of how you have reacted, and what egoic tools you use with these storylines. This awareness is how you can begin to recognize when and how these storylines surface. This awareness empowers you to make different choices in your thoughts, behaviors, and belief systems. To explore further how you personally react to your egoic storylines, please answer the questions in the *Companion Workbook* for *Section II, Exercise 6*. You may notice that, in your stories and resulting egoic behavioral tools, there are themes such as separation from others, fear, and a sense of lack. These are the defining characteristics and belief systems of the ego. This is the point at which you are hopefully questioning everything you think you know. The belief systems that emanate from the mind are from the ego. Every time you think you know *why* something happened, you want to question that thought and get comfortable with not knowing. It is the ego that believes it must know in order to feel comfortable and in control. That is not who you are. You are the observer and experiencer of all that life brings you, and you cannot know all the *why's*. Your ego will not be comfortable with not knowing the *why's* and meaning of things. Get comfortable with not knowing. This is one of the things you must surrender to have self-mastery. These egoicly-perceived *knowings* are illusions anyway. Your ego will likely try to convince you with fear or other ideas about what it must mean if you don't know the why's or meanings. Get into your heart-centered higher self, and choose to refocus away from the ego's fears and ideals of what *should* be.

Being in your higher self and navigating rough waters with calmness, skill, wisdom, courage, and the other qualities of the higher self is what will get you through rough waters. Accepting life and others as they are is not something that the ego can deal with well, but it is the starting point for the higher self. The higher self takes others and life as they present, and then makes choices about how to navigate what is presented with the higher-self qualities, none of which include judgment, fear, or attachment.

Chapter 10

Getting to Know Your Higher Self

Remember that, in all of this, you are the boss of you, and you have the power to control your mind. You must exert that control and mastery, and that takes conscious awareness and effort to move away from the default of the ego. As with all things discussed in this book, this mastery is about balance. Controlling the thoughts in your mind does not mean suppressing uncomfortable thoughts and emotions as if they don't exist. That just creates more shadow. Instead, the mastery and control over our own thoughts and emotions is about being aware of them, seeing where they are coming from, seeing the truth instead of the storylines, and choosing to focus on healing the thoughts instead of continuing to replay and live in them. We acknowledge them and from where they came, but do not stay focused on them. Mastery means nothing comes into your mind without your awareness. Mastery requires conscious choice as to whether you focus on and give repeated attention to whatever comes in, or you choose differently.

This process of learning mastery will allow you to start relating *to* these thoughts and emotions instead of *from* them. When you are relating from them, it will seem as if you are wrapped up into them as part of your identity and as defining your experience of that moment. You can feel consumed by, and with, them. Observing and seeing them with awareness immediately moves you out of being wrapped up in them. Taking a step back from these thoughts and emotions as if you can see them in the observer state allows you to see what is happening within your mental and emotional bodies. It is only from this position of awareness that you can make true choices and achieve self-mastery. This is the state of your true self—your higher self.

It is only from this higher-self awareness state that you can see the untruths in the ego's thought-stream, which is what triggers the emotions. Therefore, it is only from this higher-shelf state that you can lessen the strength and grip of both the thoughts and the elicited emotions. The exercises in the Companion Audio and Workbook will guide you through getting into and BEing in your higher self. Some additional tips for shifting into your higher self include the following:

- Take a moment to feel whatever attachment you have emotionally and energetically. Notice it as an observer.
  - ✓ Where do you feel physical sensations in your body? Stomach, jaw, gut, heart, head, shoulders, and back?
  - ✓ What does it feel like? Tight, tense, pulsating, empty, or withdrawing?
  - ✓ Be with the attachment to explore it with curiosity, interest, compassion, and hearing what it has to say, as you relate to it like a parent to a child.

- Notice the attachment, but don't be upset about it or judge it. Recognize that the thought or emotion is part of being human and having energies run through you. You can choose to neither continue to focus on it nor judge or condemn it or yourself for having the attachment. This is the balanced position of being a neutral observer. The refocusing and release loosens its grip without creating a wound or a suppressed shadow element.

  ✓ Recognizing that you have the power to control where your attention goes.

  ✓ Refocusing away from attachments allows you to step into your power to choose, and not to be controlled by them.

- Broaden your awareness to whatever else is present in addition to the thoughts and emotions, such as, what is in your environment, and notice that:

  ✓ Is the sun shining?

  ✓ What sensations and sounds are in your environment?

    ➢ These refocusing efforts are not designed to suppress uncomfortable thoughts and emotions, but rather to help you break the grip of attachments that may be consuming your thoughts and emotion. You must take a step back from them in order to break their grip over you.

- Notice what is present on a more subtle aspect. This subtle aspect is where the true self lives.

✓ What feelings do you have as you are refocusing on something beautiful in your environment, such as the sun, flowers, pleasing scenes, and so on? Love, peace, relaxation, awe, or a sense of beauty? Can you identify with those constructive feeling states and experience them right now? Identify what that feels like in the body.

This awareness is what will facilitate your healing and transition into your higher self with a greater sense of acceptance, joy, self-mastery, allowance, and peace. When you can observe uncomfortable thoughts and emotions instead of being in the midst of them, you have greater control over your choices and responses. You can refocus on more productive, functional directions. When you can give your attention and focus more to the sensations and feelings associated with the higher self, such as love, truth, compassion, peace, courage, and so on, you will align yourself more with these qualities and with your higher self, instead of with your egoic thoughts and storylines that elicit the heightened and imbalanced use of emotions. This continued awareness and focus on the more subtle feelings of the higher self facilitates your ability to choose and put your higher self in the driver seat more often.

We are often faced with challenging moments in life, and those are when it is most important to respond from our best and highest self. If we are being triggered to be in our egos, it can produce suffering through those challenges. It can also be exceedingly difficult to move from our ego into our higher self in those challenging moments, unless we have a technique to make this shift quickly and easily. From some of the earlier guided exercises, you have experienced the difference between responding from your higher self and reacting from your ego. You will want a shortcut exercise that you can turn to in these moments, which you can find in the *Companion Audio for Section II, Exercise 7*. This exercise will guide you through to getting intimately in touch with your higher self and learn the shortcut image or phrase that most resonates with your own higher self. This will be very personal and unique for each person. You can start using this shortcut or image immediately.

As you become more intimate and familiar with your higher self, and you see how BEing in your higher-self consciousness affects your thoughts, emotions, feelings, words, and behaviors, you will become increasingly adept at moving in between your egoic state and your higher-self state. When you are in the consciousness of your higher self and state of BEing, you will embody the qualities of the higher self that are listed earlier in this book. Familiarize yourself with those qualities, and notice when you embody them. Notice, also, how it feels physically in the body when you are acting from that higher-self state. Below is a partial list of perspective changes you will likely start noticing about yourself when you are in your higher self:

- You see life as it is, and accept it as it is, without regret or lamenting.

- You are willing to investigate, heal, and release limiting beliefs, negativity, and untruths in your thoughts and beliefs. You are more willing to engage in self-analysis and discovery.

- You begin to master controlling your emotions with less of the negative, knee-jerk, hateful, blaming, and angry thoughts and emotions.

✓ When such a negative thought enters your head, you instead observe it with curiosity and dispassion, looking at the underlying truth of the facts of the circumstances. You begin to identify untruths and egoic fears, allow the thoughts to move on through you, and allow the emotions to fade without indulging them.

- You see life as an adventure.
- You seek the truth, whatever the truth is, even if it is not what you want to believe. This is wanting the truth more than you want to be *right*.
    ✓ This requires courage, fearlessness, and surrendering of attachments.

- You welcome challenges for the growth opportunities they represent. This results in the following:
    ✓ BEing courageous through having to face your fears
    ✓ BEing patient and persevering through being tried
    ✓ BEing responsible through being given responsibilities, often times initially being irresponsible before learning and growing into responsibility
    ✓ BEing compassionate through experiencing lack of compassion from others
    ✓ Becoming able to control anger by being angered
    ✓ Discovering strength because it is demanded through challenges and the process of self-mastery

✓   Discovering endurance by being tested and having to persevere

✓   Discovering wisdom by first being foolish, and then becoming relied upon to reason through circumstances

✓   Discovering understanding by first misunderstanding and being misunderstood by others.

Your attitude about a challenge determines your experience of it and your ability to receive the gift, lesson and growth opportunity that the challenge represents. Resisting it will make it seem more difficult. Your attitudes are grounded in your beliefs. *Therefore, your beliefs determine your experiences of life.* The more attuned you are to the awareness of your thoughts (instead of being caught up in thinking the thoughts), the more attuned you will be to the subtle feelings of the joy of just BEing. When you are attuned to an awareness and the subtleties of your BEing, this is when the higher self will be more available to you, along with its tools and characteristics. This internal joy is not the same as the elation or exaltation of emotions, which will pass as circumstances pass. This internal joy of the higher self is the happiness of the heart, which is an ever-present joy that you must tune into to notice it—this is a state of BE-ing.

When you are in your higher self, you realize and appreciate that difficulties, challenges, and triggers are actually your friend because they stretch you, challenge you, and force you to develop your inner resources of awareness, detachment, strength, wisdom, patience, and all of the other qualities of the higher self. As a result – and only through these challenges – you become stronger, wiser, more patient, more responsible, more resilient, and you begin to embody all of these qualities of your higher self more regularly. In order to receive this growth, strength, courage, and more, you must be in your higher-self consciousness to be able to receive the blessings from the challenges. You will, then, start seeing the egoic mindset for what it is, and your choices will become increasingly easier as you see through the ego's illusions and conditioning. You start seeing the edges of your ego's colored lenses, and your experiences become more filled with joy, gratitude, and growth.

Chapter 11

Recognizing the Egoic Consciousness and Its Experiences

Moving into an observer state with your egoic thoughts offers an immediate awareness of what is happening in both your mind and body due to the ego running with unfettered autonomy. This awareness is key, and is the first step to develop your self-mastery in order to break out of the ego's grip and power. In addition to having something external to break you out of the grip of your egoic thought-stream, it is also helpful to have an internal intellectual awareness trigger to break your attachments.

What follows are some examples that indicate you are in an egoic mindset.

The Egoic Consciousness and its Expressions

One of the most obvious indicators of an egoic consciousness and mindset is any thought that has "I," me," "my," or "mine" in it. These are the core indicators of the ego because the ego is about self-identity. The identities of the self are created by the ego, and the ego believes it is responsible to protect and project those identities outward to define who you are. Being in the ego isn't necessarily a bad thing if we use our ego constructively. The constructive use of our ego involves ensuring that we are standing up for ourselves as worthy individuals against discrimination, bias, oppression, and similar attempts to dismiss or take advantage of us. Where we want to be careful is how we respond or react to those oppressive circumstances. We want to be sure that we respond with a balanced and integrated ego with our higher self, and not with the reactive tools of the ego. If we allow our ego to go rogue, its negative, judgmental thoughts will illicit corresponding emotions that get used destructively in an imbalanced reactionary expression of aggression or submission using the ego's sabotaging tools. The ego's constructive value is limited. Therefore, we want to appreciate the ego for what it can help us with, but make sure it stays contained and doesn't operate independently of our higher self.

Examples of where the ego often goes beyond its scope includes the various opinions, subjective theories, and conclusions it makes based on limited circumstances and biased conditioning. The ego will always believe its subjective opinions, and so will label them in our thought-streams as conclusions. The snowy weather example earlier in this book is an example of this subjective and false leap to conclusions based on limited circumstances. This is what may be the most challenging to see and distinguish in our mind. Where is the distinction of our intellectual activity assessing truthful cause-effect apart from our egoic motor-mind conditioned thought stream activity? The more you go through the exercises of observer inquiry with the intention of seeing the truth more than wanting to be right, it will get easier to see this distinction and where the edge of your egoic lenses live. Following are some typical egoic mindsets to get you started with your observer inquiry process:

- Opinions
- Thinking that you know:
  - ✓ What others think
  - ✓ What others feel
  - ✓ What you or others *should* do
  - ✓ What is *wrong* with the world or others
  - ✓ What will happen tomorrow, or what tomorrow will be like
  - ✓ What an experience will be or feel like
- Suppositions or conclusions about why something happened, or why someone did or said what they did, or what it means about you, them, or life.

Anytime you make a statement that portends to know something that is included in the list of what the ego wants and thinks it knows, that is a sign of the ego's desire to know and to be right more than it wants the truth. These statements are nothing more than subjective opinion, however, even if there is a single instance or partial truth being reflected. Opinions are just examples of the "I think" or "I believe" thoughts in the motor mind created by the ego and its conditioned beliefs and storylines. They usually represent overreaching, and overarching conclusions based on a relatively small number of circumstances with the ego's characterization of those circumstances. I want to distinguish between opinions and preferences here. Opinions come from the ego, but preferences—when not predicated on thoughts, labels, characterizations, conclusions, fears, and conditioning—are more about alignment with our nature and our physical senses. For example, a preference is "I prefer to be outside rather than inside most of the time, even on a hot day." Whereas an opinion is more of a conclusion, or definitive statement, about the nature of something outside us, such as "Being outside on a hot day is annoying and a bad way to spend a day." The former expresses a personal preference, while the latter makes a false conclusion and label of that activity for all. These are very simplified examples of the differences between both preferences and opinions.

This distinction can get murky, however, when our opinions, preferences, and perceived *facts* get more sophisticated and start leaning on partial truths to draw larger conclusions. The ego will take a small set of circumstances that may (or may not) represent truths in a moment and turn them into being foregone truths for all future circumstances. The ego can go off the rails when it often misinterprets circumstances through its tinted, conditioned lens. Nearly every shadow-triggered behavior is such an example of the ego going off the rails in a misinterpretation of the truth of a moment. It is helpful to remind you here of the earlier example of the daughter's interpretation of her being of lesser value, which she interpreted to be validated by the mother's soliciting of the brother's preferred dinner choice. The daughter misinterpreted a present circumstance in order to validate the ego's false storyline of her lesser value to the mother. Both her interpretation of that moment's events and the larger conclusions were incorrect. This is the ego and shadow at work.

You may ask, "How do I know what is truth versus just opinion or part of my ego's storyline? Here is the uncomfortable part: Being able to discern the truth requires several heavy doses of *surrender*. In order to see the truth, you must surrender your belief that you already know the answer. The ego hates the concept of surrender because it considers that to be both a weakness and vulnerability that poses risks to the ego. The ego always wants to be in a position of knowing because that is far more comfortable and secure. *Knowing* is also an indication to the ego of being worthy with its knowledge and understanding. As a result, the ego will rarely be able to perceive truths unless it is fully integrated into and with the consciousness of the higher self, with the higher self in the driver seat. The ego, when left on its own, sees only through its colored, conditioned lenses, which will always distort the reality of the circumstances.

The ego will always want to be right more than it wants the truth, so you can never trust the ego's perspective. Instead, you must access your higher self in order to discern and see truths. It is only your higher self that would rather see the truth than be *right*. The higher self does not hold judgments or opinions about things, people, or situations because the higher self accepts what is and goes with the flow, allowing all to be as it is in that moment. Since the higher self doesn't have an investment in, or attachment to, a particular agenda, it can see things, people, and situations as they are without coloring, characterizing, labeling, blaming, or shaming. In order to allow your higher self to be at the forefront and be the driver of your state of being to see truths, here are some of the things you must be willing to *surrender*:

- Your desire for others to be different
- Your desire for others to believe differently
- Your judgment of others because they are different or think differently
- Your attachment to a particular outcome or result
- Your attachment to others being *wrong*

- Your attachment to yourself or others you label as part of *us* being *right*
- Your desire for, or attachment to, any characterization or label of yourself
- Your desire for or attachment to any characterization or label of others
- Your attachment to your beliefs about yourself
- Your attachment to your beliefs about others
- Your attachment to your beliefs that you know anything about others or their beliefs, perspectives, thoughts or how they will respond or act
- Your attachment to your beliefs that you know anything about the future
- Your attachment to your beliefs that you know how you will respond or react to anyone or anything in the future

In order to see truths for what they are, you must suspend all opinions, beliefs, and characterizations to see what *IS* instead of what you WANT, THINK, or BELIEVE. In essence, you must surrender your ego. The ego's desires, thoughts, and beliefs will always get in the way and color truths as it looks through its colored lenses. You will always see the sky as green when looking through your ego's yellow lenses while another will always see the sky as purple as it looks through its red colored lenses. If we cannot release and surrender our ego in favor of our higher self, we will never allow ourselves, others, or life to show up as how they are in truths. This book is about how to surrender the ego, master it, and remove those colored lenses so that we can see truths and allow our higher selves to be in the lead to see and experience the truths of the blue sky.

Remembering who we are is about allowing our higher self to drive our perspectives, its actions, and behaviors from its place of clarity, discernment and truth.

Not everyone is ready to surrender their ego. Over the course of presenting this curriculum live to participants, I have watched the battle take place in some people. It is natural that we all will ebb and flow in between our ego and our higher self, but some people's egos are still in a control stronghold over their consciousness. I've observed several people in active battle mode between their higher selves and ego fighting for the driver seat. I watched some people's higher-self drive them to attend one or more sessions, only to see their ego suddenly take over as if they were a different person when their ego was threatened by some of the triggering that came up in the class for them. I watched one girl continue to fight for her higher self to be in the lead and stay in the curriculum as her ego continued to beat her down and tell her all the reasons why she couldn't, shouldn't, or didn't want to stay with it. I could see this dynamic happening in her, and all I could do is stand there with my hand out asking to be allowed to help her. She would reach out her hand figuratively to take mine when she allowed her higher self to surface, but she couldn't let go of the other hand gripped by her egoic hold like a Stockholm Syndrome sufferer. She even recognized some of this herself. She ended up deciding to go the route that her ego told her was easiest and most comfortable. I retain hope that she will make a different choice next time. Fortunately, most others walked through the surrender points to achieving great progress in both their healing and mastery.

This ego and shadow mastery will take both courage and the strength of the higher self to override our standard ego operating system that does not want to be overridden or placed in the back seat. All heroes and masters are forged from the fire of courage. This journey of learning to understand and master the ego, its shadow, and remembering who you are is no different. At the end of this journey, if you stay true to the task with the intention and desire for truth more than validation, you will be your own hero and master. Once you go through this process, you cannot un-see certain truths about who you truly are. From there, it is a matter of focusing on the light at the end of the tunnel and continuing the work. Each time the ego tries to take you back to the old, you want to refocus your intentions on the truth, healing, and liberation. Know that you may lose focus from time to time, so don't beat yourself up when it happens. Remember that you're moving up the frequency dial, and you will still ebb and flow and hear the noise of the neighboring lower frequencies. You will also hear higher frequencies and see the light on the higher side of your dial, too. Just renew your dedication to the truth and to your higher self, and then you will continue your way up the frequency dial to mastery.

Breaking the Egoic Consciousness.

Breaking the egoic consciousness is the first step in being able to recognize the ego's process in yourself. Recognition and awareness is the first step, and it is a powerful one. That awareness is a critical eye-opener. You cannot achieve mastery through an intellectual exercise alone. You must participate in the experiential nature of these exercises to have this awareness of how the ego reveals itself in you on a personal level. Only with this personal awareness will you have the recognition of when you are faced with the choice of continuing in an egoic consciousness, or shifting into the higher-self state. It is this awareness that gives you the choice. Without that specific awareness of your particular egoic expression, you cannot know when that choice opportunity is present. In other words, you can't think your way to ego, shadow, and self-mastery. It is the awareness of the experience of the ego in you that gives you the signs that can wake you up out of the ego autopilot. To see how your egoic mind process works in you, access and listen to the *Audio Companion* for *Section II, Exercise 8*. This Audio Companion will take you through a guided exercise that you can then record in the *Companion Workbook for Section II, Exercise 8*.

You may ask, "Why does the ego fight so hard to prevent the higher self from being in the lead within us if our higher self is better at acting in our best interests?" That is a very good question. To answer, we need to look at the nature of the ego. The nature of the ego was outlined and discussed earlier in this book in detail, but we can sum it up in one sentence: *The ego was born of the world of duality (or separation), and its purpose is to survive at all costs.* This basic tenet means that the ego believes that it is separate from, and must maintain this separation from, others in its self-centric, self-important effort to survive and thrive in what it sees as a world of separation that is predicated on threats of limitation and lack.

In order to surrender the ego, you must also be willing to surrender these thoughts of separation, lack, limitation, and duality and see the unity of all those in the world. When you see unity instead of separation, you can't help but see others with compassion and see abundance because you no longer see those with, and those without. You no longer see *them's* but rather see everyone as one family, connected with the natural world. Each of us is simply a different, unique expression of the one, not unlike how your right pinky toe and left thumb are different expressions of one body with different functions for the whole. When you can suspend your egoic beliefs in separation, it is easier to see that when your pinky toe is cut and becomes infected, it affects your entire body, as the ripple effects to your left thumb by the blood that circulates throughout the body brings the infection of the pinky toe through the blood supporting the left thumb as well. It may not be obvious to the eye that an infection in your right pinky toe is affecting your left thumb, but when the infection becomes so severe, your entire body becomes sick. Your body may even become weak, stumble, and fall, spraining or breaking your left thumb in the fall. You may not associate that left thumb injury with the right pinky toe, but the ripple effects of that right pinky toe infection are real, whether or not you are conscious of those causal ripple effects.

Seeing unity from the perspective of our higher self is no different. Our ego sees disparity and separation and will try to talk you out of believing in any sense of unity or connectedness as naïve or simply false. All differences and separations in our society can be viewed in a similar light as the differences between our left thumb and right pinky toe. The key here is not to view unity as the same, but instead to view it as connected. The ego will feel threatened by any sense of unity or connectedness because of its attachment to separation (Ironic, isn't it? The ego is filled with the irony of creating problems that it then thinks it needs to solve). When you can start to view all as connected to you, and you to them, then it necessarily takes you out of the egoic state that believes in separation and the polarization of *us* and *them*.

Resisting the Ego's Commentary—Its Need to Label and Characterize. In a later chapter, I'll go into more detail about tools and techniques to enable you more easily to see the facts of the circumstances and eliminate all thoughts and statements about what the circumstances must mean about who you are, who others are, and how life is. You want to look at only the facts of what was done, and what was said. That's it. Those are the facts of the circumstance. Everything else is just the ego's commentary and the ripple effects of that commentary. *How you experienced those facts of the circumstances is based on the storylines your ego told you about those facts.* Thoughts such as, *She is a mean person, He doesn't care about other people, She is a horrible person, He doesn't love me, I am unlovable, I am always irritating, I can't do anything right,* and so on, are only the ego's commentary.

These are overreaching characterizations and illusory conclusions that are the foundations of the ego's stories based on what the ego believes are the *reasons why* something happened, or didn't happen. This commentary turns into storylines based on the *ego's characterizations and expectations* of what *should or should not* occur or what is *good or bad* based on its ideals, values, objectives, conditioning, personas, and so on. We've already seen that the ego's values, objectives, and experiences are distorted and dysfunctional. So, naturally, the ego's stories about why something happens, and what something must mean, are also going to be distorted when seen through its conditioned lens. Think of the ego's commentary like a sportscaster's commentary on individual plays and players of a game. The sportscaster is only commenting on what things look like to him from her limited, subjective, outside vantage point and perspective.

Since the egoic stories that make up our conditioning are just commentary made through a subjective, dysfunctional, and colored lens, the view from that place can only produce lies, misinterpretations, misunderstandings, and leaps of judgment with half-truths at best. Yet, we go through life believing these stories that an ego with the sophistication of a toddler perceived, absorbed, and became identified. When we identify with our ego, we are allowing ourselves to become identified with those egoic storylines as well. When we start to see the reality and truth of those circumstances, as distinguished from the ego's characterizations and commentary, it starts to become easier and more obvious where our ego is sabotaging our thoughts and beliefs.

It may even start to seem so elementary and juvenile that we would fall for the ego's tools and tricks. Be careful here, however, as that could be the ego again sliding into a role of *if you can't beat them, lead them* by telling you how stupid and gullible you are for falling for it. This is how the ego tries to maintain control, even when it is exposed. The ego is tricky with many tools in its repertoire. We must see the ego, its tools and tricks, but never vilify it or condemn yourself in the process. Those are the tools of the ego, not of who you truly are in your higher self. Don't allow the ego, with its belief in fear and lack, hijack your path to truth and illumination by allowing it to continue using its tools of judgment and condemnation to beat you down along the way. This is just the ego trying to distract you, keeping you under its thumb of control and with a dysfunctional notion of protection.

As we know now, when we continue to replay over and over again the same storylines, just like any lie that we tell or hear repeatedly, it seems to become more and increasingly more true each time we hear it and give attention to it, especially when we've elicited the aligning emotions to it. We end up looking for all the reasons why it IS and MUST BE true. This is just another example of how the ego would rather be *right* than see the truth, even if it means misery. The ego being *right* is its solace in its misery. If it isn't *right*, it fears that it may become completely meaningless and without merit if it is both miserable and *wrong*. What the ego doesn't comprehend, just as any two–year–old can't comprehend repercussions down the line, if the ego is wrong, the truth and the misery actually ends. When in our more sophisticated, mature, and adult minds, who wouldn't give up being right to see the truth that allows us to be happy, joyful, loving, and receive love in return? When we give up the egoic consciousness in favor of the consciousness of our higher self, that is exactly what we get.

Chapter 12

The Egoic Mind Versus the Rational Brain and the Tug-of-War between the Ego and the Higher Self

In addition to the distinction between the egoic and higher-self consciousness states, we also need to learn discernment between our egoic minds, with its thought stream commentary, versus our rational, analytical mind. Our egoic mind can usurp our rational mind by slapping a label of *fact* on something that is merely opinion, commentary, or storyline based on half-truths, assumptions, and misinterpretations. We see our societies filled with perspectives from people not understanding that many of their beliefs are just opinions from their ego's perspective, and not fact, or rational brain analyses. Our world is currently being driven by the egoic consciousness, its need to be in control, and to know *why* something is happening. This is more of the ego's need to be *right* rather than see the truth. To the ego, if anyone disagrees with its assumptions, they must be *wrong*. That is the ego's way of continuing to reinforce its "rightness" by polarizing everything. To the ego, you are viewed as either *right* or *wrong, good* or *bad*, and either part of *us* or *them*.

I'd like to relay an example of this egoic polarized perspective as fact from my own experiences. As part of my Stephen Ministry training many years ago, the entire class took the Myers-Briggs Type Indicator®. This test assesses personality types in terms of how people perceive and interact internally and with the outside world.[13] Many of you have probably taken this test that assesses whether you are more extroverted versus introverted (E or I), whether you focus on taking information in through sensing or intuition (S or N), whether you make decisions based more on thinking or feeling (T or F), and how you take in external sources of information either by judging or perceiving them (J or P). My instructor decided to illustrate the differences in the elements of sensing versus intuiting information by picking the highest "S" and "N" in the room. I was the highest "N" in the room.

The instructor picked up a blackboard eraser and asked the woman with the highest "S" score to describe that item. At this point I was thinking, "Are you kidding me? How many things can you say about a blackboard eraser? Clearly, we're going to say the same things . . ." The woman with the high "S" began her description with "it is black, about 5 inches–by–2 inches–by–2 inches . . ." I about fell out of my chair. I was shocked. This woman was describing its physical characteristics. That had never occurred to me. It had never entered my realm of perception to *see* its physical characteristics. What I *saw* instead in that blackboard eraser was its function. My description was, "It is a utensil designed to erase writing so that

[13] https://www.myersbriggs.org/my-mbti-personality-type/mbti-basics/home.htm?bhcp=1

you can rewrite on the same surface." Wow. How different our responses were, and yet we were both equally correct. What felt like a slap in the face to me was the fact that someone else could be equally right as I was, even though I had never perceived even a hint of her perspective as a possible *right* answer. Yet, it was staring me in the face; I just hadn't *seen* it.

This experience created both an exhilaration and fear in me. Both my higher self and my ego were responding and reacting simultaneously to this experience. I was exhilarated about gaining a new perspective that made me excited now to ask others about their perspective to *see* a fuller picture, realizing that my perspective would be skewed towards the intuitive. My ego, however, was fearful in trying to determine what it meant that there could be a whole host of possibilities out there that represented truths that I didn't see. That was very scary for my ego that I could be looking right at a truth and not see it. My mind started thinking, "How do I overcome this limitation so that I can see all the truths that are out there to be seen?" You can see here how the ego and the higher self can combine to motivate the constructive highest good, but overthink it through the ego. Together, they can still come up with actions for improvement, such as ensuring there is diversity in the room.

As my experience above reflected, most of us have our egoic thought-stream, our higher-self inspirations and our rational brain analyses - all working simultaneously, alternating back and forth. Understanding and recognizing each element of our being is critical to developing the mastery to ensure the higher self is driving our state of consciousness as often as possible. Some of the most challenging efforts will be discerning between the intellect of the rational brain and the egoic mind thought-stream. Unlike the rational intellect process, the egoic thought process places a judgment on everything in order to categorize and label it. The difference between the judgment of the ego and the assessment of the rational brain is the difference between placing a moral value on it from the ego's judging thoughts and ideals versus having the neutral, matter of fact observation assessment of the rational intellect without regard to or attachment of an ideal of *good* or *bad*.

The ego is compelled to label everything it encounters. Because the ego has a need to separate itself from others, this usually results in the ego using labels of polarizing opposites, reinforcing its position in the *right* and *good* box, hoping to *win*, and labeling everyone as either part of *us* or *them*. The ego sees no balance, middle ground, or compromise. It is a zero-sum game with the ego and its perspective. The ego also uses derogatory labels such as stupid, silly, jerk, and so on, all of which carry a characterization instead of factual representations.

We want to understand these egoic tricks and tools so that as we look at our stories and conditioning that get triggered, we can more easily see our ego and when it shows up. We want to be able to shift into our higher self's use of our rational brain and see the traps of the egoic mind that keep us boxed into our conditioning, continuing to cause us suffering and sabotage. In the Companion Workbook and Audio, you will be able to dive into the details of questions that pull out your shadow triggers and egoic storylines to lead you to discover the signs of your personal ego versus your higher self. Many of these signs are physical. Our physical bodies are indicators of the consciousness we are in at any given moment, and are particularly helpful in identifying our egoic or our higher-self consciousness state in any moment. As you have already experienced with the earlier Companion exercises, you will have a particular set of physical sensations that accompany each thought, emotion, and consciousness. As you move through this process and replay thoughts in your mind, continue to pay close attention to the physical sensations you feel in your body, particularly in your breathing, jaw, forehead, neck, shoulders, chest, and gut areas. Write them down, and become familiar with those sensations as you go through each exercise, noticing how they change as you move from the egoic storylines and its thoughts to the higher-self consciousness.

As you become more familiar with your physical sensory responses, you will become more aware and conscious of them in your daily life. This is key, because this will this help you recognize when you are in an egoic consciousness that you want to shift. This awareness will put you in the observer state, which is how we can shift away from the ego's thoughts and into the higher-self state. This shift to the higher self will immediately change how you experience your circumstances of life to those of more joy, gratitude, and acceptance. As stated earlier, this process of self-mastery is about changing the nature of our relationship to our thoughts and emotions.

When we are in the consciousness of our higher self, accompanied by our rational brain, our response to our shadow triggers and egoic conditioning will be the following:

- We can see the facts of our circumstances as distinguished from the commentary of the ego's stories and interpretations, allowing us to see truths instead of fabrications about ourselves, others, and life.

- We can more easily see the falseness of the ego's thoughts about who we are, who others are, and how life is that flowed from the ego's commentary of its interpretations and stories.

- We can allow emotions to flow through us without them parking in our bodies, knowing that they were elicited by our own thoughts. When we see that the thoughts were not truths, this observation deflates the power of those thoughts, which simultaneously deflates the strength of the emotions attached to those thoughts. This more easily allows them to dissipate and flow through and out of us with minimal impact.

- We can acknowledge that the uncompassionate thoughts and emotions that flowed through us were a result of our own egoic thoughts, and not anything externally, so we stop blaming others for our emotions and experiences.

- We can see that there is no reason to try and suppress the uncompassionate thoughts or emotions from the ego's painful storylines, because we see that they do not reflect who we are. With these thoughts and emotions no longer being unwanted or *bad*, they don't need to be shoved in the shadow closet, and they cease to have the power and scariness they once had.

- We can understand more easily that, by shoving the ego's painful thoughts and emotions into the closet, thereby creating its shadow, the ego was trying to protect us from this pain. This is how we can have compassion for the ego instead of vilifying it.

- With the understandings above, we can more easily allow these thoughts and emotions simply to pass through without judgment of them being *bad* or *wrong*, since we know that they are simply untruths that were understandably created by our childlike egos with limited knowledge, limited perspectives, and an unsophisticated, unevolved consciousness trying to do its best to serve us.

It is important to note here, that while this process will do much for your healing and ability to see the falseness of your painful stories, it does not mean that doing this only once will resolve all of your pain and conditioning. Your ego will still be alive and active within you, and it will continue to try and draw you back into its stories and conditioning. Remember, your ego always wants to be right, so it will continue to tell you that this healing process is just nonsense, and that it was right the first time. The deeper and more painful the conduct of others was, the longer and more often your ego will try to pull you back into its stories, and the longer and more frequently you will engage in the tugging and pulling between your higher self and your ego. However, don't be discouraged. Each time, through the process of shifting into your higher self and seeing through the ego's operation, it heals more, gets less painful, doesn't last as long, and you suffer less and less.

As you are engaging in your ego and shadow inquiry for greater awareness and discernment of truths, it will be valuable to ensure you can identify the ego and shadow when they arise. The unhealthy ego and shadow reactions often include:

- Continuing to push the uncomfortable thoughts and emotions down;
- Attacking the thoughts and emotions as *wrong* or *bad*;
- Blaming yourself for having these thoughts and emotions, for continuing to have them, and for not having better mastery; and
- Feeling sorry for yourself, or otherwise lamenting having these thoughts and emotions.

You will ebb and flow between your ego and your higher self, and that is normal. You will likely have to revisit the egoic and shadow thoughts, beliefs, and emotions to heal them in layers that have been created over the years. Each layer of pain that you see through and heal will make each layer less painful as it comes to the surface. With greater attention to the truths, the less severe the ebbing back into the ego and shadow will be and the greater and longer the flows into the higher self will be. Therefore, don't be upset or criticize yourself when you ebb a bit and fall back into the pain of the ego's storylines.

The easiest way to get out of this backtracking is to put yourself in the observer state with the egoic thoughts and emotions, and to look at them (versus relating from them) as if moving outward from looking at a single tree to looking at the full forest. You want to distance yourself enough from these thoughts and emotions to hold them out in front of you, looking at them, without burying them back into the closet, and without enabling and engaging in them. See that these thoughts and emotions are not you, and that you are more than any of them. Remember, *you are more than any of your thoughts or emotions.* Go through this process again as often as necessary to refresh yourself in the truths of the circumstances. Once you have been able to put distance between yourself and your thoughts and emotions enough to observe and be aware of them, you then have a true choice. You have the choice either to stay with the truths, or to go back and roll around in the ego's storylines. This is a choice. Choose wisely.

Mastering your ego and your shadow is about changing the nature of your relationship to your thoughts and emotions in order to give yourself the space to choose your thoughts and experiences by choosing you higher-self consciousness. You can be wrapped up into these thoughts and emotions, or you can be at arms-length with them, realizing they are just energies running through you, brought about by your egoic self. While your egoic self is responsible for these thoughts and emotions, they are not *you*, or who you are. To remain balanced, you must remember to keep a balanced distance from the egoic thoughts and emotions so that they are not shoved in the closet or wrapped up so integrally in you that you can't tell where they end and you begin. Your ego will be with you for your entire human life because it is the operating system of being a human. Therefore, you will have to continue to recognize how it operates in you, and when it tries to drive you.

At first, the ego will be more identifiable, but it will operate more subtly when you think you've gained mastery over it. You will have to continue to be the parent to your ego's desires and fears, not allowing it to drag you back into your box of conditioned stories. You want to remember that where your attention goes, your energy flows. So, the more attention you give to the recognition of truths that you learn through this process, the more those truths become your experience. As you experience more in the truths of life's circumstances, the more the ego's stories will die out, or at least fade into the background. The thoughts and emotions to which you give your attention will grow and take root. Therefore, it is critical that you choose carefully which thoughts you focus on and allow to linger in your thought-stream.

Everything you do to stave off the ego's desire to be in control must be done with a parent's compassion. You cannot suppress or bury the ego's stories and think they will just disappear. Both tactics produce an imbalanced shadow force within you that will throw tantrums for attention. You must acknowledge the ego, give it gratitude for trying to help you, and then allow the higher self—the parent—to be in the driver seat, reassuring the ego that it, too, will benefit from the higher self being in the lead. At the end of the day, the ego is just a frightened, desirous toddler whose view of the world is distorted and centered around it. Treat it with the compassion a parent would for a toddler, but without indulgence. See it, understand it, recognize it, identify it as just a small part of an integrated you, distinct from who you truly are as your higher self, and walk hand in hand with it as your higher self leads.

Mirroring.

It is important to include a note here about a common concept discussed in many psychology, spiritual, New Age and Enlightenment circles referred to as *mirroring*[14]. The term means somewhat different things in each of these circles, but the basic principles are similar. Mirroring is usually referred to as a mimicking and displaying back to someone a mirror of their gestures, emotions, energies, behaviors, and other values being conveyed by that person. This mirroring is often done subconsciously, but can be done consciously either to reject another's energy by returning the same back to them or to be supportive, or even manipulative, in giving the impression of aligning with or providing security to that person. In psychological circles, mirroring is viewed mostly as a positive behavior and as a natural survival instinct begun in infancy in order to learn, connect, and create empathetic tendencies towards others, as well

---

[14] As best as this author can determine without an in-depth research effort, the mirroring concept was originated by Sigmund Freud. However, I have not studied nor researched this psychological concept in any depth, and do not intend to make this psychological concept a central theme here.

as to learn social behaviors.[15] In spiritual and enlightenment circles, mirroring is viewed as an *empath* quality exhibited by those who, as *empaths*, have a heightened sensitivity to the energetic output by others. In these spiritual circles, it is believed that empaths instinctively perceive the energies projected by others and mirror them back to them with similar energies as their own energy emissions - as if holding up a mirror to them. In most all these circles, mirroring is considered a positive, constructive practice. I agree in part and disagree in part.

In all forms of mirroring, I see it as connecting to the consciousness state of another, whether it is a psychological, emotional, or physiological act through their physical actions, emotional, or other energetic states. Mirroring is another example of the energetic principles reflected by the Newton's Cradle. If someone is mirroring another's higher-self state, that is a constructive behavior. If the mirroring occurs with another's egoic state, that is not constructive behavior. To the extent that we need to function in a society that is still run primarily from our egoic selves, then the psychological aspect of mirroring, which is used by babies to learn survival and human skills, establishing connectivity to another's belief systems, emotional states, and egoic identities, then I agree that mirroring has that usefulness to understand, but not necessarily to follow. This is also how family lines of dysfunction get passed down through those lines, which we want to heal, not perpetuate. In many cases, mirroring is still connecting on an egoic self basis, not on the higher-self level, depending upon the state of the initial actor. In both the psychological

---

[15] I am not, and do not claim to be, an expert or studied in the formalities of the psychological profession, its research or its theories. This general Wikipedia cite can give the reader some general descriptions with various works cited: https://en.wikipedia.org/wiki/Mirroring

and spiritual uses of this term, I believe mirroring is often simply just another form of ego-based communication. Psychology is, after all, the study of the human psyche, its resulting behaviors and cognitive function, which is predominantly the egoic self.

I want to make both a distinction and clarification here concerning the psychological concept of *reflective listening*. This way of communication could be viewed as a form of mirroring, in a nontechnical sense, because it is the act of verbally reflecting back to the person what we heard from them to show that we understood what they conveyed. While not officially labeled as mirroring in psychology, this is instead termed reflective listening. This reflective listening is a valuable technique that incorporates a mirroring effect and can be an effective tool in communication while in our higher-self consciousness as well. While this book will not dive deeply into psychological theories and concepts, I nevertheless wanted briefly to address how some of these concepts can intersect with our process of mastering our egos as we evolve into a higher consciousness beyond our egos.

Since our egos are the operating system of being humans, there will always be a need to understand the egoic self. Everyone will still see their egos operating, at least from time to time, even as we evolve our coping skills and consciousness states. However, I think it is valuable to understand and remember that when we engage in psychological tools, techniques, and concepts, we are talking about managing and understanding the egoic self, which is only our superficial self. This superficial egoic self, or the *small self*, often masks our higher self, therefore, we must be adept at understanding and mastering our egoic self, so we can better live from our higher self and know our true selves.

The ego does have a consistent, standard mode of operating, and we will always have to deal with it as our operating system, therefore, psychology will always have value, but our egos are not who we truly are as beings. Our egos are not our only, or our even preferred, drivers of thoughts and behaviors. Our egos are something to be understood, mastered, and controlled as to when and how we utilize the value of the ego in being human. The greater value, however, is in recognizing both our higher selves as distinct from our egoic selves, and learning how to operate from the higher-self consciousness as much as possible, even in our mundane, everyday human circumstances.

Compassionate Detachment.

The higher-self response to circumstances and to our own egoic sabotaging thoughts, emotions, and behaviors will come from a place of compassionate detachment. This means detaching from the thoughts, emotions, and stories so that you can observe and relate to them, and not from them, in a nonjudgmental and compassionate manner. Compassionate detachment and the higher-self state will never include using egoic energies and behaviors, mirroring, or our own ego–and shadow–initiated tools. Our higher-self response will always involve compassion, while maintaining firm boundaries.

When those who instinctively pick up on another's energies, see and feel others' egoic control, manipulation, and negatively used emotional energies mirror back to that person a similar egoic energy and behavior, they are not acting out of their higher selves. Instead, it is just another example of the Newton's Cradle and an auto-piloted, knee-jerk egoic reaction. Acting out of our higher selves is instead sending the energy of love, compassion, and empathy, knowing that *hurt people hurt people*. Choosing the enlightened *healed people heal people* response, rather than giving them a taste of their own medicine (whether consciously or unconsciously) as a mirror, is the higher-self response. This higher-self response is and must be a conscious choice. This is not to judge ourselves or others in our knee-jerk reactions, but rather it is to say that we cannot use anything as an excuse or justification for not acting from our higher self. Mirroring others' expression is the ego hijacking us. We must see this in ourselves and learn how to choose differently.

To be clear, being compassionate does not require that we submit ourselves to being a victim. Allowing ourselves to be a victim would enable sabotaging behavior in others, as well as in ourselves, and that is not what compassion is about. We can enforce boundaries, while refusing to allow ourselves to be victimized by others' behavior with our loving compassion, instead of with condemnation, judgment, and anger. This is what compassionate detachment is about. Detachment is not rejection, judgment, (aggressive expression), withdrawal, or withholding (submissive expressions). Compassionate detachment results when we stop identifying with egoic stories about both ourselves and others, and we move into an observer state where we can see and respond to the circumstance from a higher-self state instead of from an egoic state. Compassionate detachment maintains a boundary where we do not allow others to cross, nor do we identify personally with, or feel a need for, a particular thought, emotion, behavior, or outcome of a scenario, and we do so without judging or withdrawing.

To illustrate the difference between the state of compassionate detachment where we maintain boundaries with compassion versus a submissive egoic state where we enable victimhood, allowing ourselves to be directly impacted by another's state, I would like to focus on the difference between the concepts of empathy and sympathy. Several years ago during my Stephen Ministry training, the difference between these concepts was illustrated by two different images. In one image, you are standing on the top of a cavernous ledge, holding out your hand to help someone out of the cavern into which they've fallen. In the other image, you jump down into the cavern with them and stand next to them. When you are empathetic, you are on the outside of that cavern, standing in a secure, stable place from which you can pull someone up. When you are sympathetic, however, you have jumped down into that cavern along with them, and now you are both stuck down there.

If you are empathetic, you might say something such as, "I see that you are upset, and I can understand how you must be feeling so hurt by this. How can I help you through this? Would you like some help thinking through this, or would you rather me just be here to show you love and support? Can I offer to take you out for a nice dinner to get you out of the house, and just offer you some compassionate company?" These responses serve to remind that person that he is greatly valued and loved, and you feel compassion for him and for what he is experiencing. If you are sympathetic, you might say something such as, "I know what you mean. How could they do that to you??!! They are so awful, aren't they?!! We'll get them back. That is just so miserable. You have every right to be sad and angry. I'll help you think of a way to show them who they're dealing with!" This response engages in the same mindset as that person, commiserating with him in his cavern of despair with both of you down there, just reinforcing and perpetuating the same dysfunctional, sabotaging energies.

You can see here that mirroring behavior is the sympathetic reaction, whereas the empathetic response (which also uses reflective listening techniques) is the higher-self response of compassionate detachment. The empathetic response can help someone heal and transcend their state, whereas the sympathetic response is just the Newton's Cradle continuation of the same energy where you both have fallen into that crater of dysfunction, wallowing in the cesspool of sabotaging thoughts and emotions. Empathetic behavior can help pull someone out of their dysfunction, but sympathetic behavior enables it. Empathetic behavior is the higher-self response that reflects a compassionate detachment that maintains the boundaries to prevent victimhood, allowing you the stability to help others more effectively.

If someone is looking either to pull you into their dysfunctional state (misery loves company), or to manipulate you into an egoic state reaction to make themselves appear powerful and feel superior, compassionate detachment may feel like withdrawal or withholding to the other person in their egoic consciousness. Boundaries always feel offensive to someone in their egoic state when those boundaries are enforced against their ego encroachment. Their ego will have little respect for anything outside its own desires. Another's egoic reaction could show up as entitlement, which is an aggressively imbalanced shadow reaction to their own shadow story and fear of a lack of self-worth, or their own refusal to accept responsibility, which to the ego, feels like blame and judgment. You may also receive another's projections through accusations and blame. I have often seen (and received) accusations and projections of blame and ill-intentions only by setting firm boundaries. Don't let another's shadow offenses pull you out of your balanced boundaries. Their response is about them, not you.

It takes conscious intention to resist the knee-jerk mirroring reaction, and, instead, go into our heart space of our higher self to send out a more compassionate energy response. Being in our higher selves and being aligned with the qualities of the higher self that include love and compassion is what true enlightenment and empathy is about. This conscious choice of a higher-self response is something we all must continue to practice through our intentions by catching ourselves when we fall into our conditioned egoic mirroring behaviors. I look forward to the day when we do not need to connect so much through our egos, where we can focus instead on connecting through our higher selves, with our egos firmly in the back seat. When we arrive at that place, the more manipulative, superficial use of mirroring to learn and manage social and empathetic skills will not be necessary for successful relationships. The higher self is, and always will be, far more skilled and connected to achieve successful relations than our egos.

Some people may object to this compassionate detachment as a kind of numbness, but that is not the case. Being numb would be not to feel anything, which is a form of suppression. Instead, compassionate detachment is about acknowledging what is flowing through you without justification, rationalization, *honoring*, or judgement. This allows you to experience the emotional energies, but on a lighter scale that does not grip you or drag you down. Instead, with compassionate detachment, the emotions are allowed to flow through you and be released without having them stick or swirl around creating suffering. This flow speeds your evolution and healing without allowing yourself to be dragged around in the mud of the dysfunctional emotions and conditioned stories.

Chapter 13

The Inner Critic

The false stories of the ego and its conditioning, which are steeped in judgment, fear, and attachment, will inform and create the false ideals of who the ego believes you *should* be and how you *should* behave. These ideals are then enforced by our own inner critic, who blames and shames us when we fail to meet these unrealistic, falsely-based egoic ideals with subjective definitions. The emotion at the core of the inner critic is shame. Before we delve too deep into the inner critic, however, please go to the *Companion Workbook* and answer the questions in *Section II, Exercise 9*.

One of the ego's common ideals concern *success* and *failure*. The ego establishes these ideals and uses the inner critic as its enforcer. The ego will create specific targets and ideals, as its definition of *success*, which, if not met, the inner critic will then label as a *failure*. As we've discussed throughout this book, the ego lives in the poles, and therefore, it sees only one end or the other. For the ego, if something is not *success*, then it must, therefore, be *failure*. The ego's definitions for success will be based on its superficial values and objectives, and will often involve financial, power, status, material items, and achievements. Because the ego also believes in separation, it must, therefore, be separate from others, meaning it must be first, or best, in order to feel successful. This will involve constant comparison to others. As we've already seen with other ego scenarios, the ego defines itself in context to others, whether that means being successful, a victim, a bully, a wallflower, a know-it-all, and so on. Its identity is constructed based on its relationship to others outside itself.

Below are some common concepts of success to the ego and to the higher self:

- Egoic Concepts of Success (Thought-stream based)
  - ✓ Involves finances, power, status, and/or material things
  - ✓ Compares self to others
  - ✓ Establishes relationships that are designed to increase power and wealth and the other superficial ideals it establishes
  - ✓ There will always be more to obtain
- Higher-Self Concepts of Success (Heart-based)
  - ✓ Accomplishing what it is meant to in this lifetime
  - ✓ Produced by subtle urges of the heart that produce joy, gratitude, love, peace, and sense of well-being
  - ✓ Establishes relationships that are supportive to heart-driven initiatives
  - ✓ Makes no comparisons to others, recognizing different purposes for different people

The higher self's motivations are felt more subtly in the body, and are known on a deeper level than thoughts in the thought stream. When the higher-self motivations are expressed, they produce the constructive, positive, and peaceful feelings that are both inspiring and gratifying. The higher self's motivations and inspirations represent your personal truths, and these give you peace. The false stories and ideals enforced by the ego's inner critic do not give you peace because they represent false ideals. Lies can never give you peace. The ego's objectives and desires will produce more exaggerated highs and lows with heightened sensations in the body that represent the poles of the ego.

The ego will use the inner critic as its judge, jury, and executioner, and will judge the inspirations and motivations of the higher self as being a *failure*. The reality is that the concepts of *success* and *failure* are subjective, as there are no absolute truths of either. If we allow the ego to convince us of the appropriateness of its ideals, we will feel suffering if we don't meet those egoic ideals which arise from the ego's inner critic judgments. The inner critic's judgments will then further elicit emotions of shame, guilt, and other unproductive and sabotaging uses of emotions that keep us attached to the past or the future. The ego's lingering thoughts and emotions will continue to grow and punish us through the ego's inner critic' repeated judgments. This is what happens when we allow the ego's thoughts to drive around in circles in the parking lot of our mind.

When we allow our ego and its inner critic to continue to bash us with the ego's shame and unrealistic ideals, it allows our ego to solicit the sabotaging emotions and turn them into a personal storyline. These storylines become stories about "I," "me," "my," "mine," creating a lingering connection and identification with those emotions that have turned toxic. If we allow them to linger long enough, they become planted in our psyches as an identity. This is what the ego wants. The ego wants to identify with these toxic emotions in order to validate its storyline. When the suffering gets too painful, it can lead to more shadow creation, as the ego then tries to shove those painful thoughts and emotions into the shadow's cellar. The inner critic becomes both the executioner and the warden, keeping us tied to our jail cell with those thoughts and emotions. These thoughts and emotions keep us out of the present moment, and handicap us from our ability to handle our present circumstances with the qualities of our higher self. We want to release these egoic and inner critic thoughts. With the release of those thoughts, the emotions will dissipate out of our emotional energy fields, along with those thoughts.

Now, let's meet your personal inner critic in one of the most healing exercises of this book by accessing the *Audio Companion* of *Section II, Exercise 10* which will guide you through a very powerful exercise, along with the accompanying questions in the *Companion Workbook* for *Section II, Exercise 10.*

When meeting your inner critic, as guided in Section 11, Exercise 10 of the Companion Audio, you can begin to see your inner critic as an element of your psyche and ego that is not who you truly are. The inner critic in all of us is a construct of our ego. It does not reflect truths about us. It is merely the ego's most effective henchman, designed to keep us in line with the ego's ideals, like an oppressive ruler. As we continue to see and meet our ego and its tools face to face, despite the oppressiveness and bullying nature of our ego, I want to repeat that it serves no constructive purpose to demonize and vilify the ego or its inner critic. Instead, as mentioned, it is both more effective and constructive to view the ego as the toddler child that has been allowed to run rampant, throwing tantrums, demanding that we cater to its every whim. When we have not stepped into and supported the parental role of our higher self, we have enabled that toddler to continue this dysfunctional behavior. With its every successful hijacking and oppression of our higher self, the ego becomes more emboldened, even becoming more and more oppressive the more we allow and enable its behavior by catering to its demands without questioning it or imposing discipline and boundaries on it. The inner critic is one of these egoic creations. None of this warrants blame or shame, so be careful not to resort to the ego's tools for failing to see through the ego's tools—that's just more circular egoic behavior. For every instance of egoic thoughts and behavior, we want to see it with compassion and forgiveness, as a parent sees a struggling toddler in a tantrum, demanding to have its way.

In the same way that fear becomes either easier or more difficult to overcome with each time that we transcend or succumb to it, the ego will become more or less powerful each time we either enable it or enforce discipline and boundaries on its fears and false stories. With that parental structure and boundary-setting, however, the ego can be a well-behaved, disciplined child with a purpose. The key to this discipline and ego mastery is to see it for what it is, when it is present, and the ways in which it is showing up so that it is not mistaken for being *you*. This is when we start to see the edges of the lenses that make up the ego's perspectives and stories.

When your consciousness and state of being is aligned with the fear, lack, and negativity of the ego, you will feel the tension in your body. This tension and impact on your physical bodily sensations is your indicator, and you have identified how those reveal themselves in you personally through the exercises in this book. Those physical sensations are your signs that you are aligned with the ego instead of the higher self. Negative thoughts about yourself, others, or life is also an indicator that you are aligned with your egoic consciousness instead of your higher self. Too often, people think that the solution is to banish the ego, and then just end up vilifying themselves, along with the ego, when they sense the first sign of a negative thought or uncomfortable emotion, such as fear or anger. This is a trick of the inner critic. That just creates more resistance, and therefore more shadow elements in our psyche. As we know now, suppressed thoughts and emotions do not go away, they merely hide in the shadow cellar waiting to burst out of their cell when we least expect them.

Just as we would not deal with a spoiled child by ignoring or suppressing that child, we cannot deal this way with our ego and its uncomfortable or unwanted thoughts and emotions. The key here, as with all things we've discussed, is balance. The balanced approach is to acknowledge them without encouraging or ignoring them. We must accept ownership of those thoughts and feelings as coming from our ego in our own head, and not from anyone or anything external to us—but not who we truly are. We recognize and acknowledge the ego's stance of fear and belief in lack in a way that shows compassion for the fearful child that is the ego, but we refuse to enable or give credence to it. We hold the ego and its fearful thoughts and emotions with compassion, but with discipline in what thoughts we give our extended attention and focus, just as we would with a toddler. We see the thoughts and emotions, we acknowledge them, and we make a different choice for our ongoing attention, with the understanding and compassion that our ego's fear was behind them, and not truths.

In order to show compassion to our own egoic self, we must have compassion within us to give. This means that we cannot let our inner critic rule our thoughts. The Exercise 10 of this Section II helps you to see your inner critic separately from who you truly are, so you can have this compassion for your fearful ego, and even the inner critic, within your egoic psyche. It is only when we can have compassion for an element of ourselves that we will have that compassion within us to draw from in order to give to others. Remember, *as within, so without.* If you cannot show yourself compassion, you will not have it to give to others. The judgment that you hold for yourself will be extended to and projected onto others as well. If you want to be a compassionate person for others, you must start by having it for yourself and your own egoic child. This is how you heal your own thoughts and emotions; from there, you can be a positive influence in helping others to heal themselves. *Healed people heal people.*

You can only heal your own emotions and stories by making peace with them. This doesn't mean you have to accept them as true, but you do have to acknowledge that they are there flowing through you. You see them, but you don't believe them or give them attention, wrapping up in them, continuing to let them swirl around in your mental and emotional bodies. You want to utilize techniques to see where they have come from to get at the roots of the dysfunction and discomfort. Some additional techniques of discourse, intimacy, and inquiry are discussed in the next section. As time goes on, these thoughts and feelings will feel neither bolstered nor suppressed, and they can simply dissipate and/or integrate back within you to be associated with truths you've discovered by seeing them through your higher self, instead of egoic illusions.

SECTION III

UNDERSTANDING EMOTIONS AND CONSCIOUSNESS STATE FEELINGS AND HOW THEY DIFFER

The notion of *feelings* has been muddied in the way that we experience, think and discuss them, but it is critical that we become more aware of the nuances and distinctions that are commonly referred to as *feelings*. In a similar way that the many English usages of the single word, *love*, is reflected in Greek through the use of several different words to convey the different meanings, *feelings* is similarly limited in its breadth. In this section, I will make several distinctions that I hope will enable the reader to see and understand crucial differences that are key to a deeper understanding of their own experiences and state of BEing.

Chapter 14

Nature of Emotions and Consciousness State Feelings

The Emotions

As we've discussed earlier, emotions are just energy—energy in **motion**. There are no *good* or *bad* emotions. Whether the emotions turn out to be constructive and productive, or destructive and dysfunctional, depends on how we use those energies. As the case with all energy, for it to be productive, it must flow naturally and constructively. When we keep these energies boxed in, swirling around in our minds, bodies, and energy fields, they can become toxic, dysfunctional, and destructive when they are tied to, and aligned with, negative thoughts. This emotional swirling happens when we keep the same negative thoughts going around and around in our minds, not allowing the thoughts flow out. By not letting the thoughts flow out, we also box in the emotions tied to these thoughts. The emotions that are elicited from the thoughts will align with the same energy as the thoughts. Therefore, negative thoughts will corrupt the emotions to express negatively as well. The presence of the emotions then seem to validate those thoughts, making the thoughts seem real and a truth.

The emotions, while they are real because they are present, do not represent truths. If the thoughts on which they are based do not represent truth, the emotions tied to them cannot represent truths either. Instead, these emotions tied to dysfunctional thoughts are simply bolstering the thoughts of illusory stories of the ego. Emotions represent only what is going on inside our own heads, and are not reflective of anything external. The emotions are like the audience reaction to our film strip projected out onto the screen. If the film strip is showing fear, the audience feels the emotion of fear, and if the film strip is playing out a scene of betrayal or love, we will feel the emotions that align with that scene of sadness or anger or joy that goes along with the scenes in the film strip. The more immersed we are in those scenes, the more intense our emotions will be, and the longer they will linger.

If we do not practice compassionate detachment, we cannot gain objective distance enough from the thoughts and emotions to see that our underlying thoughts are causing us the suffering. As mentioned often in this book, when we release the thoughts, the emotions deflate and flow on out along with those thoughts. With that release and outflow of the thoughts and emotions also goes our suffering. Emotions flow in and out with the ups and downs of our thoughts in the moments. The more intense our thoughts, the more intense our emotions. In order to accomplish mastery over our ego, its thoughts, and the aligning emotions, we must practice compassionate detachment. This compassionate detachment enables us to change the nature of our relationship to our thoughts and emotions. In order to heal our suffering, we must look at to what thoughts our emotions are tied and evaluate those thoughts for actual truths. The compassionate detachment approach to our thoughts and emotions allows for this evaluation without either judging, vilifying, or honoring them with justifications and rationalizations that enable them to entrench into further suffering. With this balanced approach, it is possible to use emotional energies as fuel for positive, constructively motivated behaviors because they will align to the balance of our compassionate detachment mindset.

When destructive thoughts and aligning emotions are repressed as a result of trauma, it is often a protection mechanism due to the overwhelming pain in both the thoughts and emotions that the ego has created in reaction to traumatic circumstances. As in all situations of the ego, the conclusions, assumptions, and stories the ego ascribed to those traumatic circumstances are often incorrect. Conclusions and assumptions such "I am bad," "I can't trust people," "I am unlovable," "I am unworthy," "other people cannot be trusted," and so on, are not accurate beliefs, but they often become belief systems of trauma survivors. These faulty, yet understandable, belief systems become part of the identities of trauma survivors. If we promote the philosophy that emotions need to be *honored* through validating them, they are less likely to be investigated to reveal the false beliefs that underlie those stories. Without seeing the underlying fallacies of these stories and trauma survivor identities, trauma survivors' healing will be severely limited.

As discussed earlier, this is *reframing* and seeing the truths in the circumstances that were traumatic. Unpacking the emotions and the thoughts to which they are tied is instrumental in achieving this level of healing. Healing emotions is a matter of correcting the inaccurate egoic thoughts and conclusions drawn from circumstances. Healing emotions does not occur just by validating them or retelling and reliving the past and dwelling in it, which is involved in *honoring* and *feeling the feelings*. That just keeps emotional pain alive with justifications and rationalizations. When we just retell, relive, and justify these thoughts and emotions, the underlying stories and emotional validations will continue to be part of the ego's conditioning and the colored lenses through which the survivors will view themselves, others, and life itself. This can lead people to go from the submissive unbalanced expression of absorbing unworthiness as an identity to the aggressively imbalanced expression of venting and self-righteousness. We can acknowledge the reality of having emotions without validating them as representing truthful stories.

Another truth that can help people heal from toxic emotions is to recognize that emotions, like all energies, are not owned personally. While our thoughts trigger and attract the emotional energy, that emotional energy is separate from you. As a result, one of the most dysfunctional statements about emotions is to say, "I am _____" to reference the emotion that is flowing through you at that moment. Instead of saying "I am angry," "I am sad," or "I am . . ." anything, it is both more accurate and supportive of the compassionate detachment stance to say, "I am experiencing . . ." or "I am aware that anger/sadness/ . . . is flowing through me right now." Because emotions are not you, to say that you are an emotion only reinforces the hold those emotions can have on you, if you are not firmly rooted in your compassionate detachment. Remember the energetic impact of words on water from Dr. Emoto's water crystal study.

Since emotions are tied to the thoughts that are flowing through our mind, they are more associated with the ego than with our higher self. Therefore, when we are actively engaged in being wrapped up in, and attached to, our emotions, it is more difficult for us to allow our higher self to be in the lead. Our ego will be in the lead when we are gripped by our emotions. When we are focused on our emotions, they tend to uphold and validate the ego's illusory world, so they don't deserve to be *honored*. Instead, they deserve to be acknowledged without judgment (compassionate detachment), and investigated for their underlying roots to see where the illusions and attachments are, and what are the real truths.

Summary on Emotions.

It is very important to be able to detach from and allow emotions to flow through and out of our bodies. It is often difficult to let go of negatively aligning emotions because we are conscious of just the tip of the emotional energy iceberg, and not aware of all that is actually connected to that emotion. Emotions run deeper than the surface because of their connection to the thoughts and storylines of our ego that are part of our survival mechanisms, which have both conscious and unconscious elements. Emotional reactions to our egoicly-conditioned triggers often reflect addictions to our egoic stories, personas, and fears. All addictions carry with them attachments that take conscious, focused intention and effort to break. The only way we can break the thought–emotion reactive addiction is to look at them seeking truths instead of validations, and take responsibility for growing them through our own ego, and not as the result of anything or anyone outside us.

In this effort, it is important to take responsibility for our emotions without overly identifying with them or saying they "are me" with statements, such as "I am. . . ." They are your emotions, but they are not *you*, or your identity. Like having an allergy or owning a car, they may change your situation from moment to moment, but they aren't you. The only things that are inextricably part of you are the qualities associated with your higher self, which are all of the qualities associated with everyone's higher self, because these qualities are not owned by any individual. They are qualities of that higher self vibration on the dial that reflects that consciousness. This consciousness vibration on the dial is available to every human when they tune into it, allowing it to be their lead.

Some tips on thoughts to help you move through addicting and dysfunctional thoughts and emotions include the following:

- I can get through this; it won't last forever.
- I've felt this before; this too shall pass.
- I'm more than my emotions.
- Ask yourself these questions:
  - ✓ What am I thinking when experiencing that emotion?
  - ✓ What do I do when I experience this emotion?
  - ✓ What are my bodily sensations when I experience this emotion?

When you're focusing on the bodily sensations, you're not giving attention to the stories, which is where the suffering is born. Moving away from the voice in your head will help, whether you focus on bodily sensations, or just sit with the emotion while exploring it. (Useful exploration techniques to diffuse the impact of the emotion are discussed in a future chapter. Any time you stop identifying with the stream of thought behind an emotion and focus instead on something else in the present, that emotion will also recede. It takes discipline, inner strength, and maturity not to act on emotions that have aligned to negative thoughts. Self-mastery, peace, and happiness are the primary goals of the master instead of the default reactionary path of the ego's imbalanced expressions that result in sabotaging venting or repressing the emotions.

As we continue to discuss how to heal and master emotions, we don't want to replace one set of false beliefs with another set. Emotions are not bad or to be avoided. They are just energy. Some energies are helpful to bring into our field, but we don't want to bring into our experience unnecessary energies to be used in harmful, or dysfunctional, ways. Generally, all emotions are valuable because they tell you about your beliefs. One thing to remember, however, as frequently mentioned, is that emotions do not reveal truths or reality. Instead, they only reveal our internal state. We want to acknowledge the reality of our emotions, but not as a validation of truths, and do so in a way that does not resist or suppress them. We don't want to repress or ignore our uncomfortable emotions. Instead, we want to look at the eliciting thoughts. When we resist uncomfortable emotions, we create more shadow and, ironically, create more attachment. Avoidance and repression of emotions creates a clinginess and addiction to the dysfunction that motivates us to continue our dysfunctional relationship to the emotions through avoidance, blame, suppression, and fear. This includes perpetuating the addiction to our personas that help us maintain, and attach to, the illusions of the ego.

To heal and master our uncomfortable emotions, we must turn toward them without judgment. Healing and mastering our emotions enable us to become more integrated and whole within ourselves, without the shadow, blame, or separation from, or within, ourselves. This mastery results in communion with ourselves and healing integration of our spiritual, energetic and human parts. This communion, mastery, and healing is not transcending yourself or your ego. To the contrary, it is actually integrating yourself to create wholeness. When you reclaim your whole self in your full expression in a constructive, healthy way, this is healing and self-mastery.

Mastery of your emotions is a process. Mastery is not just a release of something in a moment. Your thoughts and emotions have history, conditioning, attachment, storylines of thoughts and fears, often with social factors, that contribute to the conditioning and storylines that your ego creates. As you become more intimate with and aware of your emotions and the thoughts to which they are tied, all this becomes clearer. Learning how the emotion manifests in different parts of the body helps you with this understanding and awareness. As you go through this process, remember that challenges provide you opportunities to transform. Challenges can transform you into the hero and master with greater strength, positivity, wisdom, patience, compassion, endurance and all of the qualities of the higher self.

If you don't master these feelings, they will be the master of you, and you will have little peace. If you do not master your emotions, you end up allowing others to influence and manipulate you through your emotions, and therefore your experiences. The truth is, however, that others can affect you only if you allow them. Not understanding your own thoughts and emotions will allow others to manipulate you through these unlocked doors to your behaviors, whether knowingly, or unknowingly. Having this awareness and understanding of your own thoughts and emotions allows you to change the nature of your relationship to them and locks them down into your own choice and control, not available for manipulation by others because you are in control of yourself. This is self-mastery—taking back your power and remembering who you are.

Our Consciousness Feelings.

Whatever state of being and consciousness we have in any moment will come with feelings that are tied to qualities that are characteristic of that consciousness. For ease of reference, I will refer to these as feelings, feeling states, or consciousness feelings. These reflect how we feel while in a particular state of being, which is tied to our consciousness. Emotions are energy in motion and are tied to the rise and fall of our thoughts, whereas, consciousness feelings are reflective of the state of being and consciousness you are in at that moment. These feelings tend to be cumulative in effect and endure longer than just a moment in time or circumstance. The consciousness feelings can be either from the higher self or from a more negative egoic lens that comes from the ego's conditioning. The consciousness feelings are not as attached to the thoughts as are emotions. These consciousness state feelings shape how you view what is happening in that moment, and can affect the thoughts that trigger the emotions.

The consciousness feelings do not take you through the highs and lows that emotions do because they present a more subtle, constant set of experiences. Consciousness feelings come from a deeper state of being. When the consciousness feelings are from the higher self, they are balanced and present with a sense that nothing is missing and all is well. When the consciousness feelings come from a deep-rooted state of the egoic self, it feels as if everything is missing, and nothing is well.

Much more will be discussed later about gratitude and how moments of gratitude can add up to become a state of consciousness of gratitude when we practice gratitude about various things in our life, such as food and shelter. Gratitude can lead us to having our higher-self consciousness become more dominant where gratitude becomes the lens through which we see all things in our life. If we are not aware of our thoughts, emotions, and consciousness states, we can just as easily create an egoic consciousness state of sadness, fear or anger from repeated eliciting of those emotions. The relationship between emotions and consciousness state feelings are cyclical, where they become both bolsters and triggers of one another.

What follows is a deeper look at some of these higher-self qualities, states of being, and feelings states.

Wisdom. Wisdom is the knowingness that seems to come from nowhere that you can identify. It is a gut knowing and may include the higher self's learnings and assimilation of experiences (not to be confused with the ego's overreaching conclusions and perspectives based on a small set of experiences). Often, this wisdom knowingness is intuited. Intuition is the method of receiving and knowing, and wisdom is the subject of that intuition. It is the sense of knowledge that aligns with your higher self and its values, objectives, and perspectives. It is the deep inspirational source (not through prolonged, ruminating thoughts and weighing of pros and cons) that tells you to take a risk on a new venture, relationship, or how to handle a challenging circumstance that aligns with these higher-self qualities. It is the source that tells you to use temperance and compassion in your responses to others. None of these courses of action might seem to be logical, based on thoughts ruminating in the thought stream, but for some reason, these inspirations and motivations come from the deepest parts of who you are. This wisdom is an inspiration that represents the *whether* or the *how* of implementing the higher-self's qualities of courage, compassion, perseverance, and so on.

Courage. Courage is the willingness to face your fears and continue on a path that your wisdom is telling you is the course that is most aligned with your higher self. The ego will be trying to talk you out of this path. Your higher self bolsters you with the strength and courage to forge forward, despite the ego's perceived threats, difficulties, or other reasons why the ego feels threatened and believes that is not a good idea.

Strength. Strength is the willingness and capacity to adhere to and stand up for love, kindness, compassion, unity, peace, acceptance, and tolerance. It is also a contributing source of the courage mentioned above. Strength supports our courage to follow through and persevere with courses of action that are aligned with our higher self's values of love, kindness, compassion, unity, peace, acceptance, and tolerance. The ego will also fight for what it believes is the truth in its stories, but the ego's *truths* are just its conditioned storylines that underlie its overreaching beliefs and superficial values. The higher self— the true self—stands up for universal truths that are not based on perspective, thought, opinion, beliefs, or other subjective aspects of life. Learning the difference between the ego's stories versus the universal, actual truths represented by the higher self is one of the challenges that we must master in order to fully master our egos and live from our higher selves.

Incorporated into this strength is how you fight for these truths. How you use your power matters, and determines whether you are embodying the strength of the higher self or using the default, knee-jerk programmed tools of the ego. Using the egoic tools of anger, hostility, judgment, war, and other conflict-related tools can turn any strength we have into an imbalanced egoic tool of struggle. Standing up for universal truths does not happen on a battlefield. Instead, it is living life in a way that love and peace are held more valuable than egoic values and goals. In short, strength is a way of BEING. Holding strong to compassion, love, peace, acceptance, and goodness in the face of forces moving against these values is what strength is all about. Warring battles are designed to promote separation, and do not keep you safe. Love, compassion, and connection do. Love and compassion build and sustain societies, allowing them to flourish through cooperation, building a world of encounter instead of confrontation.

Our greatest protection is actually connection. It takes far more strength to seek to understand someone with differing thoughts and perspectives than it does to revert to the egoic default of separation into *us* and *them* categories, conflict, and competition for *rightness*. This is why war is never a sign of strength. It is instead a sign of weakness because it stems from fear and greed, which are, by their very natures, succumbing to the false stories of the egoic consciousness. Mastering the ego and becoming our own heroes requires the strength of surrender. To be a master and hero and live from our higher-self state of BEing, we must surrender all of the ego's fears, ideals, and its stories. We must surrender all that we *think* we know in order to BE in a place where we want the truth more than we want to serve our ego's need to be right. This takes true strength.

Perseverance. Perseverance is the continued walking down the path of the higher self, while also continuing to show strength and courage, following the wisdom of the higher self and its truths. It is not trudging up a hill with the feeling of being put upon, dragged down, or feeling like a pack mule pulling a burdensome load. Instead, it is more of a trusting in life and in those universal truths of the higher self, regardless of the challenges of the circumstances. Even during difficult times, the perseverance of the higher self can keep us walking the path because of its love and trust, which has the effect of lightening the load as we walk the path.

Patience. Patience is the surrendering of expectations and attachments to outcomes, allowing life to present itself in its own way and timing. This does not mean complacency or laziness in not contributing to the best outcome. Patience says, "I accept whatever happens, and then I will respond as life occurs." This response may mean trying different things, or the same things in a different way, and allowing what occurred to be your teacher. When we can live with life as it presents itself, and respond to it as it comes, it removes the anxiety of attachments to our fears about the future and our expectations and *needs* (which are, by definition, attachments unless they are for basic human survival of food, water, and shelter). Patience allows us to receive undesirable circumstances as both lessons and guides to a better, higher place, and to do so without the anxiety of the ego.

Gratitude. Gratitude is one of most powerful, accessible qualities and feeling states. Gratitude opens your heart, which opens you up to perceiving, and therefore receiving, love and joy. This opening up of the heart puts the higher self in the driver seat, allowing you to receive all the other qualities of the higher self. Gratitude is also the most effective and easiest way to move from an egoic consciousness to the higher-self state. There is always something you can view with gratitude, whether it is the fact that you have shelter, clothes, food, or other basics for survival. From that point, you can often find many other things for which you can be grateful. There is always someone who doesn't have what you have, and for that you can be grateful. This shift, and move to gratitude, instead of what you think you lack, will also shift your perspective, which, in turn, shifts your thoughts, which shifts your emotions, all of which reflects and helps you to maintain the consciousness of your higher self. Opening this gate to gratitude is the most valuable thing you can do for your self-mastery process.

You can engage in a gratitude exercise at any time, and you would benefit from doing so often. The more you do this, the more frequent your shift to your higher self will be, and the longer you will be able to stay in this higher-self consciousness, rejecting the egoic perspective. Below is one such gratitude exercise.

- Thank anything, and everything, in your sight—the trees, flowers, furniture, your clothes—anything. Experiencing gratitude and offering a "thank you" is a choice of intending that love, peace, and joy be your experience of life in that moment.
  - ✓ Notice how it feels, and where in the body.
- Make a list of things for which you are grateful. Look at this list each morning and every time you are feeling angry, sad, frustrated, fearful, and so on.
  - ✓ Add to your list each day something for which you were or can be grateful.
- One of my personal favorite gratitude practices is to keep a gratitude box or jar.
  - ✓ Each day, write down what you were most grateful for during that day and place it in the box or jar. On days you have challenges, open the box or jar and read some of your past gratitude statements.

✓   Ultimately, you will be able to see the positive fruits that come from your challenges, and you will then begin to have gratitude for the challenges, even while in the midst of them.

Note that this practicing of gratitude is not just putting on rose-colored glasses that pretend to look at things with a delusional blush. For instance, the basic facts of clothing, food, and shelter are real things for which you can be grateful because others do not have what you have. When you gain some distance from some of your challenges, and you can see how they led you to a better place with growth, learning, new opportunities, and so on, you begin to learn that your challenges are doorways to growth and new opportunities, even if uncomfortable ones. When you look at your challenges this way, you stop fearing, resenting and condemning them and others involved. You also want to remember that if everything in your old circumstances were always warm and cozy, you would likely never end up leaving those circumstances to move into better ones. The key here is to allow yourself to walk through a new door, instead of fighting to stay in the old circumstance.

Joy. Joy is the higher self's lens of love, compassion, and gratitude through which you view the world. It is the feeling of deep happiness that is often brought about as we also feel gratitude and love. Joy is not dependent upon a moment, an event, or an occurrence of anything. It is a perspective about living, about others, what they and life bring, and in just enjoying and seeing others enjoying life. Unlike the emotion of elation, joy does not rise and fall with momentary occurrences. Rather, it is a state of BEing, deep within our core that is produced as we contemplate and feel the gratitude and love of our higher self.

Love. Love of the higher self, like the other qualities of the higher self, is a state of BEing, or a feeling state, more than an emotion that rises and falls with the moment. Many languages are inadequate to describe the love of the higher self, as distinguished from the love we say we have for something, or even someone special in our lives. Love, like joy, is the lens of the higher self through which we see everything—the earth, animals, and humanity. This love appreciates, respects, and wants the best of life to flourish. The love of the higher self sees with compassion, even those things that are not representative of the highest, best expression of others. This is not a love of enabling, acquiescence, or victimhood. It is a love backed by, and steeped in, strength, courage, and the wisdom of knowing the true nature of all things, irrespective of what is being expressed through them at that moment. It is a love without conditions, expectations, or judgment, with the courage and strength to stand up and support life and all beings with compassion, respect, and loving boundaries when and where appropriate.

This discussion of the feeling of love that reflects the higher-self state of BEing is not intended to discount the emotion of love that can come in and flow out of us based on relationships and moments of heightened or more passionate energies. These emotions of love also exist, but these energies are different from the heart-focused feeling state of love that is more of a state of being in which we have a deep appreciation for how we see others and life. The emotion of love is a passionate, or momentary, high that is associated more with a particular person, moment, or occurrence.

Peace. Peace, like patience, is an allowance of life to be as it is without expectation or attachment. Also, like patience, peace does not imply complacency or laziness in not acting. Peace comes from the trust of life and the patience that life will be what it will be. Peace reflects the knowledge that, when we are operating with our higher selves in the driver seat, we will be inspired and motivated to the actions that are in alignment with the highest, best outcomes of life. This peace allows others to do and be who they are and will be, knowing that when we are in our higher selves, we will be able to encounter others in the highest, best way, considering the circumstances. We have peace that these encounters will produce the highest outcomes, knowing that sometimes these highest outcomes result in lessons for ourselves that enable us to grow and evolve to higher and better places. This peace allows us to receive gratitude, even for the lessons. When we are in peace, we have no attachments or expectations, so there is no sense of lack.

Kindness. Kindness is the way we view, feel, and think about others that produces the resulting behavior we exhibit when we live in our higher selves and feel compassion for others. Kindness is the perspective we carry, and the resulting behavior for how we live our lives when we live in our higher selves. This kindness, again, does not require victimhood to those who intend us harm. Kindness is a product of the compassion that defines the higher self, and we can enforce our boundaries with kindness and compassion for others, instead of with fear, judgment, and hatred.

Below is a brief chart comparison on some consciousness state feelings for both the higher self and the ego. You may see that many of the higher self feelings also reflect qualities of the higher self that were discussed in a previous chapter. These higher-self qualities are both qualities that we exhibit as well as conscious state feelings that we "feel" internally, and that also have physical sensations associated with them in our bodies.

Higher-Self Feelings	Egoic Feelings
Joy	Depression
Peace	Anxiety
Hope	Discouragement and Hopelessness
Compassion	Disdain
Contentment	Discontentment and Agitation

The Body as an Indicator of Your Consciousness

The Exercises in the Companion Workbook and Audio focus on identifying the physical sensations that are present as you experience different consciousness states and emotions. This is because our bodies are indicators of what consciousness, or state of BEing, we are in at that moment. Our bodies are not just human casings for our higher selves and egos to be housed. Our bodies are like antennae for, and reflectors of, the energies that we emit and receive. By paying attention to the physical sensations presenting themselves in our bodies at any given moment we can interpret where we are on that radio dial. Are we in a more peaceful, calm state in the higher 100's on that dial, or are we in a restricted, contracted, tight state in the lower nineties, or somewhere in between? If we are in a contracted, tight state in our bodies, our ego is in the driver seat. If we are in a peaceful and relaxed physical state, our higher self is in the driver seat. As our thoughts, feelings, and emotions fluctuate in between those two states, our physical sensations shift as well with that ebbing and flowing between our ego and our higher self. Our body sensations are one of the best tools for determining and discerning whether our thoughts, feelings, and emotions are coming from our higher self or our egoic self. Your work in the Companion Workbook and Audios in identifying your particular bodily expressions of your consciousness will be important so that you experience, and then understand, how your body reflects the various imbalanced expressions of the ego and the balanced expression of the higher self.

As you practice catching yourself in an egoic consciousness state with its thoughts and emotions, your physical sensations will be one of the best techniques and indicators for you to catch yourself before your egoic state escalates. When I mentioned earlier in this book that the ego will try to talk you out of your higher-self behavior (such as being compassionate will be weak or make you a victim), your bodily sensations can help you discern the truth of the situation. Your thoughts will lead you astray, so your body will be the best indicator for the truth of the situation.

When you find yourself in an egoic state, which you can identify through your physical sensations, you will want to use your higher-self short cut that you identified through an earlier exercise, and review your circumstance through that heart–centered (instead of thought-centered) place. You'll want to be aware of and observe the physical sensations of your body as you contemplate different scenarios and behaviors. The one that produces peace and calmness in your body will be coming from your higher self and is what represents the truth without the ego's illusory stories, objectives, and perspectives. The key here is to recognize how YOUR body responds to the egoic and higher-self states. There are frequently common reactions for each state, but there are also differences in how each person's body responds to their respective states.

Now, let's work through some examples designed to show you the differences between your egoic and higher-self state. To do so, *Please access Section II, Exercise 1 in the Companion Audio and Workbook.* In this exercise, you will be guided by the Companion Audio through what it feels like in your body to be in the following contrasting states. The first is the egoic state, and the second is the higher-self state. Some of the egoic states listed here in this exercise are submissive, and some are aggressive imbalances. Your body will often have a slight difference between the aggressive and submissive imbalanced expressions of the ego, as you learned in an earlier exercise. The differences between an egoic state's physical sensations, whether aggressive or submissive, will be notably very different and distinguishable from the physical sensations of the higher-self state. These states also represent *feelings*, or feeling states of being, as discussed above. The feeling states we will explore in the Companion Audio include the following:

- Strength vs. Domination and Control
- Perseverance vs. Struggle
- Patience vs. Complacency and Disconnection
- Peace and Contentment vs. Agitation and Discontent
- Kindness vs. Resentment
- Trust vs. Distrust
- Joy vs. Depression

When you notice that your body is telling you that you're in an egoic state, you will want to make a shift by moving into your higher self. One of the most effective tools to shift back to your higher self is using your shortcut, and thinking of the higher self qualities and its objectives, such as compassion and gratitude. This will help you shift your consciousness and state of being, and your body will be able to validate for you your current state of being. If you have been able to put your higher self into back in the driver seat, your bodily sensations will immediately change to the peaceful, relaxed calmness that you experience when you are in your higher self.

Comparing and Contrasting How Emotions and Feeling States Work Together

As you digest the interplay of the short-term rise and fall of emotions tied to your thoughts with more enduring feelings of your consciousness states, consider the difference between sadness and depression. Sadness is an emotion triggered by an event that rises and falls with the moment where we are thinking sad thoughts. Whereas, depression is a state of being that comes from our perspectives on life and ourselves, whether in relationship to others, life, or both. Depression lingers in us, whereas sadness, without an accompanying and lingering depression, will be event-specific. Feelings that represent a state of being do not rise and fall easily and stick around, contributing to the lens through which we view ourselves, life, and our circumstances. Just as the consciousness state feelings of our higher self and ego will manifest differently in our bodies, so, too, will the emotions versus consciousness state feelings. To understand how these manifest themselves in you personally, please access *Section III, Exercise 2* in the *Companion Audio and Workbook* and complete its written and audio guides.

As you will discover in doing these exercises, the bodily sensations of emotions typically have a heightened nature about them and will rise and fall as if you are on a roller coaster with high highs and low lows. In contrast, the consciousness state feelings have a more constant, less volatile nature about them. The previous Exercise 1 of this Section III took you through an exploration of your bodily sensations experienced with both egoic and higher self feeling states of being. You have also experienced earlier exercises where some of the emotions flow through us in balanced and imbalanced ways. The exercises here in this Section III, Exercise 2 distinguishes for you emotional energies versus consciousness state feelings.

Some of the feelings and emotions that in this Section III, Exercise 2 are characteristic of the ego, and some are characteristic of the higher self. However, emotions themselves are not tied to either state because they are energies that move through us that are aligned with our thoughts. We can use sadness and anger in both states of consciousness of the ego and the higher self. We saw that also in Section II, Exercise 3. The same emotion will manifest differently in the bodily sensations, depending upon our state of consciousness and whether it is balanced in the higher self, or imbalanced in the ego, and whether that imbalanced egoic state is in the aggressive or suppressive expression.

The emotion/feeling state juxtapositions we explore in this Section III, Exercise 2 include the following:

- Joy (feeling) vs. Elation/Excitement (emotion)
- Depression (feeling) vs. Sadness (emotion)
- Perseverance (feeling) vs. Endurance
- Struggle (feeling) vs. Disappointment

In this list, both egoic and higher-self feelings states are represented. These feelings states reflect the different lenses through which you can view your circumstances. They reflect the perspectives and consciousness you have as you experience your life's circumstances, and as you view yourself and others. These feeling states, perspectives, and lenses tend to direct your thoughts, which then elicit your emotions. A regular eliciting of the same emotional energies can create, or contribute greatly to, the entrenchment of your feeling states that then will drive your thoughts, emotions, and experiences. You can see now how this circle of self-fulfilling storylines spawn self-creating feeling and consciousness states that feed on themselves to create perpetual endless cycles. If we don't break out of the ego's grip, we create perpetuating cycles of struggle and suffering. Your consciousness state will determine your feelings, which tend to direct your thoughts, which then elicit the corresponding emotions, and the more those similar thoughts are triggering those emotions, the more likely it is that you create or entrench that consciousness feeling state that will continue to create the feelings reflecting the perspective and lens that will color everything. This continues to shade the thoughts which trigger the emotions, and on and on around the circle you go. This becomes like a snowball rolling down the hill, getting larger and larger, and more and more difficult to stop.

I want to take a moment here to address what psychology and psychiatry defines as clinical depression that is often treated with medication. I am not intending to discount or counter any medical or psychiatric recommendation for anyone's diagnosis or treatment. What I will say is that our dysfunction in our consciousness feeling states, thoughts, and emotions can create physical dysfunction if it goes on for too long at levels that the body can no longer sustain and remain healthy. This may possibly include resulting synapse connection issues as well as chemical imbalances in our bodies. Some physiological signs of clinical depression could reflect the physical ripple effects of more severe lingering feeling states, thoughts, and emotional imbalances from the ego that have gone unaddressed and untreated for a longer period of time. These issues can be explored with a medical provider, as I do not intend to diagnose, suggest treatments, or otherwise comment on others' diagnoses or treatment plans in this book.

As alluded to above, there is a close causal connection between emotional energies and the consciousness state feelings. As a result, some of the feelings can also be emotions on lighter levels. When these emotions amount to consciousness feelings, it is because the emotions have been felt so frequently and intensely, that it creates a consciousness state perspective that becomes the lens of your state of being. Just as repeated moments of sadness can produce the more prevalent and lingering depression, allowing the emotion of fear to come into your energetic body regularly and linger can produce a regular lingering consciousness of fear that becomes part of your lens that sees everything from the perspective of fear. This is also true of anger. You can create a fearful, angry, or anxiety-riddled regular state of being if you continue to allow your ego to run fear-based or angry thoughts repeatedly in your head that continue to elicit those corresponding emotions that linger over and over, longer and longer, to where they just take up residence inside you. Don't let your thoughts do donuts around and around in your mental parking lot because this can create consciousness state feelings that will be more challenging to break.

Emotions, Feelings, and Qualities are
Not Yours—You Receive Them.

Throughout this book, I've conveyed the fact that you are not your thoughts or emotions or labels, personas, or other identities you give yourself. A similar notion is also true for the higher self qualities and the feelings that, in fact, represent states of being. The qualities and the feelings of the state of being of the higher self, the wisdom, courage, strength, perseverance, and so on, are not *yours*. You do not create these qualities, and they are not unique to you. Instead, through your state of *Being,* you <u>allow</u> them (or not) and <u>receive</u> them into your consciousness and energetic bodies. You receive and *embody* them. When you are in your higher-self consciousness, these higher self qualities and feelings naturally flow to you. This realization facilitates the understanding of how we are all from the same source of the higher-self. These higher-self qualities and feelings are from that same source, whether you call it the divine, source energy, or whatever you believe about the origins of our energy essence. When your position (the frequency) on the radio dial is aligned with your higher self, you resonate at a place where those qualities and feelings can be pulled into your energetic body, and you can receive them, and therefore embody and express them in your own individual way through your consciousness, your energy and your behaviors.

This is how the Law of Attraction[16] works, though we will not discuss that concept in this book. You must resonate at the correct energetic and consciousness state to attract these qualities into your BEing. When you are not resonating with these qualities, you are at a different place on the radio dial (frequency), and you cannot perceive, receive, or attract those qualities to you. There is a lot I could say about the *Law of*

---

[16] The term "Law of Attraction" appeared in print for the first time in Helena Blavatsky's book, *Isis Unveiled* in 1877, and it is commonly referred to in various New Age circles. More information can be found here: https://en.wikipedia.org/wiki/Law_of_attraction_(New_Thought)#cite_note-11

Attraction, the *Law of Manifestation*[17], the feminine and masculine energies, and how they work in synergy, but those are outside the scope of this book. For now, it is only important to understand the notion that these thoughts, emotions, feelings, and qualities are neither personal nor created by us, but you can embody them and express them in individual ways. This notion has wide and deep implications that can further free us from the tethers of our self-centric egoic concepts.

[17] Most references to *Law of Manifestation* see it as simply another way of referring to the *Law of Attraction*, where the manifestation is the resulting effect of that *Law of Attraction*. I have not seen any reference that makes a distinction between these two concepts as different energies, forces or partners. I believe these references fail to appreciate the subtle, but important, differences between these two concepts and how they work together. However, that is not a discussion for this book.

Chapter 15

Stages of Thought–Emotion–
Behavior Progression

First stage—The Thoughts. If you can see the intensely negative thoughts coming through the thought-stream and check them at this point, it will take the least amount of effort to stop the chain reaction of suffering and sabotage that will follow from these thoughts. The negative and sabotaging thoughts will usually be condemning, name-calling, judging, fear-based, and laced with disdain, disgust, intense anger, fear, or sadness. When dealing with the shadow, the thoughts will be as if you are saying them in ALL CAPITAL LETTERS in your head. If you can catch these thoughts at this stage, you will have achieved a great step in mastering the ego and its shadow. The intensity of these shadow thoughts will elicit intense emotions that align with those intensely negative thoughts almost immediately, with very little break between the thoughts and the emotions. This is the challenge of dealing with the shadow in the midst of its triggered expression. The moment that you have intense thoughts of visceral disgust, anger, disdain, fear or sadness, this is the time to pause and see those thoughts and remember that what you have going on in your head and thoughts is always a reflection of what consciousness you are in at that moment, and not anything outside you.

If you can manage this pause, this is the place to shift into your higher self by focusing on your heart and inserting rational thought about only the facts of the circumstance, with the knowledge that what another does speaks only about them and is not personal to you. Your heart focus can help you see them with compassionate detachment, and that can help you take a step back from your thoughts. You want to remember that, while someone else may be acting in an unkind, unthoughtful, hypocritical, self-serving egoic mindset themselves, that should not take you out of your own balance. You want to remember that *hurt people hurt people.* These types of thoughts that pull you into an egoic mindset are not constructive, don't change others or the circumstances, and only serve to pollute your own thought-stream and resulting emotional body if you allow them to linger for more than an instant. If you don't stop the ego and its shadow at the thought stage before it becomes an emotional body effect, the sabotaging impact will only increase.

If you can catch yourself at this stage with just the initial thoughts, you can observe them, acknowledge them, and see that those thoughts are out of alignment with your higher-self and service–to–others consciousness, then you will not indulge, excuse, or justify those thoughts. Instead, you will just let them flow out without giving them further attention. This interference by the rational brain and the observation technique of the higher self will have the effect of deflating the power and sabotage of the ego and shadow in that moment, which will prevent the raising up of aligning emotions that will make those thoughts seem real.

Second Stage—the Emotions. Once your thoughts have been allowed to linger, and you've given them attention by believing them, they will elicit the emotions that match the energy of those thoughts. Because the shadow operates so surreptitiously and quickly in knee-jerk, reactionary, ways, the distance between the thoughts in stage one and the elicited emotions in stage two will be very short. In many cases, because the identities shoved in the shadow have such deep-rooted and intense emotional and painful storylines, these shadow stories are inherently laced with painful and intense emotions. It is only when we can start understanding our ego and its shadow and seeing its stories and shadow triggers that we can start to put a moment of distance between the ego's thoughts and the resulting emotions. The more we practice observation, the more likely it will be that we can interject this pause at the stage of thoughts before our emotions become too strong or entrenched.

When we get to the emotional stage, we have another opportunity to stop the snowball effect of our thoughts from getting so intense that it creates sabotaging behavior in the fourth stage. Again, however, it takes conscious intention prior to the appearance of the thoughts in order to do this. Therefore, moving through the earlier steps of understanding our shadow and its triggers is critical. Once we have a better understanding of our ego and its shadow, we can see that our emotions are engaging our entire bodies in a way that makes us feel as if our entire mind and body are committed to an excited state. We, then, can see and feel that our bodies are energized and animated with an intensity that is not productive. It is like an angry bull that has been caged up, and has now shot out of its pen, wanting to lash out with a killer instinct at the first irritant it sees.

An important note here is that while this description may seem to be applicable only to the aggressive expression of the shadow, it also applies when the shadow expression is on the submissive and suppressive side. The difference is in what direction the killer horns face—internally at oneself in sadness, depression, and severe self-worth condemnation, or externally towards others in anger and venting. The internal direction being the submissive expression and the external direction being the aggressive expression. These stages of progression apply to any thought-emotion progression, whether shadow or conscious ego thought-stream. When our shadow is not triggered, and we are just having an egoic thought, the emotions may not be as intense because the thoughts are not usually as intensely negative. Therefore, a non-shadow general egoic reaction can be easier to catch at each stage than the more intense shadow reactions will be.

The key to deflating the emotions is also being able to pause the thoughts, stop their replay and justifications, and allow the emotions to deflate. Imagine that you are blowing into a balloon to inflate it. Your thoughts are the breath that you breathe into the balloon, and the balloon is the emotion. If you stop blowing into the balloon for a moment, the balloon will deflate, allowing the air to seep out. The same is true of the relationship between our thoughts and emotions. If we can stop replaying and trying to validate the negative thoughts and scenarios in our thought stream, and just pause for a moment, or think of something to be grateful for in that moment, the emotion ceases to become larger and more powerful, and it actually subsides. This is the moment when you can regain control over your thoughts and emotions before they escalate into higher intensity, producing sabotaging behavior.

This is also when you can convert what was beginning to be destructive thoughts, emotions, and behaviors into something constructive. You can divert the energy of those thoughts and emotions from the destructive to use it as fuel for something productive. If, for example, you were intensely sad or angry at the abuse of children, animals, or actions of others, you can divert this energy into something productive, such as volunteering for, or donating to, an organization, or another productive use of that anger or sadness. This is why we don't vilify emotions themselves because they are just energy that can be used in either productive or destructive ways.

Recognizing an escalating thought and emotional state is relatively easy because it consumes your mind and body. The challenge is to have the conscious awareness of your own state of being to want to, and have, the coping skills to pause this escalated state. Suggestions on tools and techniques to help you move into an observer state, enabling you to implement this pause, include the following:

- After an episode of an escalated thought and emotional state, use your analytical mind from an observer state to identify certain things about that experience that you can remember that seemed to be an intense, consuming thought, emotion, or justification for having those thoughts and emotions. You want to make a mental note that if you feel or sense that again, you want your conscious mind to call it to your attention. Use your analytical mind and observer state to replay the situation in your mind and body again, so that you can see and feel it. Doing this from the observer state, and not from the participant state, facilitates you from being identified and wrapped up in, those thoughts and emotions. You want to be able to *see* how it felt and what the experience was like, as if you are relating *to* the experience, not *from* it.

- Ask someone close to you to notice when you are in such a heightened, energetically negative state in the future, and think of a question or statement that you believe can be used to snap you out of the grip of that egoic state without antagonizing you. An example could be "What color of rose is your favorite," "What is your favorite sports team again?" or something similar that pulls your attention to something you love. That will give you enough of a break in the thought-stream action to break the force and momentum of the negative, intense thoughts, and deflate the emotions that arose in reaction. Remember, thoughts and emotions are energies, so you must interrupt their flow in order to break their strength and momentum.

Third Stage—Lingering, Continued Attention. Once you've passed the first two stages described above where the intensity and focus of your thoughts have generated the intense emotions to accompany them, you begin to enter into dangerously sabotaging territory. If you continue to give attention to these thoughts over and over, replaying them while also continuing to think of additional support and justification for your own thoughts and blaming, judging, and condemning others, and thinking of other related storylines, the intensity of both your thoughts and your emotions escalates. This is where thoughts of actions begin to form. The thoughts and emotions are becoming so intense that you start thinking of actions that are "deserving" "righteous," "right," or "justified," which are not coming from the heart-balanced, higher self, or rational brain. This is the place where people who engage in road rage and other violent or sabotaging behavior begin to form thoughts about what action they can take to right the wrong they deem appropriate. This is also where those engaged in the submissive expression of the shadow begin to contemplate self-harm behaviors. The actions being contemplated are directed externally towards others when it is aggressive and internally toward ourselves when it is submissive.

When we are at this stage of replaying our thoughts and emotions, we are fully functioning in our egoic and shadow selves with the objectives, rationales, and values of the ego. At this stage, rational brain and higher-self perspectives can be suppressed by the ego. For those people who are more rationally-based and balanced, as a normal course, this is when some of these thoughts will trigger our rational brain to say, "Nah, I can't do that . . . that's not who I am. That would be crazy." When the rational brain is allowed to filter into the thoughts, or the higher-self consciousness can move to the foreground through gratitude or compassionate detachment, the deflation of the egoic thoughts and emotions can begin to occur. How rationally-based or steeped in ego our personality and psyche is generally will often determine whether and how quickly we can engage our higher self and rational brain to stop the thoughts and emotions before they turn into actions. So often, by the time someone gets to this stage, the intensity of the thoughts and emotions is so high that the anger or sadness that have been elicited from the repeated attention to negative thoughts are hard to deflate. This is when it can turn into the behavior discussed below.

Fourth Stage—The Behavior. Sometimes, the behavior being contemplated in our thought stream in Stage 3 involves aggressive expressions toward another party. Even those with a strong, rational psyche and personality can still succumb to an egoic thought stream and emotionally-aligned suggestion that, while not directly violent towards another, still involves violence, such as throwing a plate, a drink, or something else at someone, in their direction, or just slamming it on the floor or against the wall or slamming drawers and doors. For those who often give into their impulses, the behavior will nearly always follow without much in rational checks and balances. This is when the behavior may be violent directly towards others or ourselves. For these people, it will be very difficult for them to stop the ruminating thoughts and emotions about an action from turning into that actual behavior. This is why road rage and mob rally violence are so difficult to stop once they get beyond Stage 2 into Stage 3.

The environment itself can become a catalyst and buoy for the emotional energy that moves people to Stage 3, and then into Stage 4. For those who are moved more by their egoic nature and have less tendency for their rational brain or higher self to offer a break in the thought and emotion energy in their psyches and emotional bodies, this is of particular concern. A note here about rational versus emotional tendencies. Because emotions follow from our thoughts, being a rational versus emotional person is not a statement about the passionate or stoic nature of someone. Instead, it is a statement about the state of consciousness of someone who acts from their egoic nature more than their rational mind or their higher self nature. Those operating more from their egoic consciousness allow their egoic mind to carry them away without being checked more regularly by either the rational mind or the higher self. In contrast, those with a stoic nature may have a submissive or passive aggressive nature, where they may be creating more shadow through suppression. Therefore, the key is the state of mind. The differences between men and women versus masculine and feminine energies is beyond the scope of this book, but to say that women have a reputation of being more emotional is, in many ways, a misunderstanding of the function and nature of emotions as well as what underlies being emotional.

It is important that you are able to recognize how you progress in each of the stages outlined above. It would be valuable for you to revisit *Section II, Exercise 8* to see how you progress through these stages when your egoic mind is left untempered and unbroken in its focus, especially over a longer period of time. Your awareness of how you progress from an initial thought to a ruminating thought, to arising emotions, to an intensity of thought and emotion, to behavior is critical if you want to master your thoughts and emotions. If you cannot see what you are doing in each of these stages, you will not be able to have mastery and control of yourself. Without an awareness over your progression through these stages, you will simply not have the awareness of what stage you are in, how you are progressing through the stages, and how to stem the escalation. When you get wrapped up into and attached to an egoic thought process that has begun to elicit the corresponding emotions, it can be challenging to pause and break out of that egoic state, especially when the shadow's intense thoughts and reactions have jumped into the mix. It will be valuable for you to identify tools and external triggers that can wake you from the egoic trance. This exercise will help you become aware of how the progression through different stages works in you personally.

Think of the image of a dog focusing on a squirrel or other object with an intense stare and complete focus in attention. It is as if they are lost and completely immersed into that object. If you snap your fingers in front of the dog's face, you can snap them out of the trance in which they've become lost. The dog will then have the option and choice to go back to that object that entranced them or to move their attention elsewhere. If you have another object that is more productive for them to focus on, such as a treat or toy, they might then choose to move away from the object that put them into the initial trance. This is also what you must do for yourself. You must identify ways to break that egoic trance of your thoughts doing mental donuts in your mental parking lot. If you can create that pause in your thought stream, then you will be faced with the choice to return to them or to release them from the parking lot and move onto something more productive. Changing the nature of your relationship to your thoughts and emotions depends upon both your ability to insert pauses in egoic trances and to start choosing differently as to what thoughts you give your continued attention.

Chapter 16

Understanding Thoughts, Emotions, and Feelings Associated with Our Stories

In order to heal, we must understand better our thoughts and emotions as well as how they are both generated and used by our egos. This requires that we change the nature of our relationships to each of them, so that we are in control, and not controlled by them. This is taking back our power and remembering who we are. Looking at the thoughts underlying uncomfortable emotions with compassionate detachment, so that you can see the egoic misinterpretations and illusory conclusions, is critical to healing. We heal the emotions when we heal the thoughts through reframing the actual life circumstances from illusions into truths. The egoic thoughts and stories are often deeply rooted, and so these don't always release completely on the first reframing exercise. As a result, it will require repeated work to correct our thoughts and refocus on the truths, remembering that what we give our attention to is like fuel that energizes those thoughts into emotions and belief systems.

The first line of defense to any emotion that could be destructive is to be aware of the thoughts that could lead to the destructive expression of the emotion, if the thoughts are believed. By being aware of the thought, you automatically distance yourself from it, and don't identify directly with it because the connection to that thought is distanced. This is changing the nature of your relationship to your thoughts and emotions. Experiencing the thought as just a thought energy, instead of it being *you* or part of your identity ("my thought" or "I am . . .") allows you the opportunity to choose not to feed it with your attention. Once a thought becomes a thought, identifying an "I," "me," "my," or "mine," it becomes empowered to take up residence in your mind and become part of how your ego defines you. While your ego generates the thought, the storyline reflected in the thought is not who you are. This false identification with the thoughts leads to suffering. This is also where your thoughts move to the next stage and become an emotion. Without identifying with thoughts and emotions, you experience life differently, and this is key to happiness, healing, and enlightenment, as it represents freedom from the grip of the ego, and therefore, from suffering. More importantly, this awareness represents the beginning of your acknowledgement that you are much more than your thoughts or your emotions. This freedom is the reward for breaking the identification with the mind and produces a different relationship to our thoughts and emotions.

If you become identified with a thought—which is another way of saying that you've become attached to it—and it results in an emotion rising within your emotional energy body, you will have to address both the thought and the emotion in order to free yourself from the suffering that it can create. In an earlier chapter, we reviewed the different stages of escalation of thought–through–emotion–to–behavior, and that discussion is relevant to refer back to here. If you become too identified with thoughts or emotions, meaning you become too attached to them, they will become more entrenched into your mental and emotional bodies. Your mental and emotional bodies impact your physical body. This is why many of the earlier exercises in this book focus on the physical sensations as you experience certain thoughts and emotions. Once the physical body reaction has been activated, it is more difficult to convince the mind that the emotion is not based on a truth or a real scenario. Emotions, and the physical manifestations of those emotions, will appear to be self-validating to the mind.

Instead of making a conclusion about truth derived from an emotion, we want to develop an awareness of that emotion. Just as with thoughts, having an awareness of the emotion in an observer state is critical to healing them, and not allowing them to self-validate, escalate, or direct our behavior in knee-jerk reactions. Meditation increases our ability to have this awareness, as it helps us stand back and detach from the emotions, allowing us the distance to see what is happening, so that we can choose not to be pulled into them automatically based on conditioning. It is important that you take a step back and utilize your higher-self consciousness to move into an awareness of your emotions as early as possible before your ego gets too deep of a hold on you through them, and then uses them to express either aggressively or submissively.

The way to heal uncomfortable and painful emotions is to notice them, call them out by name, observe how they feel in the body – the physical sensations – and then just allow them to flow out with the natural expiration of the tension of the moment. The key is then to release those thoughts that triggered those emotions as well. This is not a pushing them out, but rather allowing them to exist and flow with neither indulgence nor resistance, while not watering them with your continued attention. If you continue to replay the thoughts, the emotions will come back repeatedly and will tend to intensify. This is why it is critical to identify the thoughts that precipitated the emotions, so that you can see the cause of the painful emotions as soon as possible. This awareness heals.

Sometimes, the thoughts that elicited the emotions will be the memories of painful moments in certain circumstances. Remember that pain is natural, and we all experience painful moments, but suffering is not normal, natural or required. The suffering is caused by our continual replaying of those moments, and extrapolating them into even more painful conclusions and commentary that escalate the thoughts and emotions even further. Seeing this is how we heal it. Seeing its falseness helps us to surrender the continual replays and commentaries to just the facts of what occurred, while seeing others involved in the circumstances with the same compassionate detachment.

Meet your emotions with peace, kindness, compassion, and allowance, without indulgence or belief in their so-called truth, and then they will naturally relax and dissipate. Just notice the emotion, observing the experience of it. Emotions are energy, and they merely create a series of sensations in the body. It is the stories attached to the emotions that are what make you want to suppress or express the emotion to get rid of it. *The energy sensations themselves do not cause suffering.* When you stop giving attention to the stories surrounding the emotions, the sensations of the emotional energy will also die down.

Tools and Techniques for Understanding and Diffusing Your Own Thoughts and Emotions.

There are several helpful techniques for investigating the origin of your uncomfortable emotions. The ones I describe here are those that will help you change the nature of your relationship to the emotions and to your originating thoughts. Which techniques will work best for you will be individual. For some, one technique will work best, and for others a combination of two or more will produce the most effective results. I describe each in this section, along with exercises in the Companion Audio and Workbook that allow you to for you to experience each of them to determine which one(s) work best for you.

Intimacy. Intimacy, as a technique, is the process of sitting closely with that emotion to understand it, hear it, see how it reacts and ripples through your physical body and experience, and get to know it. Through the intimacy technique, you notice the emotion, accept that it is there, and experience it, while you explore it with curiosity. To have intimacy with the emotion and release and transmute it, you must be well-acquainted with it—how it feels, what it looks like, and so on, so when it arises, you can recognize it, know its details, and better respond to it. You want to be able to:

- (a) name it
- (b) understand it
- (c) identify what you're doing with it
  - ✓ Are you blaming it, venting it, repressing it, or letting it mutate into a negative state, such as hostility and ill-will?

Intimacy allows you to observe what you're doing with the emotion and how it is expressing in you. This awareness and observation allows you to take back your power and stop being run by the emotion. With this awareness, comes the power of choice. Through this awareness, you can choose how you use those emotions. This choice opportunity can lead you to use the energy of those emotions more consciously as fuel, or to simply allow them to be and then flow out, releasing them. Both options are constructive and healthy uses of our emotional energies. Intimacy allows you to relate *to* the emotion, rather than *from* it, because you are facing it instead of being wrapped up in it, consumed by it, and identifying from it. This observation position allows you just enough distance from the emotion to facilitate a balanced and wise perspective on the emotion and use of its energy. This balanced relationship with the emotion is a state where you are neither consumed by the emotion nor ignoring, disassociated from or shaming it.

With intimacy, you must be able to listen deeply to the emotion, both to what is and what is not being said by and through the emotion. This is a listening and understanding process. You listen to the emotion's communication, intentions, and comprehension, how the emotion feels in your body, and what that energy is motivating or inspiring in you as a reaction. This is both an intellectual and energetic understanding of the emotion. Once you can recognize and understand this emotional state, the healing process can begin through a higher self and rationale brain collaboration recognizing what is and is not truth from the circumstances. From this awareness position, you can more readily see what is a knee-jerk reactionary process based on misunderstanding and misinterpretation, versus a consciously chosen response based on the compassionate detachment of the higher self.

Accomplishing true intimacy with your emotions requires a willingness to engage in a deep vulnerability because it requires you to remain emotionally transparent with uncomfortable emotions. Emotions such as shame and fear, particularly, can make you feel uncomfortable with vulnerability. This vulnerability, however, is not a weakness. Instead, this vulnerability is an immense strength. Without this vulnerability, you cannot accomplish the level of deep intimacy that is required in order to understand and, then, heal your emotions. In order to achieve any form of intimacy, it requires vulnerability and a willingness to be transparent. This is reflective of your relationship to anyone, including to yourself in your own psyche and being.

As you can recall the details of your personal circumstantial history, this vulnerability will allow you to separate the historical facts from the storylines your ego told you *about* those circumstances and what they might have *meant*. It is important to see the facts of the circumstances as distinct from the ego's commentary and conclusions about those circumstances that became part of, or were derived from, your stories and conditioning. Knowing and seeing when your ego's commentary and conclusions are kicking in is part of this transparency, vulnerability, and intimacy. Through this process, you can see and know when you are being triggered and reactive, and how that triggering is connected to a past circumstance (likely from childhood), about which the ego created commentary and overreaching conclusions. This intimacy and connection will help you understand better the types of circumstances you face in the present day that can present a triggering for you. This helps you to be more aware of your own conditioning, and your thoughts and emotions. This informed awareness aids you in moving into your higher-self observer state, instead of staying in the reactive egoic state.

Having empathetic compassionate detachment in this intimacy process will allow you to stay in touch with your true, higher self, while allowing your emotions to flow through you without either getting attached to them or burying them. In no event do you want to let emotions—whether in a healthy, balanced or an unhealthy, imbalanced expression—distract you from who you truly are in your true, higher self. Staying in touch with your higher self, even while being in the midst of strong emotions, is what makes relational intimacy possible.

Inquiry. The inquiry technique engages your intellect in order to assist your higher self in investigating the emotion and its underlying thoughts. Through the inquiry technique, you can look at and investigate the genesis of the thoughts behind the emotions. By engaging the intellect in this investigation technique, you immediately move into the observer state that allows you to take a step back from the throws of the emotion. That step back defuses the strength of that emotional energy as you focus on the intellect in a rational inquiry effort. This stepping back is not a suppression or ignoring of the emotion, but is just an expansion of your view to see the forest and how that emotion tree fits into it. It is a way of uncloaking yourself from the wrap and grip of that emotion to see and understand it. This step back allows you to move into a balanced place of empathy and compassionate detachment with the emotion.

As an emotion arises, when using this inquiry technique, you start your investigation into that emotion by asking questions of it. With the intention of getting to the root of the uncomfortable emotions, you ask what were the thoughts that created or contributed to the emotion. Once you can see what thoughts were part of that emotional energy rise, you gain valuable information about your own mental and emotional bodies, as well as how the egoic thought stream created a ripple reaction. When you see this thought–emotion causal connection, it operates further to defuse the emotion, so you no longer feel the heightened nature of the emotion. When you are gripped by a heightened emotion, you are usually going to be driven either to express it in an aggressive or submissive manner by venting or suppressing it. This step back into awareness through the inquiry technique provides a dual benefit of both uncovering some egoic conditioning, as well as defusing uncomfortable and sabotaging expressions of emotions. This inquiry process is another way of allowing you to relate *to* the emotions in a balanced way in order to get at their roots.

By investigating the emotions and their generating thoughts, you can disassemble the ego's illusions to reveal the higher self and life as it really is. Understanding the truth of emotions breaks the ego's illusions, freeing you from the ego's lies and suffering. The ego's perspective is usually based on partial truths and misinterpretations. Working backward from the emotion to see what thoughts created it takes the control and power of the emotion and the ego away, giving it back to you. The ego uses emotions to validate its storylines because the emotions make those stories seem real. Summoning the rational side of the brain while in an observer state will disempower the ego and its hold over your mind in that moment.

Discourse. The discourse technique is a more interactive form of getting to know the emotion than the intimacy model, combined with an element of inquiry. In the discourse technique, the emotion itself engages with you, whereas with an inquiry, you are delving into an exploration *about* the emotion. Discourse is an inquiry **with** the emotion and the unconscious mind where the ego's conditioning and triggers reside. Through discourse, you invite the emotion to reveal the beliefs behind it that live in your unconscious mind, having been put there by the ego. For this discourse technique to work, you must surrender judgment and allow the thoughts of the ego, which are driving the emotion, to speak directly to you as you ask questions and engage with the emotion as a separate entity from you. Remember, emotions are just energy in motion, and they are not *you* or *yours*, even though it was your ego that elicited them. It's a fine line where you must take responsibility for them, but without identifying with them as part of you or your identity. In the Companion Audio, I lead you through exercises on the discourse technique, along with intimacy and inquiry techniques, in order for you to experience working with specific emotions.

As you identify the negative and uncomfortable storylines about yourself, others, and life that your ego has been telling you, you must be open to hearing truths that differ from these stories. Hearing a story and believing it are not the same. You can hear the rantings and sorrow of a toddler while still knowing that the toddler's perspective does not represent truth or reality. That toddler, however, believes those stories and perspectives and is suffering as a result. You hear the toddler out, comfort the toddler, communicate the actual truth, and then help the toddler engage in a new perspective based on truth. You don't sit there and watch the toddler writhe around on the floor in misery without trying to engage the toddler in a more productive perspective with a different truth on which the toddler can focus to redirect the toddler to more constructive behavior. This is how you want to treat your egoic thoughts and emotions.

When you can hear and see the truths of the circumstances that gave rise to the egoic stories from the higher-self perspective, seeing where the ego's lenses are, you can more easily see the actual truths, false assumptions, leaps in judgments, and illusions. Ask your egoic mind, "Why do you feel a need to protect or fear?" You can thank the ego for trying to protect you if it had fears. If the ego believed in a lack, you can identify where you see false egoic assumptions and where you have abundance in actuality. This redirecting of your mind to focus your thoughts on gratitude, love, and compassion, which are the truths of life and of your higher self, will remind you of the joy and abundance that exists in life. This is where you want to focus.

This seeing truths and refocusing on gratitude, compassion, and abundance is not about putting rose-colored lenses in your eyes to cover up, or blind you to darker realities, like an ostrich with its head in the sand. Instead, this process is a truth-seeking refocusing on the realities of your actual circumstances versus the assumptions, overreaching conclusions, and egoic projections. Do you see the beautiful flower of the rose, or do you believe misinterpreted and over-reaching conclusions that all roses are dangerous plants because some have sharp thorns? You don't have to be blind to the thorny stems on some, but you can hold the stem with gloves while you admire and focus on the beautiful flower, seeing the falseness of the story that they are dangerous plants to fear. Do you focus on that car, house, or personal accessory you don't have, thinking over-reaching conclusions that you are always lacking, never measuring up to others? Or, do you focus on the closet of clothes and car that you do have, which allows you to come and go as you please, for which you can feel immense gratitude, knowing that things do not equate to success or self-worth?

Every emotion has a life span, so letting it go and have its natural life span without focusing on the egoic stories that elicit those emotions is key. The stories and emotions will take on a life of their own if you allow them to linger, or worse – bolster them with more stories and attempts at validation. Emotions can morph into other emotions such as anger, shame, and blame. The ego, then, will generate additional stories to justify and rationalize those emotional extensions. That emotional snowball will just get larger and larger, as well as more and more powerful and forceful as it rolls down the hills of your mental and emotional bodies. Taking responsibility for your stories does not require you to roll around in them. You simply acknowledge: "My ego did that; I see that now. I have the power and authority to let this go now, and I choose to let it go." *This is taking back your power.* Otherwise, you continue to be the dog being wagged by the egoic tail, as well as by others' behaviors, as you get pulled into egoic behaviors in a knee–jerk reaction to others' egoic behaviors. Being in the egoic state of mind is like being that flimsy box strewn about in the rapids of the flow of life, instead of being in your sturdy kayak with the sturdy oar to steer around the boulders and through the rapids.

You *always have a choice* in what you think. Therefore, you always have a choice in the emotions that arise in you, as well as in how you act and behave in response to them. The question is whether you see that choice. If you are in your egoic mindset, you will rarely see that choice point. However, when you are in your higher self, you will be able to see the ego's work in the situation, and, therefore, you will always be able to see that choice opportunity.

Dealing with the Pain of Learning Experiences.

There is no denying that there are times in life when we are presented with very uncomfortable situations, whether of our own making, or just from the rapids of life that we come upon. These circumstances will often produce painful experiences. Our challenge in those circumstances is to see where we have lessons to learn, and where we have to be at peace and allow the flow of life to present itself while we respond to it as best we can in that moment. The key to being at peace with whatever presents itself is to surrender our desire for things and people to be different. The next step, then, is to have gratitude for the lessons and growth opportunities that may be present within those circumstances. The attitude we have as we go through inevitable, uncomfortable circumstances will determine how we experience those circumstances. We can either be miserable in suffering or choose to have gratitude for the gifts that are always present, even in the midst of undesirable and uncomfortable situations. When we are in our higher-self consciousness, our strength, courage, compassion (for self and others), along with gratitude, will ease the pain and prevent suffering.

Suffering will linger as long as it takes for you to shift into the direction of gratitude, love, peace and harmony—which is the truth of the nature of life and of who you really are as your higher self. Remember, pain is natural to experience in life, but suffering is not. Suffering is the misery of regret, shame, anger, resentment, resistance, and fear of life combined with the thoughts that underlie those emotions. Pain usually comes from the sadness or sorrow of a loss or the recognition that we may not have been our best self at some point. However, this pain can be converted into something positive, such as gratitude for the awareness of a lesson from which we become better, and channeling that emotional pain energy into ways we can help others. Wishing for life or others to be different and lamenting things as they are will always produce suffering because we cannot change what is in that moment. The good news about suffering, however, is that once we've had enough of it, we will look for a different path, which will eventually lead us to seek a different way of BEing that can lead us to more joy, love, compassion, and peace. How long we engage in suffering thoughts and emotions will always be a choice of either continuing to blame others and life, versus taking responsibility for our own attitudes, egoic thoughts, emotions and behaviors, even in the most uncomfortable or undesirable of circumstances.

If you feel you are suffering with lingering sadness, shame, blame, recurring or regular anger, or other heavy emotions and negative thoughts during a life episode, look at what your thoughts entail, go through the inquiry, discourse, or intimacy techniques and see where you can identify lies, exaggerations, overreaching conclusions, and similar egoic storylines that are making you suffer unnecessarily. Remember that the ego's judgment and blame are tools it uses to avoid looking at its own thoughts, fears, and expectations. Look underneath those surfaces to address directly these illusions brought to you by the ego. Joy, wisdom, love, and compassion are still always available characteristics of our higher self, even in the midst of painful and uncomfortable situations.

The voice in your head—which is the ego's thoughts, beliefs and storylines—can distract you from the joy, wisdom, perseverance, love, and compassion of your higher self. These higher–self traits are the qualities you most need during challenging times. These higher–self qualities will allow you to draw from those circumstances the valuable lessons and growth that they represent. The voice in your head—your ego—does not have wisdom, love, or clarity. It is filled only with the programming of the storied and colored lens of the ego's conditioning. When you are distracted by the ego's thoughts, fears, resentments, judgments, and angers, you cannot be present in your higher self to draw upon its valuable qualities in the moment, which are the only qualities that can lift you through challenging times. This requires a trust in life, in your higher self, and in the motivations and inspirations of the higher self.

The ego and its thought stream will try to talk you out of the higher-self motivations and inspirations with its justifications, rationalizations, and fear–based thoughts and suggested actions. A key indicator of whether you are being distracted by the ego's thoughts is the physical sensations your body is experiencing in a given moment. With the exercises you did in the previous chapters, you are becoming more familiar with those sensations. Another important indicator of your ego's state is the use of its self-centric thoughts involving "I," "me," "mine," or "my" being dominant in your mind. Use of these pronouns as a central factor in the thoughts of your mind indicate the ego's spin of the circumstances around the identity that the ego has created for you. The stories spinning in the egoic mind are the film strip, or virtual reality, that the ego has created for you.

When you access your higher self, it will see through the fears and judgments of good and bad from the ego. Because the ego is attached to a particular outcome and desire, when life does not present the ego's specific desired circumstance, it will view the circumstance as *bad*, and something to be feared. This egoic belief in a circumstance being *bad* will induce thoughts of victimhood, woe-is-me, anger, resentment, sadness, or other negative and dysfunctional thoughts and resulting emotions. The ego will want to change things that it cannot, and wants life to be different than what it is. This is where the suffering arises. The higher self will see the truth that, in every undesirable circumstance, there is always something positive for which to be grateful. This could be a lesson for growth that gives us greater wisdom or strength, or it could be a path that leads to something unexpected that gives us a different opportunity of some kind. With the perspective of the higher self, any circumstance will be accepted and be seen for the truths of the positive aspects that it represents. The higher self will view these circumstances from the perspective of the silver linings, growth, strength, and lessons that are always present. We only need to approach the circumstance without attachment or resistance in a desire for something different in order to see these truths.

The egoic perspective on undesired and uncomfortable circumstances will include lamenting, resisting, and resenting the circumstances. As a result, the ego cannot perceive the lesson. Further, when the ego cannot perceive the lesson, the egoic consciousness prevents us from growth, strength, perseverance and many other pearls left by the ebbing waters of the flow of life. Let me state this with crystal clarity: *no change, healing, or growth can occur when we are in our egoic consciousness* where we are both resenting and resisting what life presents to us. I hope that this statement alone will help you look at your suffering and uncomfortable circumstances differently and help you release your attachments, resentments, and resistance to your circumstances, and shift into a higher self perspective and consciousness.

Part of egoic resistance to life's circumstances includes when we judge, shame, and blame others. This is part of our suffering, whether we realize it or not. When we have these judgmental, blaming, and shaming thoughts running around in our heads— even when about others—it is a form of suffering. These thoughts about others result in our suffering because it causes us stress, anxiety, and negatively used emotional energies of anger in the aggressive expression and sadness in the submissive expression. Only when you can allow life and others to be as they are will you be able to receive the highest good from a situation, whether that is a lesson and growth, an opportunity, or other benefit. This allowance of what is does not, however, require that we be on the resistance's opposing pole of complacency. To believe that if we are not resisting what we don't like, we must be, therefore, complacent is the egoic perspective of the extremes of the imbalanced poles. Allowance, without complacency, is like living out the Serenity Prayer.[18]

> *God, grant me the serenity to accept*
> *the things I cannot change,*
> *Courage to change the things I can,*
> *And wisdom to know the difference.*

The Serenity Prayer represents the balance between resistance and complacency, reflecting the higher self perspective on our circumstances. We must be careful, however, in how we define the circumstances that we can change for which we want courage. We don't want to insist that we can change situations that, in truth, amount to simply just resisting what is. That will be one of the ego's tricks for control. When we seek to invoke courage for change, we must engage in this initiative initially with an acceptance and acknowledgement of what is without resentment or resistance. It does exist, and we cannot change what is in the present moment. We can simultaneously accept what is while making efforts to change it. We must be certain, however, that we are seeking change from the balanced approach of the higher self, so we do not become attached to a particular outcome or develop a need or attachment to things being different. This courage to seek change must always be balanced by the wisdom of knowing what we cannot change in our circumstances and in others. This wisdom comes from our higher self. Meditation can help you access this wisdom with you higher self, using your body sensations for confirmation.

---

[18] The **Serenity Prayer** was written by the American theologian, Reinhold Niebuhr (1892–1971).

Chapter 17

Taking Responsibility for Our Own Thoughts, Stories, and Emotions

We want to have the intention and be willing to take full responsibility for everything that we do, say, think, emote, and feel. Simultaneously, we want to have the intention and willingness to surrender both our expectations for ourselves and others, as well as our ego's tendency to view others' actions to be a statement about us. This taking responsibility for our own thinking, behaviors, and conditioning is similar to our discussion on taking responsibility for our own projections discussed earlier, but has deeper and wider implications here.

In this dual effort of taking responsibility and surrendering, we need to express compassion for ourselves, as well as others. Without having this compassion, we will likely fall into blame, shame, and judgment—whether of ourselves or others—and we will not be able to see truths. When you can see your own egoic conditioning, you can take responsibility for it, hold it more lightly, and not put it above love and relationship with others. Some common thoughts and stories we think and tell ourselves, which are actually coming from our egos, that cause suffering and sabotage with dysfunctional uses of anger, resentment, and irritation towards others include the following:

- *Others are so rude.*

- *Others are so inconsiderate.*

- *These people are so stupid [or other fill in the blank for how you view others regularly].*

- *The world is a dog–eat–dog, heartless, rough and/or terrible place.*

- *I can't believe someone would do this _____.*

These statements and thoughts come from the ego from either taking another's behavior personally or being attached to another's actions. There are several important factors to remember about others' behaviors:

- Another person's behavior is not about you, despite how personally affronted your ego may be from their behavior, and regardless of whether another's behavior is or is not directed towards you.

- Another person's behavior never causes your emotions. Your own thoughts, expectations, and attachments cause your emotions. This is true regardless of how unkind the behavior of another may be. Remember, this is not about blame or shame – whether of yourself or others. Another's behavior may be cruel, but we always have the choice as to how we react or respond to this behavior and what commentary we create regarding it, even where we think our expectations are reasonable and *right*. This does not relieve another of their own responsibility in their own unkind behavior. Responsibility and blame are very different thought processes. The former has no moral judgment of *right/wrong* or *good/bad*, but the latter does. Blame comes from the ego, and is attached to expectations. Maintaining attachments to expectations will not serve us in achieving balance or in allowing our higher self to be in the lead. This taking responsibility for our own thoughts and emotions is part of taking back our power. We are liberated from the pain, anger, blame, shame and sadness when we can release our need to be justified in victimhood, even if we were, in fact, victims of another's behavior. Without taking responsibility for our own responses (even if natural and understandable), we retain an attachment, unwittingly, to the pain and suffering. With responsibility for ourselves comes liberation and empowerment because we remove the power of another to cause us emotional and mental suffering.

- The behavior of others is a reflection of what is going on inside their own internal state of their thought stream and their storylines. As a result, while your behavior may be a trigger for someone else, the way another reacts to you is still a reflection of their own storylines and shadow triggers. They will react to anyone else in the same manner, so their behavior is never going to be personal to you. This is true of your behavior being a result of your own state, whether your higher self or your own egoic storylines and expectations. Another's behavior may trigger reactions in you, but they are your triggers, and therefore you need to take responsibility for them, and not blame your triggers on another's poor behavior.

When we can view others from the eyes of our higher self, we can see them with eyes of compassion, instead of the judgment, blame, and condemnation of the ego. So, if your reaction to them is one of judgment, blame, shame and condemnation, this will be a reflection of your own egoic storylines and shadow triggers that reveal your own ego's areas for investigation, healing, and mastery. If your shadow triggers and egoic storylines are being seen, healed, and well-mastered, and you can experience the circumstance while in your higher self, your response will be one of compassionate detachment. You will not feel attached to, or otherwise personally impacted by, another's actions, and you can see both yourself and others for who you each truly are with genuine compassion.

If you meet unkind behavior with your own unkind behavior, you contribute to the downward spiral of the collective egoic consciousness that feeds off and escalates dysfunction and negative personal relationships. I remind you again of the Newton's Cradle balls. You are either contributing to the energy and consciousness of the ego or to that of the higher self in yourself and others. There is no neutral position because we are always giving off our own energy, and everyone is impacted by the ripple effects of our own state of BEing. You will also find that when you can respond to another from your higher self state, you will also feel better because the energy and state of BEing of the higher self is one of peace and compassion, which will always feel better than anger and irritation.

As you work towards the integration of your egoic self with your higher self in the lead, you will move through an ebb and flow. The learning experience you go through as you recognize when you are in your ego versus being in your higher self will develop a maturity in you that enhances your growth and strength. Only after you've experienced an unproductive and uncomfortable experience can you grow from that to better mastery. This principle holds true for all of our growth experiences. We learn compassion and love through others', and even our own, unkind behavior.

Our ego's default reaction to another's unkind behavior will be to return that unkind behavior, which usually includes labeling them with unkind characterizations and personas. This has several destructive effects:

- When we impose a label onto another, we reinforce that label and that behavior, both subconsciously and energetically for that person. This reinforcement occurs both in our own psyche and in that of the others'. This contributes to their addictions to their own egoic state and dysfunctional personas and emotional energies.

- Because projecting labels onto others reinforces those labels within our own psyches, we reinforce these storylines in our own egoic mind, and we will perpetuate that egoic storyline and lens. This reinforcement and perpetuation of labels will reinforce our own internal film strip, so we will continue to see that behavior in others. As a result, this storyline will continue to be reflective of our experiences.

- The negative, destructive labels we use are made up of negative thoughts, so when we fill our thoughts with these negative labels of others, it increases our own negative emotions, energies, and feelings that fill our own energetic fields, mentally, emotionally, and physically.

As you can see, blaming, shaming, and projecting labels onto others has far–reaching implications for both ourselves, as well as those onto whom we project our own negativity and storylines.

Putting effort into managing our ego and prioritizing our higher-self state of being is also important when we, ourselves, may have been unkind, inconsiderate, or otherwise are facing criticism. Only when we are grounded in our higher-self consciousness can we be graceful in receiving criticism and seeing the truth of our own behavior. Even when another's criticism is laced with, or even coming primarily from, their egoic conditioning, it is always useful to look objectively at our own behavior to see whether and what we might have expressed from our own egoic conditioning that may warrant an apology or a deeper look for an opportunity for more healing and ego mastery.

As we identify thoughts that induced us to use an emotion destructively and dysfunctionally, we want to be sure that our ego does not slide into justifications or rationalizations for that destructive behavior. I will reiterate here my criticism of historical psychoanalysis practices I discussed earlier about honoring emotions. In my opinion, honoring emotions is tantamount to rationalizing and justifying them much of the time. I am in no way suggesting that we want to demonize or suppress them either. The balanced and healthier way of dealing with emotions, in my opinion, is to acknowledge that those emotions arose within you—which is NOT an honoring or other rationalization of them—and then look at the thoughts that triggered those emotions. Emotions are not truth-sayers.

The triggers for our emotions are our own thoughts, so we want to look at the facts and truths of the situation, instead of any labels, characterizations, assumptions or conclusions derived from our thoughts. Acknowledging that we had those emotions, but without attaching to, suppressing or demonizing them, requires, and is an embodiment of, a compassionate detachment from those emotions. Compassionate detachment allows us just enough distance from the emotions to gain perspective on them and the situation, without dismissing them, as if we are looking at the forest and how a particular tree fits into that forest. This compassionate detachment holds those emotions loosely and with compassion.

Conversely, to honor our emotions, in my opinion, is to offer an attachment to and justification for them. This honoring attachment and justification is not taking responsibility for them, and is not healthy or conducive to having awareness and perspective on our own thoughts that elicited the emotions. Instead of detaching from them with an arms-length ability to observe them, when honoring them, we end up living from them, being immersed in often destructively used emotions. The notion of honoring our emotions functions as an encouragement to keep our mind focused on them, which fosters the attachment to them as a form of justification. This honoring does not heal or release them. What is needed for healing and functional mastery is to see what incorrect conclusions about events underlie the emotions. Healing and compassionate detachment doesn't lead us to demonize the emotions or ourselves, either. Compassionate detachment allows us to acknowledge their presence while we look under the covers and see from what these emotions arose.

This compassionate detachment approach to traumatic experiences is particularly important when our traumas were experienced as children. Children do not have the sophistication of an adult, so they are more susceptible to the destructive egoic storylines. Children, in particular, often blame themselves for unkindness or abuse by adults. The abusers and oppressors will project blame onto their victims. Children will often adopt the submissive expression of that egoic storyline, drawing very dysfunctional and destructive conclusions, labels and stories about who they are, who others are, and how life is. Some common conclusions and storylines the child ego creates include:

- *I can't depend on or trust people for my survival because those people don't love or care about me.*
- *I am unlovable.*
- *I am a bad person.*
- *I am unworthy of respect.*
- *I am without worth, talent, or value.*
- *I fear for my survival.*
- *I deserve(d) the unkind treatment*

When people suffer from traumatic events, the storylines and thoughts like those listed above will continue to define their perception of their identity and how they view others and life. Those who suffer trauma often have deep, dysfunctional emotions associated with those events. It is understandable that traumatic experiences would produce dysfunctional thoughts and emotions. Being understanding of those emotions is not honoring them, rather it is having compassion for them. Compassion and honoring are not the same thing.

In my opinion, this honoring and feeling the feeling greatly interferes with the ability to heal from these destructive trauma stories and their associated emotions. When we look back at the facts of the circumstances with detachment, we can often see where the conclusions, labels, and assumptions that we drew as children, and continued to reinforce and perpetuate as adults, were actually false. When we do this with compassion, along with that detachment, we can see the egoic pains of others as well. This changes how we view those circumstances and allows us to see those circumstances with the truth that others' actions resulted from their own pains and were not personal to us. Instead, we can see that others' behaviors were reflections of their own internal state, and we can deflate the anger, hurt, and beliefs in unworthiness. This is the reframing that we talked about earlier.

The truth for these victims is that there is nothing at all wrong with them. They simply lived through circumstances of abuse perpetrated on them by another because of what was going on inside that perpetrator. Part of the beauty and benefit of going into the shadow is the opportunity to reframe past circumstances that created false, painful storylines in our egoic psyche that were so painful that we could not deal with them. Shadow work allows us to integrate and heal through uncovering the falseness of these stories and our fears about them. This is freeing, and releases a huge weight from our minds, souls, and spirits. Doing this shadow work is not just about opening old wounds, or thinking we'll be faced with and must deal with our own darkness, which can be scary. Instead, *shadow work is about finding our gifts and truths and letting go of the illusions and secrets that keep us sick in an egoic consciousness of suffering and struggle.*

The traumatic events spawning storylines often spur ego–created identities for us steeped in the justification for those emotions and storylines. These persona archetypes often center around being justified in our anger or sadness or resentment, or worse, that spawn dysfunctional and suffering chain reactions if we don't heal them. We are responsible for healing our own traumas and suffering. It does no good to continue engaging in any blame, whether of others or ourselves, because that just results in perpetuation of our own suffering, even if our egos feel validated.

Chapter 18

Relating to Others and Our Relationships

Accepting what life presents to us in any given moment without resistance, while still seeking change where we can, is more than just how we approach our life circumstances. This acceptance of life without resistance is also how we must approach others. We will suffer if we cannot accept others as they are, or if we are attached to a desire for others to be different. We want to be accepted for who we are, so we need to be able to do that for others. The ironic thing about this is that we cannot accept others for who they are until we accept ourselves for who we are and stop the inner critic from taking a hold of our thoughts and emotions about ourselves. Being able to accept others for who they are, enabling successful and functional relationships, is just one of many reasons why we want to address our own inner critic and stop rejecting ourselves. Remember, that accepting others for who they are does not mean we cannot simultaneously address unkind, inconsiderate, and sabotaging behavior in others. Balance, and the manner and intention motivating or inspiring our thoughts, words and behaviors, determines whether we are engaging in productive or destructive activities.

Accepting others as they are is the natural effect of living out many of the lessons we've discussed thus far. It requires an acknowledgment that our lack of acceptance and resulting judgment of others is a reflection of our own judgment and lack of acceptance of ourselves. In order to change how we view and treat others we must change how we view and treat ourselves. It also requires an acknowledgment that our own emotions about or towards others is a result of our own thoughts, expectations and attachments, not others' actions. It is our own thoughts of wanting or needing to be respected, loved, and treated with kindness that produces painful experiences when that expectation or desire is not met. If we didn't care about how another viewed or treated us, we would not feel pain at unkind treatment. We want to hold these desires and expectations lightly because it is often our attachment to a need for others to like and respect us that underlies much of our suffering. When another is unkind to us, we must remember that their behavior reflects their internal state and not our worthiness. When we can fully absorb and integrate this teaching, we will recognize that attaching to the need for respect, affirmation, or another specific treatment from others is futile because it is entirely unrelated to who we are. What matters is knowing who we are without attachment to another's view or treatment of us. I want to note here that holding lightly any expectation or desire for certain treatment from others is different from maintaining boundaries of what we choose to accept from others. We can maintain strong boundaries without attaching to an expectation or desire, so if someone does not align with our boundaries, our pain does not impact our identity of who we think we, or they, are because of the misalignments.

Since we control our own emotions, consciously or unconsciously, we control how much judgment we render or how much love and compassion we give. If we don't feel love or compassion in a relationship, that is something that is on us, not the other person, just as another's lack of love and compassion is on them. It may be that another person for whom we do not feel love or compassion treats us or others unkindly, but that does not mean that we cannot feel compassion for that person and a basic love for that person as a fellow human. We can decide that this person is not aligned with what we choose to have in a relationship and the boundaries that we choose to maintain, but these choices do not mean that judgment and unkindness is a natural, or necessary, result of our choices when others do not align with them. This is another example of the role of compassionate detachment. When we detach from the need or desire for another to be different than who they are and what they present, it is easier to view them with compassion as a fellow being with their own higher self, who may be experiencing their own suffering and lessons.

Withholding love and compassion from another is a reflection of not only how you withhold love and compassion from yourself through the self-judgment of your inner critic, it can also be a tool that the ego uses to get what it thinks it needs or wants. The ego may believe that it gains control, power, superiority, safety, or some other benefit or advantage by withholding love and compassion, rendering judgment instead. This is classic ego. When we are in our higher selves, we can express this compassionate detachment by surrendering our desire for someone to be different. The ego is averse to surrender in any form or for any reason. The ego is about control and "winning," which it values more than love. It is uncomfortable for the ego to surrender its desires for others (or life) to be different and express compassionate detachment.

Here are a few tips for how to engage in this surrendering:

- Surrender the thoughts that start with "I want . . .," "I wish . . .," or "I expect. . . ." When those thoughts enter your mind, notice those thoughts, and become conscious of them as an observer, with an awareness that these are sabotaging thoughts that you must surrender in order to release the suffering.

- As you move into the observer state, look at what emotional attachment you might have to those thoughts. Emotional attachments come from your thought attachments that get replayed repeatedly in your mind. Because your emotions stem from your thoughts, if you have an attachment to a thought of wanting or wishing someone to be different, then you will likely have an emotional attachment as well.

- Choose a different thought to move your focus and attention to acceptance, gratitude, love and/or compassion. An even better tool is to release all thoughts, imagine yourself in your favorite place in nature, and just be there in your mind. The belaboring of gripping thoughts will create increasing suffering as they linger long enough to grow deeper roots that elicit corresponding emotions that seem to validate these dysfunctional thoughts, growing in intensity as the thoughts linger. The thoughts that have a hold over you will continue to grow into additional justifying thoughts that will only deepen and widen the emotions and suffering.

In order to accomplish these steps, you must have the willingness and intention to surrender gripping thoughts of attachment. Wanting the truth more than you want to be right will be key to being able to surrender those thoughts away from the ego's grip. An important thing to remember, here, as previously mentioned, is the fact that our inner thoughts and state becomes our external experience—*as within so without.* What we give our internal attention and focus to is very powerful, so we don't want to empower negative thoughts, as those will create negative experiences. When we take responsibility for our own ego's thoughts and experiences, we can respond to acts of unkindness from others with our own higher self's compassion, instead of retaliatory or reactionary egoic unkindness (aggressive expression of the ego) or sadness (the submissive expression of the ego). Finding fault is easy and is the default of the ego, so we must use conscious choice and awareness to break out of the ego's gripping thoughts and reactionary behaviors.

As we learned earlier, we are always creating ripple effects from our thought and emotional energies. Therefore, a loving internal state will create a more loving external expression, and will evoke a more loving response from others whom you touch with your energy. Love begets love, while judgment begets judgment. This is another energetic causal relationship fact that we learned earlier. If we are judgmental to others, it is just a reflection of how we are judgmental to ourselves, which we absorbed in egoic stories from being judged ourselves. It is a continuous cycle of triggering ripple effects that will perpetuate through your relationships.

While your unloving thoughts and actions may stem from how you were treated by others, once you reach adulthood and have the sophistication to see and understand your own ego's thoughts and emotions, you have the responsibility and accountability for the choices you make at that point. You either choose to continue the default programming of the ego, engaging in *hurt people hurting people,* or you choose the accountability of your own role in your conditioning and make a different choice. This is healing. This healing helps you, as well as others, to see the path to healing for their own conditioning and dysfunction. *Healed people heal people.* Are your ripple effects perpetuating a cycle of dysfunction and suffering, or creating a cycle of healing?

The extent of your own healing and happiness in your relationships will be dependent upon the extent and ability to which you can set aside your egoic desires, demands, expectations, judgments, fantasies, and ideals about a person, versus just simply BEing with the person with love and compassion. Your own thoughts are the source of your happiness versus unhappiness, your judgment versus acceptance, your anger or sadness versus compassion, and your irritation versus peace. No one makes you anything. You make yourself everything you experience or feel based on your own thoughts and egoic lenses or higher-self truths, each of which create your experience. Just as others are not responsible for your thoughts and expectations, you are not in control of, or responsible for, others' stories, beliefs, judgments, and expectations. When someone is judging you, realize their judgement is not personal to you. Their treatment of you is really about them, so don't take it personally. You can maintain your boundaries and still let others know that their judgments are not appreciated without return judgment and dysfunctional emotion.

In all situations, it is important and valuable for each person to hear others and discern whether there was an unkindness given (and not a shadow reaction of a perceived slight), but no one is responsible for another's thoughts, emotions, or experiences. As a result, it is important to recognize and accept that no one can change another, either. That means that you cannot be anyone's savior, and no one can be yours. Everyone must save themselves. You can help others see a different path for themselves through the ripple effects of your own walking in your higher self, but you can only offer yourself as a lead example with your loving and compassionate treatment of them while you maintain your own boundaries. You cannot do the healing work for anyone else. You can only give them love and compassion as you walk your own higher self path. Since the corollary is also true that no one can do the work for you, either, but can show you good examples and energetic responses through their higher-self consciousness leadership, it will help you to be conscious of the company you keep. If you are around others in their egoic state constantly triggering you, it takes more effort on your part to maintain your own higher-self state.

Showing another love and compassion who is in their sabotaging, conditioned state does not, however, require you to allow yourself to be subjected to their dysfunctional behavior. You can accept others as they are with their differences in conditioning, without accepting unkind treatment from them. It is important to remember that in order for us to see truth apart from the ego's conditioning, we must be in our higher selves when we are determining whether we are receiving unkind treatment, and whether that person's conditioning and ideals are merely different from ours. The ego sees differences in conditioning of others as "wrong," "bad," "inferior," and could even justify it as unkind, or inconsiderate, because others don't cater to or align with our own ego's expectations and ideals. The ego, with its rationalizations and justifications, can be very slippery and tricky.

Relationships will be only as strong as both parties' ability to surrender their egos. This isn't about sacrifice or subjugation of either person, but recognition that love is possible only when both are willing to put love and the relationship first, and deal with issues from that point. Most conflicts are about differences in egoic conditioning. If one person begins the surrender, usually the other will follow, unless one party in the relationship is so steeped in their egoic consciousness that their desire and intention for domination over others is too entrenched in their psyche. If that is the case, you will not be able to have a functional relationship with that person until he or she can access their higher self more often and more readily. When one person can trigger the other into their higher self, it can result in both parties putting down their egoic weapons. This is when peace and love is possible. The battles of conditioning and egos is a personal one where the battle is really inside you and with your own conditioning. The ego demands the other to be more like you and comply with your likes, dislikes, expectations and ideals. When you release your ego's addiction to its own expectations and ideals, you can put the relationship and love first. This surrender, however, is never to be taken to such an extreme that it amounts to one–sided sacrifice. As with everything we've discussed in this book, it is about balance and boundaries.

We each must take responsibility for our own thoughts, emotions, and consciousness state feelings internally, and engage with others about our emotions and feelings only after we've taken responsibility for them, which we ourselves have created. A productive conversation is to identify the issue and how to resolve it and is *not* the "*this is how I feel*" or "*how you make me feel*" conversation. Instead, a more productive statement and sentiment would be: "I know I am responsible for my own thoughts and emotions about this, and I'm working through those, but can we discuss this and try to find another path to make it easier for me?" Engaging with others while taking responsibility for your own thoughts, emotions, and consciousness state and using a practice of evoking qualities of the higher self, such as truth, love, compassion, and so on, will produce more constructive interactions. This type of encounter, versus confrontation or judgment and blame, will produce more positive interactions, both from you and from the other person.

Dealing with Others in Emotional States.

When others are in an egoic state with heightened sabotaging emotions, if you allow their emotion to just be, whether in you or another, it naturally relaxes, and dissipates without incident in its own time. This is how an emotional exchange between people diffuses. You allow their emotion to just be, without engaging with the other person to fight, disagree, or change. This is showing compassionate detachment. When you do not practice this compassionate detachment of observance and allowance without judgment, there are many possible ways you can react to someone you interpret as being unkind to you:

- Victimhood
- Anger
- Resentment
- Self-righteousness
- Judgment

When you are in your higher self, you can maintain the compassionate detachment, and this results in compassion for them in having a struggling, or suffering, egoic moment.

You have no control over how others see you, or how they respond to you, or what they say to you. You can only choose how you respond to them. Your own inner climate will determine how you respond or react to them. If you are in your egoic self, you will engage in knee-jerk reactionary behavior likely using one or more of the first five reactions listed above. If you are in your higher self state, you will respond with the compassionate detachment, knowing that their behavior has nothing to do with you, but is rather only a reflection of their own internal state

Chapter 19

Working with Specific Emotions and Consciousness State Feelings

Now that you know more about emotions generally, let's delve into some of the most common emotions to aid you in working with your own use of these common emotions.

Anger

Before we get into the details of anger, what it represents and how to work with it, it will be best for you to explore your own use of anger. Please answer the questions in the *Companion Workbook, Section III, Exercise 3*. It will be most helpful for you to answer these questions on your own use of anger before proceeding.

As with all emotions, anger arises from our thoughts. For our thoughts to evoke the emotion of anger, our thoughts will typically be thoughts of expectations that were not met. These thoughts could be expectations of entitlement or expectations of boundaries that we expect others to respect or abide. These boundaries could be our own personal boundaries and behavior expectations with respect to ourselves, or it could be expectations we hold for behavior with respect to others (which may be the same or different from those we hold with respect to ourselves).

Just as with all emotions, how we deal with anger can be either balanced or imbalanced on the aggressive or submissive side. When our thoughts are based on the egoic values and ideals, or about what we expect or feel entitled to from others, our use of emotions will nearly always be imbalanced. For example, if our anger stems from thoughts about our entitlement, which is an aggressive expression of a lack in self–worth, the anger will often be used in a similarly aggressive way. It is important to note here that there is a difference between entitlement (aggressive) and a balanced sense of worth and confidence with balanced boundaries. If our boundaries are based on a balanced sense of worth and confidence, we still have the option of using our anger in an imbalanced way on either aggressive or submissive sides. For example, we could have imbalanced expectations to be treated with preferential treatment because we think our needs are more important than those of others. This expectation is based on an aggressively imbalanced thought about our own superiority and a failure to appreciate others in the ego's typically self-centric way. Therefore, these expectations will usually use aggressively imbalanced anger energies when these expectations are not met. If our "expectations"[19] were based on a balanced foundation of our boundaries, we have a stronger base from which to use the

---

[19] I use "expectations" in quotes because having expectations—even about our boundaries—can be an egoic hijacking of our higher self's sense of worthiness and confidence, if not tightly balanced, which is what would then lead to an imbalanced use of anger if those boundaries were violated.

emotion in a balanced way. However, even though we could have a balanced boundary for being treated with equal worth and respect, we could still use our anger in imbalanced ways of venting or suppressing it just to get along when those boundaries are violated. When we suppress our anger by tending to be more submissive to another's behavior and story line, we tend to have weaker boundaries, and then fail to stand up for ourselves to enforce those boundaries, often in a conflict-averse belief that you need, or want, to get along in order to keep the peace.

Now, let's do more work with your personal use of anger. In this next exercise, you will need to think back to the scenario(s) that were the basis for your answer in Question 1 of Section III, Exercise 3. Please access the Companion Audio for *Section III, Exercise 4* for the guided part of the exercise, which will guide you through answering the questions listed in *Section III, Exercise 4* of the *Companion Workbook.*

The outwardly aggressive expression is what is commonly thought of as anger. This common notion of anger ignores the options of the submissively imbalanced use of anger and the balanced expressions. As a result, anger has received a notoriety that has demonized anger, and resulted in an increase in submissive expressions of anger from people believing that anger is *bad* by its very nature.

There are also institutionalized aggressively imbalanced uses of anger through another unhealthy application of honoring and feeling the feelings, in my opinion. There remains today a belief as well as a therapeutic practice of aggressively venting the emotional energy of anger through means such as hitting pillows or other aggressive venting expressions that portend to promote a healthy *feel the feeling*, or release of the emotion through venting. In my opinion, there is nothing healthy about venting of emotion in this way. This practice does not address the underlying dysfunctional thoughts that created the anger, and instead only promotes an aggressive expression of anger through this venting exercise. The practice of venting encourages attachment through justification and rationalizing thoughts that just perpetuate the same thought–emotion creation cycles. If the underlying thoughts creating the anger were themselves balanced, it is highly unlikely that the anger would be still around needing to be expressed outwardly in this venting. If the emotional energy was balanced, it would flow in and out with the rising and falling of the moment and/or be used as fuel for constructive acts. If the thoughts giving rise to the anger were imbalanced to begin with, and the anger lingers, this venting does not provide for a mechanism to convert that negative aligning anger energy into a balanced expression. Again, emotional energies begin and end with our thoughts and the nature of our relationship to them. Therefore, mastery and release of our emotions starts and ends with our thoughts, not an aggressive expression of venting. Even if anger has been dysfunctionally bottled up and suppressed, moving anger from the suppressive submissive expression to the aggressive expression is no healthier. It is just moving from one dysfunction to another.

While there is truth that the energy must be allowed to flow out, the aggressive venting of that anger goes beyond just allowing the anger to flow out naturally. Instead, that kind of venting of the anger energy moves us to interact from the anger instead of relating to the anger, and seeing how it is connected to our thoughts, or how we have dysfunctionally bottled up the anger in our bodies (likely along with bottled up thoughts that are doing donuts in our mental parking lot). The balanced use of anger is either to allow it, along with our thoughts that elicited that anger, to flow out naturally as the moment falls, or to use that energy to motivate us into functional and balanced action. Balanced action can include things such as donating your time or money to a cause devoted to helping maintain the boundaries and behaviors you align with and that anger you when violated, or participating in a demonstration (mindful of how demonstrations can be emotionally charged into an aggressive expression), or other act that is mindfully directed towards improvement of some kind. In many cases, anger is the result of aggressive expressions of entitlement and expectation. Without addressing these dysfunctional thoughts and stories in our egoic minds, we will experience an endless cycle of anger imbalances. Therefore, we must deal with the underlying issues of our thoughts and egoic stories. Nothing else will heal, and everything else is just a temporary anesthetic.

Let's now experience your personal anger in each of the imbalanced states of aggressive and submissive expressions as well as balanced anger. Please access the *Companion Audio* for *Section III, Exercise 5* and it will lead you through exercises that you will also answer in the *Companion Workbook* for *Section III, Exercise 5.*

Most emotions have a tendency to morph into additional emotions from an escalation in our thoughts. Shame, blame, guilt, resentment and anger all tend to derive from another emotion and easily morph into another. In order to heal and use our anger constructively in a balanced way, we must have an understanding of it. Any of the techniques of intimacy, discourse, or inquiry that we discussed previously can provide this knowledge of our emotion. We must understand from where it is derived, and what it does while in our energy bodies. Not only does this understanding of our emotions help us in our own healing, but it helps us deal in a balanced way with others who project their anger or other emotion onto us. When we understand our own thoughts and emotions, we have greater control, and are triggered less into our own dysfunctional use of anger by another's imbalanced expression.

In order to understand your own anger, please access the *Companion Audio* for *Section III, Exercise 6*, which will lead you through the intimacy, discourse, and inquiry exercises to get to know your anger in detail and answering the questions in the *Companion Workbook, Section III, Exercise 6.*

Common Anger Morphing Expressions

Anger Phobia. This is demonizing of the anger emotion itself. For those who suffer from this thought process, they believe that anger itself is bad, and that to feel anger, especially to express it, whether aggressively or balanced, is a sign of being uncontrolled and immature spiritually, mentally, and emotionally. People with this belief system view anger as synonymous with the aggressive expression and morphing of ill-will, hostility, aggression, and hatred. This belief system induces people to keep the peace at all costs, and they tend to have weak boundaries as a result. The spiritual communities have a high degree of this belief system running through it. This belief system represents and produces the submissively imbalanced expression of anger, and is equally dysfunctional as the aggressive expression.

Because of the suppressive nature of this submissive expression, people tend to create a deeper, wider, and more powerful shadow to their egos involving anger. This can also produce morphed aggressive belief systems of blame, shame, and other negative labels about themselves and others who they view as exhibiting any anger energy, whether balanced or aggressive. This becomes a passive aggressive expression. The more we fear and reject anger, the more susceptible we are to having weak boundaries, submitting to others' story lines and projected behaviors, allowing ourselves to be victims. This can extend to the dysfunctional, submissive belief system that having open boundaries is a sign of spiritual maturity and getting along, living from a place of love and compassion. The truth instead is that this belief system often reflects a submissively expressed ego and shadow that still requires healing. There often will be wounds from previously abused boundaries and other submissive storylines about lack of worthiness. Saying "No," and having boundaries that we enforce with compassion and courage is how our higher self can encounter circumstances in a balanced way.

Hostility. One of the aggressively morphing expressions from anger is hostility. When our anger escalates from our thoughts of unmet expectations that balloon past anger into actual ill–will towards another, hostility will result. Hostility is a result of us not catching our thoughts or emotions in Stages 1 or 2 of the Stages of Progression discussed in a previous chapter, and it ends up getting to Stage 3 from continuing to recycle thoughts of our anger, offense, and violated expectations. When we get to this stage, we have greater difficulty in controlling these thoughts and emotions, and this often leads to Stage 4 of sabotaging behaviors.

Hatred. Hatred is the next escalated stage of hostility, if left unchecked. This level of ill–will projected onto another is a more intense, deeper version of hostility. It will often involve an egoic belief in *us* and *them* characterizations and judgments. As a result, there typically will be more deeply-seated negative egoic storylines and ego commentary and characterizations involved that reinforce the *us* and *them* labels. This level of emotion and belief system is based on subjective judgments about the *them* being *bad* or *wrong*, while the haters feel self-righteous, and therefore superior in their judgments, belief systems, emotional energies, and any resulting behaviors. This kind of emotion and storyline is usually based on an aggressive shadow expression of their own lack of worthiness that must lower others to raise itself, along with the aggressive expression of entitlement.

This level of emotion is challenging to stop in Phase 3 and prevent from extending into a Stage 4 sabotaging behavior because of its intensity, commitment to the hateful thoughts, the emotions behind it, and the need to validate its egoic beliefs. The egoic commitment to the storylines may prove challenging to dismantle. Without a desire to see the truth more than wanting to be right, this is unlikely to be healed or seen other than through the egoic lenses until a brick wall of continual suffering or compassion shown by the hated *them* provides a breakthrough willingness to see others and circumstances differently. Remembering *as within, so without* reveals that haters first hate themselves, so showing them compassion without indulgence is something they don't show themselves.

Without this intention for truth over being right, the attachment to the stories and emotions will be too strong and addictive, and will not provide space for either compassion or detachment. It is important to catch yourself with anger in a healthy, healing way (not a suppressive way), so that it does not escalate. Anger can be one of the most sabotaging thought and emotional states, but it does not have to be so. When expressed aggressively, it can produce dangerous, violent behaviors, and when expressed submissively, it can produce dangerous, internally violent thoughts and behaviors that produce emotions of intense sadness that can lead to depression consciousness states over time, and even self-harm.

Impatience vs. Patience

Impatience often is more than just a momentary emotion of the circumstance. It is also often part of a consciousness feeling state. When circumstances of the moment produce the impatience emotion from our thoughts, it would be like being in a hurry, running late, having a deadline, getting delayed, or having to navigate hurdles to get a task accomplished. When it is more of a feeling state of consciousness, we would tend to have little patience for others and circumstances generally not performing as we want. This can be a milder form of entitlement, but always involves judgment. With impatience we have an attachment to particular outcomes. Below are frequent characteristics of both impatience and patience.

Impatience
- It is a sign that you're caught up in the ego's perspective of life.
- You take it personally when life doesn't go your way.
- It is a judgment–based egoic story about what is *wrong* with life or others that interferes with the ego's desires.

Patience
- A willingness to surrender the egoic will to the flow of life and accept what is in that moment.
- Allows the present flow to govern.
- You are present, and therefore happy, loving, and peaceful.
- Love and compassion are natural in the moment.

Jealousy and Envy

Both jealousy and envy are based on a belief that someone is better or less than another. It is based on both attachments and judgments. These attachments are based on subjective ideals and the judgments of being *better* or *less than*. They are not concepts based in objective reality and are untrue measuring sticks that change from moment to moment and person to person.

Resentment vs. Gratitude

Resentment more often tends to be a circumstantial emotion, but can become a consciousness state feeling like impatience. Gratitude is often both an emotion and a consciousness state feeling as well. We can have a moment of gratitude in the circumstance, but when we are spending more of our time in our higher-self consciousness, we will have a general disposition and consciousness of seeing things with gratitude, which is a reflection of how we look at all circumstances and people in our lives. Below are some typical characteristics of both.

Resentment

Resentment is classic resistance to what is in the moment because of an attachment to a particular desire or ideal that is different from where the flow of life has taken us. We have resentment because we are attached to, and unwilling to surrender, our desire for something to be different. This attachment can be to a life circumstance or to a person who has something we want but don't have, and therefore we wish ourselves to be different in comparison to others. In all cases when we outwardly blame another, this just masks our blaming of ourselves for not being better. Resentment is produced when our ego is unwilling to release our desire for circumstances or ourselves or others to be different, and we use blame of another or of life as a way of releasing us from our own egoic story of blame and our responsibility in the circumstance.

Gratitude

Gratitude is appreciating what is in the present. If you are feeling the emotion or the consciousness feeling state of gratitude, you cannot be experiencing sadness or anger. Therefore, thinking of the things for which you can be grateful is a pathway out of despair and discouragement. Gratitude is an incredibly powerful tool of mastering the ego. When you intentionally practice gratitude for even the basic things in your life such as shelter and food, it starts having ripple effects throughout your consciousness. Through gratitude you can see optimism, hope, and positivity, which takes you out of your ego and its negative thoughts, emotions and stories. Gratitude opens the heart, making all other qualities of our true nature— our higher self – more available and experienced.

When practiced daily, gratitude becomes a way of BEing that changes both our inner and outer worlds. When our inner world changes, and therefore how we experience life changes, our external life changes. Gratitude is the easiest entrée into our higher self. This higher self observer view leads us to the qualities and skillsets enabling us to better cope with life's challenges. Therefore, you want to replace thinking negatively about yourself and your woes with thinking about gratitude, even if only for the smallest of things. Through this gratitude, a change in consciousness will start to take hold in that moment.

Each moment adds up to create more and longer moments, which ripple into a more constant state of BEing. Giving attention to gratitude, instead of the ego's thought stream, can change your life.

Sadness and Depression

Sadness is brought about by the thoughts of wanting a circumstance to be different than it is. We find that occurrence undesirable, either because we think what happened *should not* have happened or we are attached to that event not happening. You might recognize the similarity between what causes sadness and what causes anger, or resentment. Anger is elicited when our expectations are not met. Sadness is elicited when an event occurs that is different from what we want and to which we are attached. Anger is the aggressive expression to an unmet expectation circumstance, and sadness is the submissive expression of an undesirable event. Sadness and anger are often the opposite sides of the poles of undesirable events. The former is based on a mindset rooted in requests and desires, whereas the latter is based on a mindset rooted in entitlements and expectations.

Just like anger, the word, entitlement, also often has a negative connotation, because it is often used in an aggressive expression of our expectations of others, and how we relate to them. The reality is that when we have balanced and reasonable boundaries, they are based on a balanced holding of a right to have boundaries and to say yes or no to anyone's requests of us. This is the literal definition of an entitlement. When we are balanced, we believe we are entitled to have reasonable boundaries, and we enforce them with compassionate detachment from others' expectations of us and others' senses of imbalanced entitlement. When we have our boundaries violated or threatened, if we are balanced, we can simultaneously feel a slight degree of the anger emotion as we maintain firmly our boundaries, as well as a slight degree of the emotion of sadness at being treated with disrespect and having to rebuff another's overtures against our boundaries. Those balanced energies rise and fall in the moment as we realize that another's actions are not personal. We may also sense these emotions so distantly that they barely register in our energy fields. The degree of energy these emotions emit will likely be related to the degree of our connection to the person threatening our boundaries. We must be careful about our expectations, however. Expectations, like entitlement and anger, can be easily imbalanced. If we aren't in our balanced, higher self, our expectations, even about our boundaries, can be an egoic hijacking of our higher self sense of worthiness and confidence. If not tightly-balanced, our ego could lead us to an imbalanced use of both expectations and anger if those boundaries were violated.

When we move into the submissive expression of a circumstance, it moves into a more one-sided sadness that has more of a victim or sorrowful perspective. It is natural to have moments of sadness at an undesirable circumstance, such as a death or other loss, but the ego's attachment to a different reality makes those sad, wishful thoughts linger, increasing the intensity of the sadness that can then produce suffering. Sadness is often about the past that we bring into the present with us, so when we are sad, we are not living in the present fully. You may question this since you may believe that it is because of the present circumstance of being without a loved one that causes the sadness. The reality is that when we think of the loss of a loved one, we are remembering that person being with us, wishing that they still were. It is an attachment to the loved one in the past, which inhibits us from seeing the present for what it is, enjoying it in the moment. We are sad for what we think we are missing, instead of being joyful and enjoying the moment as it is. Sadness, like any other emotion, is based in our thoughts. If we are in our higher-self consciousness state, any sadness about a departed loved one will be soon muted to more of a loving emotion energy about that person, and we can still feel the joy of life as seen through our higher-self lens.

Many believe that if they are not sad at the passing of a loved one, they are not honoring or exhibiting love for that person. This, again, confuses attachment with love. When we love another, we celebrate them and the times we shared with them more than cling to their loss with sadness. When we mourn deeply, or for long periods of time, it is really a self-centered activity of the ego where we are focused on our own wants, needs, and attachments that are either not being met, or we fear won't be met. That is the opposite of love. We may fear being alone or missing someone in the role that this person played in our life.

It is natural to miss the presence of a loved one, but the natural, balanced expression of this sadness will be limited in both duration and extent when we are balanced and firmly seated in our higher self's love and gratitude. This does not mean that we won't still love and miss that person for the rest of our lives. It is the sadness emotional energy that will release its intensity with time, if we are balanced with it and allow it to flow out and not attach to it. When we are balanced and seated in our higher-self consciousness, we will feel more love, gratitude, and joy when we think of that person, instead of the sadness of what we feel is missing from our lives.

I'd like to share an example of this from the experience of a man who had lost his wife who participated in one of my live curriculum sessions. As he put it, when he experienced a med-itation to view his sadness from the perspective of his higher self, "The sadness was still there, but it was just there sitting with me without it causing me any suffering. It was much more in the background without it being actively painful." As I've frequently stated throughout this book, pain is normal, but suffering is not. The suffering comes from our attachments to particular outcomes, to our own expectations, to fears about the future, to lamenting and shaming the past, and to wanting something different from what is in the present.

The higher self's relationship to sadness is different than the egoic relationship to the sadness. When we experience sadness through our higher self, we will notice the emotion arise, but we are in our observer state that doesn't experience emotions through the suffering of the ego. When we are in our higher selves, our thoughts are not about attachment, so the emotion doesn't rise to the same level of intensity, but merely brings about a set of sensations. Our higher-self emotion ex-perience takes place in the moment, allowing the energy to pass through, and is not connected to a story or meaning as interpreted by the ego. Therefore, the emotional energies don't linger for long periods after the moment of sadness passes. This isn't a suppression or denial of emotions, but rather an evolu-tion of them, letting them naturally pass through like cars on the highway just driving through.

When emotions turn into consciousness state feelings—Depression.

When emotions become frequent visitors and stay for extended periods of time, they can become more entrenched, and can shift our states of being. When this happens, these become feeling states that are not just circumstance-dependent, rising and falling with those moments, as emotions do. Instead, they become more the lenses through which we see everything. They become the feelings of our consciousness state.

When intense and lingering sadness emotions over one or more events moves into a deeper consciousness state, it is because we develop a deep belief in the ego's negative story about self or circumstances that we don't want, and we feel powerless to do anything about it. This comes from a continuous, or repeated, lack of alignment with the higher-self consciousness, creating a negative feeling and perspective on life, ourselves, and others. This intense, distorted, and repeated storyline then shapes our experiences, producing more sadness from more events. This regular and repeated state does not allow people to heal or follow their higher-self hearts. Instead, when allowed to take root, this repeated sadness turns into a consciousness state that can induce people to create a life that is steeped in the ego's state of suppressive expressions of continual sadness without joy. This becomes a state of depression. Depression can leave a person very vulnerable to more negative emotions and life experiences.

Please note that this discussion of depression is not intended to discuss, describe, discount, or dispute any psychiatric determination of a chemical, or other physiological malady, in the mind or body that recommends medication or other therapies. While our mental and emotional bodies do connect with and ripple into our physical bodies, often causing our physical maladies, there may be circumstances that recommend medication to manage the present physical effects of depression. Sometimes, treating the physical body may aid in breaking the cycle to then being able to address the mental and emotional aspects of depression.

Chapter 20

Fear

Fear, as the core characteristic of the ego, warrants its own chapter. Fear has many faces and morphed states. To begin with, it will be valuable for you to explore and experience your own relationship to fear; therefore, please answer the questions in the *Companion Workbook Section III, Exercise 7* before proceeding.

Fear, as an emotion, is anticipated pain. It is anxiety about the future. As a basic starting point, we can see how the ego's fear and self-centric perspectives have derailed us in our society and lives today. The ego's fear has translated into fear of just about everything. The ego now has a fear of the unknown, a fear of others, a fear of diversity, a fear of others succeeding for fear that others' success means our lack of success, or even failure, and on and on. The ego's fear keeps us either paralyzed or driven to extremes, while interfering with our quest for love, compassion, joy, and peace in life. If we are in fear, there are many qualities and experiences that we cannot be in simultaneously. In addition to the obvious lack of peace when we're in fear, we also cannot be in a state of experiencing love or compassion.

Fear vs. Love

Fear and love are mutually exclusive. If you are feeling and thinking loving and compassionate thoughts, then fear will not be a part of that internal conversation or the emotions you feel. Your loving emotions are consciousness feelings and sensations that will take up all the space of your thoughts and emotions, leaving no room for fear. You simply won't worry about the "what if's" imaginary stories when you're in a state of love. You may be inclined to question this if you believe that it is your love for another that makes you fear the possibility of certain outcomes, such as danger or abandonment. This is similar to the earlier discussion on sadness and love. The reality is that while you may love someone, the moment you fear a possible outcome in the future, you've moved more into your own attachment to a particular outcome or circumstance, and you are no longer sitting with the love.

When we feel love, we do not feel fear. We think that we fear because we love, but this is not true. This is one of the ego's most effective illusions—to use fear as justification of the illusion that it is a loving protector. The reality is that when you are feeling the emotion of fear, you are not feeling the love. Instead, at that moment, you are feeling a lack of trust for others, life, or both. Your fear is not motivated by love, but by distrust. You may say that the reason you are concerned about the mistrust of others and life is because of your concern and love for your loved one. Again, your loved one is not the source of your mistrust that you are believing in with your fear. The source of your distrust is the ego's stories about how life and others are that cannot be trusted, according the ego. The fact that the circumstances of your mistrust involves a loved one as the impact of the distrust just makes the distrust more impactful to create anxiety. The loved one is merely the object or ripple effect of your mistrust of others and life. There is nothing of love in this fear, nor any other fear.

When we feel love for others, it is the ego that steps aside. When we feel fear, it is the ego that has stepped forward. It is the ego that fears being hurt in some way. The ego views the vulnerability of either being hurt or being wrong as a risk to be feared, and therefore precautions must be taken to prevent this. This is not to say that our concern for another's health and happiness is all ego, however. When we want the best for someone, that can be our higher self's thoughts and emotions of love, but when we feel fear about the outcome for that individual or our relationship with them, that is our imbalanced ego taking over with its fears of the future. The "what if's" to the ego become larger, more realistic and looming. That is the world of the ego. What could go wrong, then, is likely to go wrong to the ego, and thus the ego produces stress, anxiety, distrust, and more fear. Then the ego starts using its dysfunctional tools to get what it wants – which is protection, oppression and control.

Because the ego is steeped in fear, an imbalanced ego will have an imbalanced sense of fear and cannot coexist with either love or trust in the same moment. If your imbalanced ego is in the lead, it will be generating thoughts and emotions based on fear (that often include a belief in the lack of availability of something, whether the affection of that individual, resources, attention, and so on.), and so will likely be morphing into thoughts preoccupied by competition, hoarding, control, or protectionism. In that moment of indulging in the ego's fear, it will be impossible simultaneously to feel or think about love, compassion, or other loving thoughts or emotions. Real love requires surrender, compromise, service to others, and vulnerability, all of which the ego and its fear view as weakness, threatening, and abhorrent. Either love or trust can be the antidote to fear. You can't love what you fear or fear what you love. Because the ego is our default programming, we must learn to practice love and trust.

Each moment is a separate, distinct opportunity for either your egoic or higher-self consciousness to step forward and drive your mental bus. It is that quick and fluid for our consciousness and focus to shift. In any moment, your ego can slide into the lead and replace those thoughts and emotions of love with those of fear. You can, and do, ebb and flow back and forth, repeatedly. The key point is that you cannot have both thoughts and emotions of fear and love simultaneously flowing through you in the same moment. You don't want to confuse your egoic attachments for love. As you continue to allow your ego's fear and your higher self's love go back and forth, you are mentally, emotionally, and spiritually on a seesaw, moving up and down. There may be moments of balanced centeredness where you have clarity of mind and thought, along with the emotions of love and compassion without fear, but those will be only fleeting glimpses if you continue to allow your ego to drive your thoughts and emotions, thinking of all the "what if's" and egoic attachments. Becoming your own master means you must start seeing the sabotaging impact of the ego's drive and attachment to separation and fear.

When we are sitting in our thoughts and emotions of love and compassion, we naturally have a sense of trust and an *all will be well* peace, regardless of what might transpire. If we don't have joyful peace, then we are not sitting in that love of our higher self. Instead, we are attached to a fear or anxiety about a future outcome. There is also a possibility that what we believe is love is not actually love, but is instead an unhealthy attachment that is more of an obsession or neediness than a true love. Even if something happens that is unexpected or undesired, the consciousness of love, compassion, and trust does not fear those undesirable results. Instead, when we're in our true, higher self with love, compassion, and trust, we know that the fears of the ego are overstated. When we are sitting with the love, trust and compassion, we sit with the present moment without worrying about experiencing painful thoughts and emotions at some point in the future. The higher self's perspective of love, compassion, and trust knows how to respond in moments of challenge, and sees those fears of the ego as little molehills instead of the mountains of fear that the ego creates. The proverbial mountain versus the mole hill is a good analogy.

The Illusions of Fear as Our Protector.

Fear believes that protection and safety come from warring, or other powerful actions. Foundational to this presumption is the false notion that military power can influence or overpower others to get you what you want, or to avoid what you don't want. The reality is that this view about military, or physical, power being the source of safety and protection is the ego's rationalization in the form of oppressing of others. Because the ego believes in lack and limitation, it requires separation in order to feel safe, secure, able to access resources, and to be free from oppression from others. The ego feels it must overpower others in order to be free of their advances and op-pression. To the ego, most everyone is, or *should* be, either a victim, repressed and controlled, or a dominator, oppressor, and controller. This is part of the ego's default polarization in a zero sum game with an inherent fearful mistrust. When left to its own design, the ego cannot see a balanced place where people are both safe and motivated by love and compassion with an inherent trust for others and life. That, to the ego, is viewed as vulnerability and naiveté, and, therefore, weakness.

The reality about influence is that, only by connecting to another's higher self, can you motivate them to do, or not do, something in a balanced way without dysfunctional, sabotaging oppression, control, or manipulation. Remember that the energy you put out will trigger the same energy back from others to you in most cases, unless the other person is firmly rooted in their higher self. Therefore, if you are using an egoic behavior such as aggression, control, or oppression, you likely will be triggering the same energy in return, which will be either an aggressive response mirroring the same control and oppression or a submissive response of fear and victimhood. Fear is the antithesis of joy or happiness. You cannot simultaneously feel the emotion of joy and fear. If you are in joy, you cannot be in fear. All of the higher-self traits are antidotes to fear because fear cannot coexist with them. Fear operates at a different frequency on the energetic dial. In contrast courage is a higher-self trait that allows you to overcome fear, while providing you with the motivation and coping skills to act, despite having an egoic fear.

When in the egoic state, we are influenced by the egoic values, and we are motivated to use the ego's tools and behaviors. As a result, fear, being an inherent egoic state, drives us to conquer, control, dominate, and seek power on the aggressive side, or to hide, withdraw, and suppress, resulting in higher anxiety on the submissive side. Being in fear keeps us trapped in the ego's consciousness and perspective, which is made up of negative thoughts and dysfunctional, sabotaging use of emotional energies. As previously discussed, when we have the same emotions regularly and continue to think the thoughts that elicit those emotions, it can turn into feeling states of being. I have discussed how the emotions of anger and sadness can turn into more pervasive consciousness states. Fear is no different. Fear about multiple things will create a fear consciousness that will shape your perspective about life, which will then translate into having fears about many things. Overcoming one fear, however, can make it easier to overcome others. The corollary is also true that if you fail to use your courage to overcome one fear, it will allow the fear consciousness to take a deeper hold, and then it will be more difficult to overcome other fears. A fear consciousness establishes a pattern of fear that will induce you to avoid circumstances and build up fearful thoughts about many things that then become belief systems. When this happens, fear becomes the lens through which you see and experience everything in life and fosters paranoias.

The beliefs that our fears keep us safe is one of the greatest illusions of our egoic stories. The reality is that if we allow our fears to run our lives, it limits our ability to access our higher self's qualities, which includes not only courage, but wisdom. This wisdom is what we need to see the truth of our circumstances that motivates us to make the choices and use the skills and tools of the higher self that result in us being safe. Otherwise, if we turn to our fears, our ego will move us to worry, and even anger, as we get lost in the thoughts of fear about what we think might or could happen. As we engage and interact with others, the ripple effects of our egoic energies of fear trigger the egoic fears of others, and, in this manner, we create a societal collective consciousness of fear. Our personal fears become societal fears, and the societal fears become personal fears. Our fears feed off each other.

Balanced Fear and Breaking the Grip of Fears.

As with all emotions, fear can have both a balanced energy and use. When we are faced with an imminent life–threatening scenario, we can experience a natural, balanced emotional energy of fear. Examples of balanced emotional uses of fear include not stepping too close to the edge of a cliff, ensuring we are not allowing ourselves to be in direct contact with predators, not allowing our toddler to play too close to busy streets, and so on. These types of imminent threats to our physical survival are the inherent purpose of the ego's fear. When our ego is balanced and integrated with our higher self, fear can be healthy and functional, but is far more limited in application than what most experience most of their life. Fear, used in a balanced way with a mastered ego that is well-integrated with our higher self, motivates us to move away from or to take reasonable precautions for life sustainability without extensive thought processes or lingering thoughts and storylines. When balanced, the moment of fear occurs only as we are faced with imminent, life-threatening circumstances, and then it flows out as we are motivated to move away from those circumstances. The fear ends as we move away from the imminence of those threats. This is the balanced use of, and the reason for, the existence of fear as an emotional energy. The ego, in its unbalanced state, however, corrupts it.

Fear, more than any other thought-stream storyline and belief system, changes the way we see life. Because the nature of fear is survival–based, its storylines are powerful and impactful in our minds, and therefore fear can be the most difficult egoic corruption from which to break free. The only way to break free of the ego's fear is to summon our higher self's courage in order to push through the fear to both experience and face life's circumstances as they arise with courage and wisdom, while taking reasonable precautions as necessary. When we see that the feared circumstances did not play out as the fear stories suggested, this can give us greater confidence and the courage to dismiss other fears that the ego brings up for other circumstances. This working of the ego reflects the proverbial *making a mountain out of a molehill,* which the ego does constantly. Fear has a ripple effect, regardless of in which direction we go with it. Overcoming it bolsters us further into overcoming more fears, while, in contrast, succumbing to one fear bolsters the ego's bullying us into succumbing to other fears.

Using the tools and techniques that you went through earlier in this book can be helpful in looking deeper into the thoughts that are underlying your fears, and see where rational thought may be missing from the ego's stories and beliefs. Just as with other emotions, once you observe the fear and become aware of that fear and the underlying thoughts supporting it, the fear will cease to have the same powerful grip over you. When you can loosen its grip over you, the fear won't be in a position to drive your thoughts, emotions, and behaviors with such control. This is when the fear can become less scary. As with other emotions, the challenge is to catch the underlying thoughts before they elicit the emotion of fear. Once the fear comes into your emotional body, it becomes more difficult to dismiss. You may need to think calming thoughts or those of gratitude to disengage the active fear and its physical sensations that make the egoic stories seem real. To experience your own relationship to fear, please go to the *Companion Audio for Exercise 8, Section III* and listen to the guided exercise that will assist you in answering the questions in *Section III, Exercise 8 in the Companion Workbook.*

The ego will think of all the worst-case scenarios that will keep you in the thought-stream and addicted to the fear elicited from those thoughts about the future. This distracts you from the present moment. The ego's fear presumes that others have the ability to hurt or affect you by their choices, which is part of the ego's conditioned stories and negative beliefs that everything that occurs around us is about us. Everyone must go through their own suffering in order to wake up. It is suffering that wakes most people up from the egoic consciousness, and everyone's journey is different. We must remember that the future is unknowable, and when we lack trust in life, it will be easier for the ego's worst-case scenarios (which are often not based in historical or rational facts) to take hold of our thoughts and beliefs. Remember, all fears are just ideas or stories about possible future scenarios that have little basis in fact; they are merely fictional storylines.

An example of the ego's irrational, overblown fear is the fear about getting hit by a bus as you approach a street. Is getting hit by a bus as you enter a street a real possibility? It is physically plausible, but the question is whether it is likely. The severity of that possibility will purport to give validation to that egoic fear, but the likelihood of your being hit by a bus is low, especially if you take the minimal precaution of looking both ways before entering a street. As a result, this fear is an irrational one not worth your time or attention, and therefore is not necessary to modify your normal behavior because of this remotely possible scenario. If you allow your egoic mind to run away with this fear, then it could drive your mind into a fear frenzy each time you need to cross a street, to the point that you become paralyzed with fear and not able to move yourself to cross that street. This is what happens in the mind with phobias. The egoic mind is permitted to run amok with a fear-based thought, so then the fear thoughts and emotion energies permeate your mental and emotional bodies, rippling into your physical body, which produces an extreme anxiety that paralyzes your ability to engage in rational intellect choices and behaviors.

If we can surrender just one fear to trust, it will help us transcend other fears that our egoic mind tells us we *should* have. Both succumbing to and surrendering our fear each has snowball effects. In each case, a single act of succumbing to or overcoming a fear acts like a snowball, creating a larger, more impactful effect the next time you face a choice point to either succumb to or overcome a fear. Fear can be polarizing in pushing us into either an upward trend of transcendence or a downward trend of succumbing to and being paralyzed by fear. However, the balanced effect of fear is being mindful of rational and truthful imminent threat to our physical being, for which we take precautions such as looking both ways before crossing a street.

It is now important to distinguish between intuition and instinct. Our instincts are usually based on our primitive egoic nature, so these will demonstrate fear as an instinctual reaction to circumstances. Our intuition, however, comes from our higher self, which does not have fear as a response to a circumstance. If there is a risk of imminent harm, both our ego and our higher self can respond to that threat. Our ego will react with fear to move away from that threat. This is the original role of our ego's fearful nature. Our higher self will respond with a wise knowingness about a path choice without more than a moment of fear being perceived, thought, or felt. These scenarios often involve sudden uncomfortable physical sensations, presuming you don't have an egoic tendency towards distrust generally. The key here is to be able to discern between an egoic consciousness state of mind versus a higher-self inspiration that knows when something is truly amiss. The inspirational response is like when a thought pops into your head out of nowhere and is not something that you have previously thought. Remembering how the physical body is an indicator of what consciousness you are in is always important. We must draw a distinction between a sabotaging egoic fear that represents an artificially created fear from the ego's illusory "what if's" versus the higher self inspiration that can sense, energetically and knowingly, when something needs to change from the path that we are currently walking. A large part of self-mastery is being able to discern the difference between the egoic thoughts and the higher self motivations and inspirations. This book provides you with the tips and tools for successfully mapping your journey through it all.

Wisdom and inspiration, not fear, is the basis of higher-self response (such as a spur of the moment change not to go down a certain path or take a plane trip, and so on). Whenever you think thoughts and experience emotions involving a fear of the repercussions of a result, you are not experiencing the situation from your higher-self consciousness. Fear is not a thought process or emotion of the higher self. Ever. Notwithstanding, however, there is no need for shame in thinking of or experiencing fear. Instead, you just want to notice it, be aware of it, thank your ego for trying to protect you, and look underneath those thoughts and emotions to see what is really there, why it is there, while remembering to trust life. You must then access your higher self to find the wisdom and courage to address the circumstance without fear.

Because fear is currently such a major element of our world's collective consciousness, we each must deal with the fears of others that are being projected onto us. It is easy for our egos to absorb and adopt the fears of others. To deal effectively with the fears of others and the collective, we must allow the courage of our higher self to lead, and avoid being swayed by others. This includes using our higher self to avoid the need for the approval of others. This is where the effects of our higher-self consciousness can ripple into bringing forth the higher selves of others to help allay their own fears and worries.

The ego uses fear to reel you back into its control and keep you busy in the thought- stream about the future in "would, could, and should" thoughts. Fear is also present as a companion to every egoic desire. The fear is that you won't get what you desire, and what that will mean about you if you don't achieve that desire. If you don't obtain that particular desire, then you just create a new desire to appease the previous desire/fear partnership. If you do get that desire, the ego will create a new desire, and the desire-fear relationship cycles around again. The ego lacks acceptance of life as it is, so it creates a vicious cycle of desire and fear. If you can make happiness the goal, instead of a certain outcome, event, or circumstance, you will start seeing the beauty in life, and the dysfunctional fears can more easily fall away. This is part of the key about detaching from particular outcomes and surrendering our attachments to our desires, as these positions refuse to accept or be happy with life as it is. The ego focuses on what it wants. That kind of mindset will never allow you to be happy because you will be constantly resisting, resenting, rejecting, and lamenting life as it is in any given moment.

Worry and Anxiety.

We can get wrapped up into the consequences and scenarios of our fearful thoughts, and this can morph into other states. Worry and anxiety is what we do with fear, as we continue to allow our thoughts of fear to circle around and around in our heads about the possibility of a future event either occurring, or not occurring.

Most Common Fears

Fear is the natural state of the ego, and if allowed, will distort and hijack even the higher-self qualities and objectives. If the ego is left unchecked, it can work to over-shadow the higher-self objectives by pairing these with an egoic fear of not obtaining a desire. Some of the most common fears are listed below. You can apply the concepts reflected in these common fears to any other fear you may experience.

Fear of not Being Loved

The fear of not being loved is essentially another way of describing the fear of being rejected or abandoned. When a child experiences behavior from a parent that the child interprets as less than loving, it often triggers a primal fear of being rejected, abandoned, and therefore not surviving. Children rely on adults—their parents or parental figures—for their shelter, food and all aspects of basic human survival. Therefore, for a child, this belief of not being loved triggers deep fears and pains about their own existence. Any perceived rejection can be viewed by a child as not being loved, which triggers these deep survival fears and resulting painful stories. Because a fear of not being loved is such a primal survival-triggering, deeply painful story, it is often quickly suppressed and repressed into the shadow. As discussed in earlier chapters on the shadow, when fears and painful stories are repressed into the shadow, it creates very sabotaging beliefs and behaviors that grow and take root outside of our conscious awareness. Those sabotaging expressions will show up later in reactionary patterns that will be either submissive or aggressive. Below are some of those shadow beliefs and behaviors that can result.

<u>*Submissive Expressions*</u>.

- *Not feeling good enough/low self-worth.* This is the underlying belief system that dictates all the submissive expressions of the fear and the belief that we are not loved or lovable. When we feel unlovable, we put ourselves into circumstances that create self-fulfilling experiences in two ways: First, we will fail to see the love that others try to give us. We cannot see love from others since we do not have or see it for ourselves, so we either miss or misinterpret love that may come to us. We essentially become unavailable to love, despite wanting it, because this lack of love and worthiness we believe in becomes the lens through which we see things. Second, because we have these negative feelings, emotions, and beliefs about ourselves, we draw to us and align with the same from others, showing others how we expect to be treated. We essentially teach others how to treat us, and draw from them the energy we exude and expect, which is that we are unlovable, and therefore should not be treated with loving behavior. We, then, exude unloving behavior ourselves to others since we don't have love for ourselves, and so do not have any to give. *As within, so without.*
  - ✓ Many misinterpret their attachments and the need to please others as loving behavior, but it is not. This submissive behavior is both

dysfunctional attachment and manipulative behavior of giving in order to receive. It is still the ego's service–to–self dysfunction. Loving behavior is doing for others without any desire, expectation, or need for anything in return. True loving behavior views others without attachment or defining that person in relation to us in any way.

✓ An example of attaching and defining another by their relationship to us is seeing them from the perspective of our actual or desired relationship to them. When we view another as *my* anything—my spouse, child, mate, friend, and so on, that is defining that person by either our actual or desired relationship to them, which usually comes with defined ideals that accompany that relationship label. Then we add a submissive imbalanced expression of fear of not being loved to this, we engage in behavior that wants to please "my [fill in the blank]," so I can get the respect, love, affection, and so on that I desire (and possibly expect making it a passive-aggressive expression) from that person performing that role in my life. This is the ego's service–to–self. An example of a balanced loving behavior would instead be doing something loving and helpful for a person because that person could benefit, with zero need or expectation of acknowledgement, affection, or even gratitude, in exchange. You do this because it is in your heart to give and do for others, not because of who they are to you, or what you might receive in return. You do it because of who YOU are in your higher-self heart in a service–to–others consciousness.

- *A need to please.* The submissive expression of the fear of not being loved and the shadow belief of being un-loved and unlovable can produce the need to please in order to get the love we think we wouldn't otherwise receive on our own merits. This belief system does not believe in our own self-worth, and so seeks and believes our value will come from others through ca-joling, placating, and pleasing behaviors, and that this pleasing others will be the only time we receive love. This behavior will, ironically, tell others that we are not worthy unless we perform these services, and that will be the treatment and behavior the person will be drawn to. This creates a self-fulling treatment in being treated with less love, affection, and respect, which will falsely appear to validate our shadow beliefs.

Aggressive Expressions.

- *Entitlement.* When the initially submissive expression of low self-worth turns aggressive, it can result in an imbalanced, aggressive form of entitlement. Depending upon the degree of entitlement, it can produce unloving behavior towards others, such as rudeness, oppression, and demandingness, along with an attachment to ex-pectations of others submitting to your priority.
- *Judgment and Superiority.* When someone has a shadow story of lacking self-worth (which most people have on some level), they have allowed, absorbed, and submitted to others' judgment of them being less than worthy of

love, and have shoved that into their shadow. Now, they judge themselves and everything they do through that lens of lacking worth and lovability. As a result, they will often try their best to reject that story consciously through an aggressive expression of being superior and projecting judgment of others harshly as unworthy as well. A large percentage of us in this current culture express our shadow story of unworthiness in this aggressive expression and projection of judging others. How aggressively someone judges others will be directly proportional to their own belief in their own sense of lacking worth, which then morphs into anger and resentment.

Fear of Poverty

The fear of poverty, like the fear of not being loved, is a fear about one of the most primal needs for survival, and a fear that we are impaired in our ability to survive. With the fear of poverty, the ego doesn't feel safe in having enough resources for survival. Below are common submissive and aggressive expressions of this fear.

Submissive Expressions

The submissive expression of this story will result in someone always feeling poor or lacking resources, and could include lacking motivation, believing it is fruitless to strive because it will never be enough. Regardless of whether a fear of poverty gets expressed aggressively or submissively, the fearful individual will have a lack of trust of others, of life, and of themselves. As a result, those under a submissive expression will take jobs they hate just to pay the bills because they don't see any other options due to their lens of distrust and beliefs in their own inability to obtain more. They are so risk averse that they will take the present circumstance over the risk of losing what they do have to obtain what they really want from their heart's desire (not just the egoic desire for more money). The submissive expressions do not believe safety can be achieved, even through hard work and sacrifice. Instead, they believe poverty is their lot in life. They submit, succumb to, and embody the identity of poverty. They are likely to feel stress and anxiety on a regular basis because of these beliefs.

Hoarding and Greed

Hoarding of money and resources in an overly protective fashion is a submissive expression of the fear of poverty because a person will be extremely risk averse, and so fearful of never having enough, and not willing to share. This person will believe they are either in or on the verge of being in lack. Therefore, they have a continuous need for more, having little trust in themselves, others, and life.

Greed has a similar mindset. Both stockpile their resources and need strong separation from others to reassure themselves that they can maintain their resources for their own survival. This fear will induce people to be stingy, lacking a spirit of generosity, refusing to give much to others. They believe they never have enough and could always be just a moment away from losing what they have. This produces regular anxiety as well as the needs both to hoard and control.

Aggressive Expressions

The aggressive expressions, on the contrary, are aggressively risk prone, willing to risk everything to achieve the big payoff.

They want to reject the feared storyline that they are in lack by recklessly acting as if all resources are expendable. For the aggressively imbalanced, their hidden rejected fear of poverty will push them to sacrifice and risk everything for the chance to acquire as much money and resources as possible through risky, reckless, and all or nothing ventures.

The Gambler

The gambler is an aggressive risk taker without moderation who wants to reject the story of fearing poverty and a lack of resources. The rejection of this fear of poverty produces both an aggressiveness and recklessness in putting his money and resources at risk, wanting to believe that he has everything under control.

All egos, regardless of which expression their shadow uses, will value money and things more than love, relationships, family, and just about everything else.

In both imbalanced expressions, this fear of poverty describes our relationship with life that is reflected in and projected out into our resources. Every fear incorporates a lack of trust, but the fear of poverty implicates how we react and relate to life itself, believing life is something with which we must struggle and fight, instead of trusting life to give us what we need. The fear of poverty and being "poor" is a state of mind more than a state of our resource pool. Conversely, when we live from our higher-self consciousness, we are motivated by our heart's goals and desires and how we can contribute to society in a service–to–others way, and not how much money and resources we can obtain. When in a balanced higher-self state, we trust life to give us what we need, and we see abundance much more easily because we expect nothing, and do not require more than what sustains us. When in our higher selves, we see things with eyes of gratitude instead of the egoic eyes of lack and fear, and we attract more for which to be grateful and experience more gratitude for what comes to us. This is what is behind the Law of Attraction.

Fear of Failure

This fear takes us back to the basic objectives and values of the ego. This fear is predicated upon illusory concepts of success and failure—the usual polarization and artificial ideals of the ego. These concepts are entirely subjective, and whatever definition or criteria anyone gives to these terms, they are not actually going to be truths in terms of what is *success* or *failure*, especially when these ideals are associated with the ego and its fears. When the ego is involved in establishing an ideal of success, it will involve the superficial values of the ego, such as the acquisition of material things and separation from others through power and position. Both of these expressions tie these ideals to the ego's identity.

Submissive Expressions

Those expressing this fear submissively don't believe they have what it takes to be *successful*, as their ego defines it, and, therefore, believe they are a *failure*. The submissive expression will induce people to give up early, or even entirely, on what impassions their hearts, believing that they cannot succeed, so they do not give much, or even any, effort towards them. This can also both limit and paralyze people from taking the risks required for achievement, growth, and evolution by taking away their courage, confidence, and perseverance. The perspective and submissive expression of this story is both self-sabotaging and self-limiting.

Aggressive Expressions

The aggressive expressions will drive a person relentlessly to achieve the egoic goals of material, power, or position. This aggressive expression often morphs into a perfectionism based on this fear of failure, arising from the underlying fear of unworthiness and the judgment that the ego expects to receive from this *failure* and unworthiness.

When we can get out of our egos and into our higher selves as the driver in our consciousness and state of mind, we can change the definition of success to be defined by the heart, based on its values and objectives (see Section I charts). While the higher self's objectives and values aren't material in nature, when you are filled with the higher self qualities of courage, confidence, wisdom, perseverance, and others, you naturally are inspired to accomplish what moves your heart, and then you behave in a way that draws both resources and prosperity to you for these inspirations.

Fear of Aging

The fear of aging, and what it means for our body and appearance, stems from an insecurity about our appearance as well as a superficial egoic value that prioritizes physical appearance. This fear stems from the egoic value and belief that our identity and worth comes in large part from our physical appearance. This fear often harbors a suppressed shadow story that we are not physically appealing, and therefore unworthy of attention, love, value, and so on.

Aggressive Expressions

The aggressive expression of this fear and shadow story will induce exaggerated efforts at improving or enhancing the physical appearance, such as plastic surgery, extensive make-up, dieting, and clothing veneers.

Submissive Expressions

The submissive expression will produce more of a wallflower approach, both believing and behaving that they are too old to do things, wear certain things, or otherwise limit themselves based on an illusory belief of what being a particular age must mean.

Both expressions are based on negative beliefs and assumptions about the physical body and ageism. These stories and beliefs become part of the ego's identity. In contrast, the higher self focuses on the benefits of experience that age brings, such as knowledge, wisdom, experience, and maturity.

Exploring Your Fear and Breaking the Fear Addiction

In the examples above of some common fears, as well as in some of the previous exercises, we explored how the aggressive and submissive expressions manifest. This is a good time for you to explore how fear feels in you, as you may express it differently at different times. Earlier, you explored its foundation in Section III, Exercise 8 with the intimacy–discourse–inquiry techniques. Now, let's explore how fear works either aggressively, submissively, or in balanced ways in you. Please access the *Companion Audio for Section III, Exercise 9,* and you will be led through the exercise to then answer the questions in the *Companion Workbook for Section III, Exercise 9.*

After you've worked through the above exercise to explore more about how your ego's fear expresses in you, it is then time to work on breaking the ego's grip and its fear addiction. The first step is to have an intention to change the nature of your relationship to your fears, which requires surrendering the ego's "I," "me," "my," and "mine" thoughts. Remember that the emotion of fear is not who you are, and the identities that the fear stories create are also not who you are. Using the information you have gleaned from the exercise above in exploring your fear, notice what attachments you have had to a fear, a story or a thought. You can even notice the degree of attachment you have to either the fear, the story, or the thoughts, and the degree of difficulty you may be having in releasing or surrendering them. When you become aware of the attachment, you are walking the path of the higher self of compassionate detachment, making the qualities of the higher self more available to you.

Make a list of the joys and things for which you can be grateful, and focus on those in your thought-stream. Remember that once you follow your courage to push through one fear, it will be easier to draw upon that courage to push through other fears. The corollary of this is also true, as it will be more difficult to access your courage if you didn't use it to overcome a previous fear. The more you push through a fear, however, the more you will see that the fear was just a molehill and not the mountain that your ego's story was telling you.

When the fearful thoughts and storylines start appearing back in your thought- stream, it is important to recognize that. Remember that when you have this awareness, you also have a choice to decide to move away from those thoughts, or to move back to running those thoughts around and around repeatedly in your mind. The compassionate detachment perspective of the higher self will allow you to acknowledge the fearful thoughts and emotion with compassion for the child-like ego's fear, but without believing the fearful story or giving in to it.

Chapter 21

Shame and its Relatives

Shame shows up often with the ego. Shame often begins as an initial foundational storyline that will morph into other thoughts, emotions, and expressions. It can also show up as a morphed ripple stemming from stories of unworthiness and lack. To begin your exploration of your own shame, please turn to the *Companion Workbook* and complete the questions in *Section III, Exercise 10*.

Shame is the emotional and energetic effect of believing that we are both inadequate and unworthy. Shame is the main emotional energetic ripple effect of the inner critic's criticisms, judgments, and other tools. Shame is not always addressed in many healing and self-help circles for a variety of reasons. First, it is an uncomfortable, vulnerable emotion and underlying storyline. Second, it almost always and quickly morphs into other emotions, imbalanced qualities, and stories in both the aggressive and submissive expressions, so is not always easy to identify and isolate. The submissive expressions of shame are particularly prone to suppression, and therefore, a deepening and widening of the shadow.

Like all other emotions, there is a balanced expression of the shame energy, but it is more accurately referred to as a remorse that comes more from the conscience or higher-self regarding our own behavior that was not kind, or not otherwise aligned with our higher self. This balanced expression inspires us to apologize and make amends, but without judging us to be *bad* or inherently unworthy. Below is a chart that reflects several aspects of the healthy forms of shame being remorse and the unhealthy and imbalanced forms of shame.

Balanced Shame – Remorse (Healthy)	Imbalanced Shame (Unhealthy)
Arises from the conscience and empowers us to take positive action	Activates the inner critic masquerading as the conscience with a lot of *should* and *should not* thoughts
Motivates—empowers	Demotivates—disempowers
Empathy and remorse kicks in from our heart	Suppresses the guilt that becomes part of the shadow
About the behavior	About the person
Is balanced, so it doesn't shift into aggression, withdrawal, or dissociation	We end up removed from the shame, as it often shifts into imbalanced expressions of aggression, withdrawal, or dissociation.
Opens our hearts in empathy and brings us into dignity	Closes our heart and takes us out of dignity by being crushed
Produces remorse	Produces guilt, along with the shame

Now, to explore how shame expresses in you, personally, please access the *Companion Audio, Section III, Exercise 11* to work through the guided exercise, which will then lead you to answer the questions in the *Companion Workbook, Section III, Exercise 11*.

If you'd like to explore how shame and guilt can morph and express when in aggressively and submissively imbalanced and balanced uses, access the *Companion Audio* for *Section III, Exercise 12* that will guide you through the exercises in the *Companion Workbook* for *Section III, Exercise 12*. You can also discover more about your shame by using the inquiry–discourse–intimacy technique to explore the underlying stories, which you can do by accessing the *Companion Audio, Section III, Exercise 13* that will then lead you through the exercise of *Companion Workbook, Section III, Exercise 13*.

SECTION IV

HEALING THE CORE OF THE EGO AND MAINTAINING THE HIGHER SELF CONSCIOUSNESS

Now that you have read this far, and, hopefully, experienced many revelatory insights into your own thoughts, emotions, feelings and behaviors, I will attempt to thread all of these concepts together here with perspectives, tips and guidance on implementing and integrating everything into your daily life. This section is my attempt to fortify you with the strength, courage and faith of knowing who you truly are and how to ensure the real *you* doesn't get lost in the midst of your day-to-day life. Being in the world, but not of it is the path of the hero and master.

Chapter 22

Achieving Mastery, Healing, and Wholeness Through Aligning with the Higher Self

The information, tools, and techniques in this book can help you to gain a greater awareness of how your ego and its shadow, as well as your thoughts and emotions, are working within you, how they cause your suffering, and how you can begin to heal that suffering. Much of your healing towards wholeness will be accomplished through using this awareness to understand your suffering and to start making different choices to change the nature of your relationship with your thoughts and emotions. This enables your higher self to step back into the driver seat as the parent to your adolescent ego. What follows is a brief list of things you can do to help yourself to move towards your higher self more regularly.

- Acknowledge your ego and its shadow when they bring negativity towards yourself or others.

- Embrace and forgive your shadow.
- Ask yourself what conditions are giving rise to your shadow reactions?
- Include a physical element and outlet such as regular exercise, yoga, energy work, breath work, reiki, and so on, to help you refocus away from your thoughts.
- Remember that projecting our judgment onto any *them* only increases our own shadow, as well as its sabotage and power over us.
- Practice meditation to quiet the ego's thought-stream and experience your true self—the higher self.
- Remember that peace isn't just a thought—it is a quality of the higher self, which requires you to be aligned with your higher-self consciousness in order to be experienced.
- Shift your perspective away from the polarizations of right/wrong, good/bad, and us/them.
- Stop judging.
- Stop labeling and characterizing.
- Surrender the illusion of and the desire to show the world that you are *right*.
- Surrender the desire for yourself, others, or life to be different.
- Practice gratitude.
- View challenges as opportunities.

When you master the ego and heal the shadow, you achieve wholeness. This mastery and wholeness can only be accomplished when you integrate your mental, emotional, and spiritual bodies with your physical body and ego. When in wholeness, we don't use the polarized labels of good/bad, right/wrong, or us/them, but instead exchange judgment for love, compassion, and forgiveness. These are the higher-self qualities. When you are in your higher self and acting from that consciousness, you operate from a place of *wholeness*. The more you can operate from the higher self, the more whole you will be and feel. This is a symbiotic, synergistic relationship where one begets the other. Just as ego begets ego, the higher self begets a higher self both for and from others, in addition to wholeness for yourself. Wholeness is healing.

This holistic perspective allows you a deeper intuitive knowingness that can continue to inform and direct your responses, behaviors and words that are in alignment with your higher self and this wholeness. Wholeness can't be realized, however, until your ego and shadow conflicts are resolved. You are living near, or at, the source of wholeness and your higher self when:

- You are at peace and cannot be shaken from your center of balance and contentment.
- You have self-knowledge because you are willing to see truths more than wanting to be *right*.
- You empathize without judgment.
- You see yourself and others as part of a whole without divisions of superficial identities or *us* and *them* labels.
- You find desires from your heart create a calmness, and easily present themselves without struggle or difficulty.
- You implore a compassionate detachment where you are not absent from, but you are not invested in any particular outcome.

- You know how to surrender:
  - ✓ Your need to know.
  - ✓ Your need or desire for yourself, others, or life to be different.
  - ✓ Your egoic desires, thoughts, and emotions.
- You see beauty and the divine everywhere.
- You do not look to the future as the best time yet to come or with anxiety, nor do you look at the past with regret. Instead, you see the present as full of beauty, opportunity, and joy.
- You no longer see or use characterizations of polarization such as good/bad or right/wrong.
- You are aligned to peace, joy, love, and qualities of the higher self.
- External conditions and acts of others do not impact you or your beliefs about yourself or life.
- You feel more connected to others, and you find that others cooperate with you more often.
- The results of your actions are constructive and positive both for yourself and others.
- You are fulfilled without having lingering desires (which is not the same as having no motivations or inspirations).

To attain these states, perspectives and experiences, there is one key: *awareness*. Seeing these perspectives, stories, thoughts, and emotional energies in the observer state is the only way you can begin to overcome the ego's default reactions. Becoming aware of what is happening in your thoughts, emotions, and consciousness state is the key to acknowledging the issues, which gives you a pause point where you can then make a different choice to align with the higher self. If you are too attached to, and aligned with, the thought-stream of your ego, you will not be able to move into the observer state that gives you this awareness and conscious choice point. Instead, you will find yourself identified with the thoughts of the egoic mind, which can be agitated, distracted, and under stress, thus inhibiting your ability to experience your higher self, whether in meditative practice or regular daily life.

Chapter 23

BEing the Higher Self, Attaining the Peace of the Higher-Self Consciousness

In order to unwind yourself from the ego's grip and BE more in your higher-self consciousness more often, it is imperative that you have both the desire and intention to see the truth more than you want to be right. The affirmation and intention in Exercise 1, Section II can help you to move into the productive head space for the journey of both finding and deferring to your higher self. It can be helpful to view this journey as an adventure in seeking the truth. You are the courageous, pioneering explorer navigating through the internal workings of your mental and emotional bodies as well as your own psyche. You must, however, first be willing to trust life, as well as to look at your challenges and egoic behaviors as both lessons and opportunities for growth.

All challenges are opportunities for growth, and it is your choice whether you let these challenges bring out the best or worst in you. When faced with the challenges of life, it is an opportunity to choose between:

- Love over Animosity
- Trust over Fear
- Optimism over Pessimism
- Strength and Perseverance over Bitterness
- Compassion over Condemnation and Judgment

The egoic thought-stream will hold a debate both with and about life. It will be angry with life, and will blame it, plead with it, and therefore breed unhappiness and struggle. The ego will make you think that you, others, and life should be different. If you are attached to your thoughts, this could dampen your happiness and divert you from your highest and best self, your gifts as a higher self, as well as the path in life truly meant for you. Every choice point in life is an opportunity for you to live your best self in joy, happiness, and peace, with the opportunities to express and experience your gifts and talents, regardless of the circumstances.

Being in the higher-self consciousness means BEing in, and having a consciousness of, love and compassion, first for yourself, and then for others. You cannot have love for others unless you have it for yourself. When your judgment is active through your internal expression of the inner critic, it will be active through your external judgment expression towards others as well. BEing at one with your higher self, however, allows you to have compassion for those who are acting unkindly, instead of being in an ego–triggering–ego relationship. When you are in your higher-self consciousness, you have compassion for the pain of others and the battle they are caught up in with their egoic conditioned thoughts and resulting emotions. You can have this compassion because you have it for yourself, and you know that, when in the egoic mindset, people *know not what they do.* As you have forgiven yourself, and have been forgiven by others, you can extend this forgiveness to others. This compassion, acceptance, and forgiveness can only be accomplished when you are in alignment with your higher self, which is your true nature.

It is from the consciousness of your higher self that you receive the inspiration about how to BE in your life that is in alignment with the higher-self qualities of courage, wisdom, peace, joy, gratitude, love, and all the other higher-self qualities. Just as being in an egoic consciousness is a self-fulfilling prophecy of seeing through the ego's conditioned lenses, seeing only what the ego expects to see, being in the consciousness of your higher self is also a self-fulfilling prophecy. It is only from this higher-self consciousness that you can see how to BE, and therefore experience life from that perspective of courage, love, compassion, and so on. This includes how to respond constructively to any unkind behavior towards you. When you allow yourself to BE in your higher self, allowing that consciousness to inform your speech and actions, then you can transcend your own thoughts and emotional suffering. You also help others to do the same through the ripple effects and the physics of your energy. This is the path to peace and healing. For those who subscribe to beliefs in the divine, Christ, or Krishna consciousness, this is how you achieve it, and how you can help others get and stay in their version of this consciousness. This is the way out of fear, hatred, and conflict.

You must remember that who you truly are is your higher self, which is not the thought-stream or the resulting emotions. When you can relate differently to these thoughts and emotions by interacting with them as an observer from just enough distance to gain the bigger picture perspective, you can find peace through the heart space, which is where your higher self resides in truth. Peace cannot be found by thinking of peace, or just intellectually understanding the concept of peace. It can be found only through experiencing it, which can be accomplished only by moving beyond the thoughts, feelings, beliefs, and understandings of peace and other related concepts. The experience of peace is in your BEing-ness. This comes from both the observations and awareness of your higher self and its ability to see what is really happening within your mental and emotional bodies. The egoic mind keeps you out of this state of peace because it keeps you at a distance from your higher self, and, instead, keeps you attached to the thoughts. Quiet the mind to just BE in the peace.

BEing in your higher-self consciousness allows you to be attentive to the natural flow of life in each moment. This is what carries you through each moment without fear, doubt, or mistrust. The quality and act that is most in alignment with life in that moment will present itself from your connection to the flow of life through your higher-self consciousness. If you can BE in the consciousness of your higher self, the quality, inspiration, and motivated act will flow through you as your naturally responsive act and speech in that moment that aligns with your higher self. When you are in alignment with your higher self, you are in alignment with life itself.

While you are not in control over how life unfolds, you are always in control of:

- Whether you accept not knowing, or not being in control of outcomes and trusting life.
- How you respond in each moment.
- How well you embrace change.

While in the higher self, you embrace life and change with optimism as an adventure.

The key to getting through the challenges of life is to stay present in them, and not be distracted by, or get immersed in, thoughts about the future or the past, as well as not rejecting or resisting what life is presenting in that moment. Staying present allows you to receive the higher-self qualities and gifts of coping, such as courage, wisdom, and gratitude for the lessons from challenges that bring forth your growth. Knowing that you don't have to figure out the future now can give you a sense of peace, if you allow it. The future is never reality. The only reality is the present.

The higher self's happiness isn't dependent upon circumstances. When your consciousness is aligned with your higher-self state, you are filled with perspectives of contentment, joy, wonder, gratitude, awe, and delight in life in both the most ordinary and extreme moments. The higher-self's joy and happiness is a different level of happiness than the emotions created by the ego's thoughts in its momentary elation over events. The higher self's joy is richer, deeper, more fulfilling, and ever more sustainable over time. The having and doing in the higher self's life is informed by the BEing of the higher self and its qualities and objectives. The egoic state's having and doing is informed by the thought-stream and its fear, lack, and desire. These two different motivators create different lives because they create different experiences.

When you're in your higher self, you don't let your ego turn thoughts into dysfunctional emotions or emotional attachments. Therefore, when you are in your higher self, there is little processing of thoughts or emotions required. The thoughts and emotions that arise when you are in your higher self remain in the simple experience of seeing the emotions that naturally arise and dissipate once the moment has come and gone. When you're in your higher self, you stay in the *here and now* and are in touch with the feelings of love and gratitude that keep you from focusing on thoughts and emotions that can bring negative reactions and energies. When you aren't telling stories in your head about your circumstances, you are more able to release the emotions that arise because they will not last longer than the natural life span of the moment. The higher self creates no stories about "should's," "could's," or "would's," and instead accepts what is, which allows detachment from the thoughts, allowing emotions to dissipate, and aligns you with the flow of life.

To evolve and continue down this path of healing and mastering the ego to live more in your higher self, you must surrender the thoughts, beliefs, opinions, desires, fears, doubt, and fantasies of the ego. Giving up thoughts and beliefs about yourself is the price of truth, healing, and freedom from suffering. You can't lose the voice in your head entirely, as you cannot kill the ego, and that is not what we want to do anyway, but you can just accept and allow the thoughts to rise and flow, while losing the attachment to them as if you are watching cars pass on the highway. This detachment from your thoughts reduces the ego's power to grab and distract you. The goal is not to kill the ego or vilify it, but rather to integrate it with the higher self in the lead. The goal is to just notice these egoic thoughts without identifying with them as *you* or *yours*.

Eventually, with repeated success in simply allowing thoughts to pass on through without giving them your attention, they will stop arising as frequently and with less strength. The goal is to stay in the present long enough to allow yourself to have the awareness of those thoughts and emotions as an observer with compassionate detachment. When you're aware of them with acceptance, and without being involved with them, this compassionate detachment removes the intensity from them, resulting in both greater mental and emotional relaxation. This is the same principle as how you relax when you are accepted by others just as you are. This is effectively showing these thoughts and emotions compassion without judging, rejecting, or indulging them by identifying with and from them. This allows them to relax and move on. As a general principle to remember, accepting things as they are allows you to stay present and take advantage of the qualities of the higher self, such as wisdom, courage, strength, perseverance, and the patience to deal with any situation.

Here is a table of principles that reflect the real truths of life, and who you really are as your higher self:

You are part of, and aligned with, life.	Life is good and perfectly designed.
You don't know very much about life's design for certain, and you don't need to.	When you don't accept life as it is, you suffer.
You are not in control of life, and you don't need to be.	Life is a school, and your experiences are your teachers through which you learn and grow.
The only things in life that are black and white are those colors.	Whatever is occurring in your life is intentional and aligned with the highest good in that moment. How you experience those circumstances is always a personal choice.
You find acceptance easier when you see everyone with compassion for their struggles.	Thoughts and emotions do not reflect the truth.
You always have whatever you need in order to handle whatever is occurring.	Difficulties and challenges are your teacher. Whatever is happening is for the highest good for your growth.

Everyone is learning from everyone else. Everyone is both a student and a teacher.	Surrender your desire to want things and for people to do or be different, and then love and compassion will flow.
Love is what heals and changes hearts.	It hurts you to hate or to push people out of your heart.
Other people are not powerful enough to make you angry or to hurt you—you make yourself feel the way you do.	Emotions arise from thoughts and often uphold the ego's illusive reality. They don't deserve honoring, but they do deserve both acknowledgment and investigation.
Your higher self knows everything you need to know about life. Therefore, you want to be guided by the higher self.	There are always different ways to look at a circumstance that can produce both positive and negative experiences. Your choices determine your experiences.

Chapter 24

Tools for Maintaining the Higher-Self State

Because the ego is the default state of being for us as humans in this physical realm, it takes conscious effort, intention, and self-aware decision-making in order to give ourselves the best chances of mastering our egos and allowing our higher selves to be our lead consciousness state. It is your BEing-ness, which is defined by the subtler feeling states, as distinguished from emotions, that define your consciousness state. These higher-self feeling states must be experienced, which means you must BE in those states. Your thoughts will not get you there, so you can't just think kind thoughts in the moment (though that is a helpful place to begin creating the consciousness shift). These more subtle consciousness state feelings can get lost when we are in active thought or *doing-ness*.

The physical sensations you explored in previous exercises are some of the best ways of gauging what state you are in because the body does not lie when reflecting our energies. Just as the words energetically impacted the water in Dr. Emoto's study, your own BEing state is an energetic state that impacts you as well as those around you. Are your bodily sensations expansive, relaxed, at ease, and are you breathing easily? Or are they tense, contracted, or agitated, with shallow breath? Your body is your guidebook. When you are considering a thought or action, see how your body reacts to it. That is your indication of whether what you are pondering is aligned with your higher self or not.

Tools to Help You Break the Ego's Grip and See the Shadow.

As we dive deeper into our ego, and particularly its shadow, we start being able to separate who we are from the stories and fears of our ego. In order to do that, however, we must have a productive, illuminating, and functional relationship with our shadow. Until we get to this place with our shadow, we will continue to be the victim of the illusions stored there. The path to wholeness, healing, and true enlightenment goes through the shadow. You cannot achieve any of these goals without going into the shadow and uncovering its secrets and deceptions. To do this takes courage, not because what we will find is scary, but because it requires us to surrender. We must surrender all the ego's thoughts and beliefs about what we think we know about who we are, who others are, and how life is. We must want the truth more than we want to be right. If we can make that choice to surrender with the intention of truth over righteousness, we will find our gifts, truths, and the treasure of who we truly are. This truth comes with the vision to see life as it truly is, as well as with the skills to help keep the ego from creating more shadow and sabotaging thoughts, emotions, and behaviors. This is the beginning of the end of our suffering, and the beginning of joy and happiness at the deepest levels. This is where happiness isn't a roller coaster ride or circumstance-dependent.

When you are sitting, observing, and appreciating the beauty of a sunset, you are just "BEing." When you are sitting still, looking across the room at beautiful flowers and smiling, you are just "BEing." When you become aware of the physical sensations in your body as you do the guided exercises in the Companions, you are just "BEing." When you are just "BEing," you are in your higher-self consciousness for that moment. This is not to say that your higher self does not inspire and motivate you to action and doing as well, but in order to become aware of your higher self's inspirations, motivations, and messages, you must distance yourself from the noise of your egoic thoughts and behaviors.

Your state of being and consciousness will drive whether and what thoughts you have running around in your head. What you have in your head is what you have to give to others in that moment. What you have to give is what you perceive as coming from others. What you perceive from others is, then, what you experience. Therefore, your state of being determines what you allow yourself to receive in any given moment. *As within, so without. You shall reap what you sow. What you give, you shall receive.* There is a reason why these axioms have been around for ions. Understanding their true and deeper meanings is revelatory.

When we can BE loving, we can give love, and then we can further perceive love in order to receive the love being shown. If we don't have loving thoughts, we can't BE loving, and so we will always see others as not loving towards us as well (*as within, so without*). If we can never see their acts as loving towards us, then we cannot receive the love they, or others, may be trying to give us. The concept of *as within, so without* means that what you have in your head is what you give, and what you give you receive in return because that is what you perceive through your ego's lens. Like the rose example, if you have negative, fearful thoughts in your head, you will notice the thorns on the rose more than its beauty. When you focus on the thorns more than the beauty of the flower, you will see the rose as a dangerous, painful plant, and thus you will not cherish it, and so will not get close enough to it to allow its beautiful fragrance to be received by you. You will therefore be less likely to see the physical appearance of a rose as beautiful, instead seeing only danger.

Below are some additional tools and techniques that can help you move from an egoic- to higher-self state in order to become more aware of your higher-self inspirations and motivations.

- Notice if and when you are engaged in thoughts running around your mind that involve "I," "me," "my," or "mine." These are nearly always egoic thoughts.

- Notice if you feel an attachment to these thoughts and how attached you feel to them.

- Notice if these thoughts have elicited any emotions that you are now experiencing. If so, name those emotions specifically. See that your own egoic thoughts have pulled these emotional energies into you.

- Move into an observer state and utilize the analytical nature of your intellect to ask yourself questions about why those thoughts are circling in your mind, *but do not make it about someone else, as if your thoughts or reactions are someone else's doing.* Remember, your reaction and thoughts are a reflection of your own consciousness, and not anything outside yourself.

✓ Continue to ask yourself, "Why do I think this?" until you reveal a fear or belief in lack. These will be the basis of nearly all your ego-addicted gripping thoughts and emotions.

- Stay in your intellect and observer state and look at the facts of the circumstances—who did or said what. The "why's" or "what does this mean?" are egoic commentary in its attempts to know and be in control, and do not reflect truths. Remember, do not look at another's acts as the cause of any of your thoughts, emotions, or reactions. Look at others' actions as simply a trigger of your own thoughts and beliefs. Look at how particular behaviors of others trigger your own conditioned reactions. Avoid and resist any desire to attribute meaning to another's acts. Keep your exploration to the observable facts of acts actually performed by yourself and others.

    ✓ See how the thoughts that you had running around in your head were attributing meaning and intentions to others.

    ✓ See that being bothered by others' actions are centered around what it meant for, or about, you.

- Ask yourself why it mattered to you? Ask your rational intellect, "What difference does it make really?" What is the most realistic impact to you in reality?

    ✓ See how the thoughts you had running around in your head likely stemmed from fears.

- See how you can reframe the circumstances, so they do not really matter as much as your ego thought they did.

- Move away from the thoughts you started with, release the emotions, and allow them to deflate and flow out.

- Focus your attention on something outside your mind, such as something in your present environment, your favorite place in nature, the physical sensations you are feeling at this moment, and so on. Note: this is not suppression, deflection, or a lack of acknowledgement of these thoughts. Instead, it is merely a reflection that you have completed your acknowledgement, but you dismiss a belief in those thoughts, so they can now flow out.

- Identify how you can have compassion for anyone involved in your original thoughts and focus on that compassion.

    ✓ If you need to maintain boundaries to keep out another's imbalanced, dysfunctional egoic behavior, identify those boundaries mentally, but with love and compassion. You can envision roses with their beautiful appearance and protective thorns surrounding you. You simultaneously show both the loving and compassionate rose flowers facing outward towards others with the protection of the thorns, so they cannot breach your boundaries. Being compassionate does not require us to be a victim. Similarly, instilling boundaries does not require us to be heartless, mean, cruel, blaming, or shaming others.

    ✓ If your mind reverts to a blame, shame, resentment, or other dysfunctional, imbalanced thought or emotion, take command of your thoughts, and move back to the thoughts of compassion or gratitude.

To put yourself in the best position to BE who you truly are in your higher-self state, here are a few more tools you can utilize described below.

Meditation.

One of the most effective tools we can use to help us master the ego and the shadow is meditation. Through meditation, we can begin intentionally to move away from the thoughts running through our mind and focus on just BEing. Just BEing—as opposed to doing or thinking—is the domain of the higher self. Meditation, as a regular practice, facilitates a *thoughtless* state where our egoic motor minds are taking a break. Early in your meditation practice, your mind will continue to try and interrupt your meditations with a variety of thoughts from "what am I going to have for dinner tonight" to more of the ego's ramblings about how to deal with this situation or an-other. When you notice that your mind has started churning, just refocus your attention on your favorite place in nature and go there in your mind to a joy, gratitude, and love for that place. Imagine yourself there, physically touching, smelling, and seeing all that is there in your mind's eye. Another great internal vision for your meditations is to go to your sacred heart space, and just sit with your higher self, noticing the physical sensations of your body, and just "BE" there with your higher self, using the image or word that reflects your higher-self shortcut that you experienced in an earlier exercise. There are many guided meditations available through many sources, including many mobile applications. The website where you will find the Companion Audio for this book contains some as well.

As you are early in your meditation practice, you may benefit from having more guided meditations to keep your mind focused and off the egoic thought-stream. As you improve in maintaining a break from the motor mind thought-stream, you will want to start practicing meditation without being guided through it, but rather just sitting in your sacred heart space or favorite place in nature, scanning your physical body, or sending love and light through your heart to the world, or something similar.

Mindfulness.

As you begin your day, whether during, or after, meditation, or just during your morning routine, have the intention that you will be aware of how your mind and your thoughts are operating today. You will want to notice when you are lost in thought about a circumstance, whether past or future. When you can go into the observer state, you remove yourself from the active ego engagement, and you can more easily see and discern whether that thought process is productive or not. If you see that you are caught up in a past replay or an anxiety about the future, recognize that you have the choice at that point to redirect yourself to a more productive use of your mind in the here and now, releasing the attachment to those thoughts and let them just fall into the background or dissipate altogether. Section II, Exercise 8, Breaking the Egoic Consciousness, is an example of how to do this. You can redirect your focus to your physical sensations, and just notice them. Then, you can move into your more productive engagement with what is in front of you at that moment.

If your body is feeling contracted or tense, you know that you are in your ego, and you want to stop, release those thoughts, go to your favorite place in nature in your mind, and then come back and make a different choice with your thoughts and state of BEing. Developing this space to pause will take some time, but your intention to be mindful will help you develop more quickly as well as with greater mastery. The only thing that will help to increase your success at mindfulness is practice. No amount of thinking, or intellectually absorbing the concept, through more books or whatever source will get you there. You must experience it and make the choices to shift away from the default programming of the ego's thought-stream.

Part of mindfulness is being quiet in the mind long enough to allow for the higher self's motivation and inspiration to be heard, felt, and known. If you allow your egoic mind to distract you with its *who, what, when, where, why anxieties, and replays*, your inspirations and intuitions will be drowned out, and thus you will not perceive them as readily. In contrast when you are focused on love, gratitude and joy, those inspirations and motivations will be loud and clear. Some other ways you can help yourself redirect your focus to your higher self is to have your favorite things around that give you joy. Having pictures of loved ones can help if these create feelings of love; however, if there is a shadow-triggering drama involved with those loved ones, these may not be helpful.

Uplifting, soothing, and inspiring music is also a good way for many people to release their anxiety-ridden thoughts in order to feel more relaxation and peace. Just as the energy of words impacted water in Dr. Emoto's study, so, too, did music. Water crystals responded differently to Mozart or Beethoven than it did to harsher sounds involving heavy metal rock music and similar genres. Below are more images of Dr. Emoto's study of water crystals showing the reaction to different music.

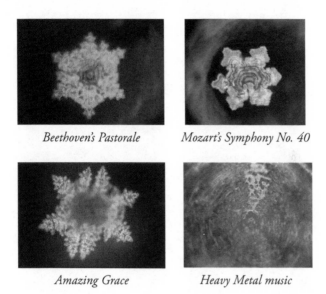

Beethoven's Pastorale   *Mozart's Symphony No. 40*

Amazing Grace   *Heavy Metal music*

Dr. Masaru Emoto water crystal study, as published in *The Hidden Messages in Water*. Reprinted with the express permission of the Office Masaru Emoto, LLC. See also, https://www.masaru-emoto.net/en/crystal/

When you can BE in your higher-self consciousness, you will experience life as indicated below:

- You can drop your thoughts on external identities about who you think you are based on your gender, nationality, race, ethnicity, job, wealth, religion, and so on.

- You don't get lost in the illusions of the egoic perspective.

- You are content, and do not need anything outside yourself to make you happy.

- You accept life just as it is, and you see the good in it.

- You no longer see yourself as lacking, struggling, or fearful, or as the odds being stacked against you.

- You see the goodness, beauty, abundance, and supportive nature of life that is available to you.

- You see the ego's view of *bad* in things that happen as just a perception or a mental construct of the ego in its dysfunctional polarization of good/bad.

- You don't take things personally.

- You surrender to what life is presenting in the moment, and you know that your higher self already has—or will be given—everything that is needed to cope with the circumstances. This does not mean you allow yourself to be a victim, or to be complacent without trying to improve yours and others' circumstances.

- You allow the ego to create its stories and emotions (not resisting the ego) without attaching to them, knowing that the real you is accepting things as they unfold, and therefore you don't have to be bothered or driven by the egoic thoughts and emotions that you recognize as just conditioning.

  ✓ This lessens the power of the ego, its stories, and conditioning over you.

  ✓ You realize that the suffering comes through your thoughts, stories, and emotions, not from the events themselves. People cause their own suffering.

- You stay within the unfolding of situations, and don't jump to the past or future, seeing it for what it is, and dealing with it more wisely.

✓ By not jumping to the future or past, you don't create the unpleasant, anxiety-laced thoughts that lead to the unpleasant emotions that take you out of the present moment and out of your wisdom.

✓ Allows you to take advantage of the qualities of the higher self, which are all different complexions of truth and love.

The power and beauty of BEing in our higher selves is not limited to only the healing and empowerment it gives us personally. The ripple effect power is in how we can impact others to shift into their own healing as well. Just as the Newton's Cradle of balls shows us, ripple effects are both real and powerful. With your own shift, you help to shift others, too. When in your higher self, your energy and actions from that consciousness state will be more likely to ripple into triggering others' higher-self responses instead of their egoic or shadow reactions.

With the true happiness of the higher-self state of being, there is no striving, driving, or struggle. Instead, the feeling and state is just one of BEing. All the doing, striving, and driving is the ego's way of trying to acquire and achieve. The ego disappears into the background when you allow yourself to just BE. When you are just BEing, you don't try to be an identity or live up to the ego's ideals. This resting of all the labels and identities you've adopted through the ego, and instead, just BEing in your own awareness state, is how you realize who you really are as your higher self. You will then realize that success and failure are just artificial ideals of the ego that keep you involved with it and its subjective, artificial, dysfunctional identities, and characterizations of its storylines. Success is a concept that will continue changing for the ego. Remember that you are not the thinker of the thoughts. Instead, you are the observer of the thoughts. Once you realize this and experience it, your ego loses the power to drive you.

As you practice this awareness mastery, remember that this choice away from the egoic consciousness and its thought-stream is not tantamount to resisting, rejecting, or suppressing it. Condemnation will not free you of the egoic state, but will, in fact, draw it to you, creating more shadow with which you will struggle and suffer. You must simply choose differently without judgment and with compassion for yourself and for your child-like egoic state. As you allow the ego's thoughts and stories to chatter on in the background without resisting, condemning, or indulging it, the more it will subside without leaving a mark.

As you are looking at the thoughts in your head and trying to release the negative, judgmental, and destructive storylines, a helpful first step can be to convert the negative thoughts into positive ones. Instead of being preoccupied with thoughts of lack about yourself, others, or life, you can focus on a list of things for which you can be grateful or appreciate about yourself, others, or life. We discussed earlier how thinking thoughts of gratitude can be an effective way to transition from egoic to higher-self states. Ultimately, however, the best state is to remove the "I" completely from your attention and focus because your true self— your higher self—is found outside of thoughts.

Who you truly are as your higher self is not an identity, an idea, or an image, but rather a consciousness that experiences life. The difference between *believing* you are loving and *experiencing* yourself as love and goodness is the difference between being in your head, with its egoic thought-stream, and just

BEing your higher self in real time. While being in a state of beliefs is not actually experiencing your higher self, there are some thoughts and beliefs that can be a bridge to help you move from your egoic state to your higher-self state. The thoughts and beliefs in your and others' innate goodness is often such a bridge to the experience of who you truly are. You can achieve this belief by realizing that the thoughts and images of yourself as flawed, bad, unworthy, inadequate, not good enough, and so on are false. Then affirm the opposite is true. The knowingness that you are from the highest good of the universe, worthy, fully gifted, and capable of all things meant for you in your highest and best self is characteristic of your higher self state of BEing. When you can see this in yourself, you can also see this in others. You can't see innate goodness in others without being able to see this in yourself. This is a reprogramming of mistaken beliefs, resulting in a breaking of the illusion of your egoic false self. Affirming that you are, and have the qualities of, the true self opens the door to experiencing who you truly are, who others truly are, and how life truly is.

However, a note of caution: just having a happier self-image is not really stepping into who you are because this self-image is still an image, which is made up of a set of thoughts and storylines. It does, however, make discovering who you are easier, and is also healthier, so that you can begin to focus on your higher self instead of the negativity of the ego. This positive self-image, however, can still be corrupted by the ego because it is steeped in thoughts. The ego can distort these thoughts into thinking you are better or more *enlightened* than others because you've just mastered a better self-image with a more successful manifestation. Again, having this more positive self-image is not always a reflection of you being in your true self—it may just be a more functional self-image.

The real you doesn't have a focus on the "I," because it knows it is part of a whole, and is interconnected as a unique expression of the ultimate highest, best source of consciousness. Some call that the divine, or Source, or God, or whatever higher power and light that people believe. There is a difference between knowing you are a reflection and embodiment of love, courage, gratitude and all of the higher self qualities in contrast to having a belief in a set of thoughts that make up an image. The former is a reflection of the higher self, and the latter is a reflection of a more tamed ego. This tamed ego can be used as a stepping-stone to the higher self, which feels informed with truths and liberated to detach from all stories and images. Through the higher-self consciousness feeling state of confidence, you know that you embody and feeling those higher self qualities.

Below are examples of transitional thoughts you can choose to focus on, instead of negative ones, that will help you be at peace and relax in the midst of a mind that is trying to stir up your emotions:

S/He might be having a bad day.	I can understand why/how she might feel that way.	I can let that go.
I forgive that.	That isn't about me and doesn't affect me.	I don't need to be perfect.
There's nothing I can do about that, so I'm not going to worry about it.	I'm doing my best, and there is nothing at which I'm failing.	S/he's doing the best s/he can, and that is OKAY.
I choose to send love and compassion instead.	I'm not going to let that be a problem.	All is well.
It's not important.	It will all work out.	This, too, shall pass.

Everything is unfolding as it needs to.	It's none of my business because it does not affect me.	I leave that up to God/the divine/spirit/ the flow of life.
Delete that thought.	Peace, peace, peace	I don't need to know/have/ do that in order to be happy.

When life is asking you to sacrifice something, ask what you might be gaining instead. Trust that you are never asked to sacrifice when you don't also gain something. The higher self looks at what is gained instead of what is lost. This is part of surrendering the desire for life to be different. When we are in our higher-self state of BEing, we are in acceptance of life, and we then have everything we need to cope. Suffering comes with our inability to accept change and challenges, ascribing a *bad* label to it. *Waking up* out of the ego and its thought-stream into our higher, true self requires that we are present and focused on the current moment. This is a core part of what people who subscribe to particular spiritual beliefs and philosophies refer to as an *awakening* or *enlightenment*. When we can surrender the ego's desires, goals, beliefs, and conditioning, we are left with our higher selves, and this becomes the consciousness that then informs, inspires, motivates, and drives our objectives, desires, and actions. When we are thinking and acting from the place of our higher selves, our actions result in more joy, love, peace, compassion and all of the other qualities and objectives of the higher self.

Just as the egoic mind feeds on itself and becomes self-perpetuating, so, too, does the consciousness of the higher self. Once you begin to experience it more, the ego's perspectives cease to interest you or have a grip on you. This loosening of the ego's grip starts with a few key choices:

- A desire and intention to see the truth versus being right.

- Making an effort to pause when you notice negative thoughts and emotions, so you can turn your attention away from those thoughts and into the higher-self observer state to investigate those thoughts and their underlying beliefs.

- Having compassion for yourself instead of the inner critic.

- Cease wanting other people and life to be different.

This process can be summed up in three words: *1. Awareness, 2. Acceptance, and 3. Compassion.* These also describe the concept of compassionate detachment.

How to Start Choosing Differently than the Ego's Default.

Surrender the Attachment to Your Thoughts. Surrendering attachment to your thoughts is the first and most important step in mastering your ego, allowing your higher self to drive your consciousness. Surrendering attachment means you not only surrender your continual replay of those thoughts going around repeatedly in your mind, but you also surrender your attachment to those thoughts as being truths. Remember the lesson discussed at the beginning of this book: *don't believe everything you think.* When you can surrender your attachment to your thoughts, you can more easily achieve the following:

- Allowing the thoughts to flow out without growing roots.

- Allowing the short-circuiting of dysfunctionally used emotions that would align with the negative and dysfunctional thoughts.

- Allowing space for the pause of conscious choice in what you believe, and how you want to respond.

- Allowing space for your higher self to drive your perspectives, values, objectives, and behaviors, especially when combined with the use of mindfulness tools.

- Surrendering the beliefs and judgments rooted in the separation of polarized perspectives and labels of right/wrong, us/ them, and good/bad.

- Surrendering the belief in lack—in you, others, and life.

- Surrendering fears and distrust about yourself, others, and life, allowing everyone and life to present the gifts of their nature without preconceived expectations.

Surrender the Desire to be *Right*, and Choose the Desire for Truth. The desire to be right more than wanting the truth is one of the biggest obstacles to us in seeing the edges of our egoic, conditioned lenses. If we cannot see our ego's conditioning, we have no hope of seeing our shadow or the source of our suffering. In order to heal, we must have this awareness. In order to have this awareness, we must be willing to surrender being right in order to see the truth. The reason that awareness heals is because truth heals. Awareness is the door to truth, and therefore healing. The other important element of this surrendering of our desire to be right is the surrendering of the desire for ourselves, others, and life to be different. Inherent in our desire to be right is our desire to see ourselves, others, and life consistent with our conditioned beliefs. In order to loosen the grip of those sabotaging beliefs, we must be willing to be wrong about those beliefs. Remember, the ego is not who you truly are, so surrendering your ego's beliefs is not surrendering who you truly are.

Use Your Choice for Truth Awareness to Explore Your Ego and Shadow. When you've been able to make the choice for truth over being right, you will start gaining more awareness of your egoic conditioning and storylines. This opens the door to the dungeon of your shadow and its triggers. Once you open the door to your shadow, you can shine the light onto the false, painful stories that the ego created, and then buried there. These shadow stories were shoved deep into, and absorbed by, the unconscious psyche, becoming part of the secret foundation of your beliefs about the nature of yourself, others, and life. This exploration illuminates the pathway to reframing the circumstances that gave rise to these egoic stories, so you can see the truths, heal, and liberate yourself from the suffering of those stories.

Surrender Use of the Ego's Tools of Fear and Judgment and its Enforcer, the Inner-Critic. Even with the desire to see the truth more than wanting to be right, and having the awareness that can illuminate the ego and its shadow, the ego's judgment can hijack the higher self by trying to reinforce its beliefs in fear, lack, and separation. The ego's judgment will try to convince you that the higher self's perspectives and objectives are opening you up to victimhood and foolishness, both of which are based in the ego's fears. In addition to judgement, common emotions and egoic tools that function as companions to the inner critic can include:

- Anger (and, on a more extreme basis, Hostility)
- Fear
- Victimization and Self-Pity
- Envy
- Aggression—whether in self-defense or attacking others

The ego will use its enforcer, the inner critic, to try and keep you and your higher self under its thumb. Don't let it do this. Remember who you are. You are the higher self, embodying all its qualities of courage, kindness, compassion, wisdom, and perseverance, as well as all its other qualities. Whenever the words, "would," "could," and, in particular, "should," appear in your thoughts, recognize this as the ego trying to trap you into its thoughts and judgments about the past and future.

Practice Meditation, Stillness, and other Mindfulness Tools. The use of mindfulness tools will be instrumental in helping you to implement the awareness and pause to choose the higher self to drive your consciousness and behaviors. Having the intention to want the truth more than being right is the first critical step. These mindfulness tools will help you develop the mindsets and behaviors to implement and realize that intention. Through these mindfulness tools, you will be able to create the space away from your thoughts where your higher self can surface and be the driver. You want to stay present, and not distracted by thoughts of past or future.

Practice Gratitude and Compassionate Detachment. There are many reasons to practice gratitude and compassionate detachment. One reason is that practicing gratitude helps to combat the ego's belief in lack. When the ego tries to convince you about what you don't have, or don't have enough of, must compete for, and separate from others to obtain— focus on gratitude. Your gratitude can include any one or more of the following:

- The things you do have
- Food
- Shelter

- Clothing
- Transportation
- Family and friends' support
- Nature
- Pets and other animals
- The money in your pocket, wallet, and/or bank account
- Experiences of life
- Lessons of life
- Life itself

As a companion to this gratitude, the importance of compassionate detachment, which has been discussed extensively in this book, cannot be overstated. The lens of compassion, with which we want to view ourselves and others, replaces the judgment that the ego wants to render. We cannot simultaneously impart judgment *and* compassion. The compassion lens allows us to see our own as well as others' actions with the truth that unkind behavior is being driven by the ego's fears and suffering. Challenging circumstances are the paths to lessons and growth, and when seen for their truths, it is easier to view these with the lens of compassion instead of judgment. When this compassion is accompanied with detachment (not to be confused with suppression or numbness), we can see that these unkind behaviors and challenging circumstances are not personal to us; therefore, they do not say anything about who we are. Then we can more easily release and prevent a build-up of painful thoughts and emotions that can blind us to truths, compassion, and gratitude. Compassionate detachment helps us to perpetuate an upward spiral, as opposed the ego's downward spiral.

Surrender You can see that the theme of surrender is key to making different choices. Choices that move away from the ego's default require us to surrender everything the ego values. Many of these values are covered in an earlier chapter, and they center around control, its beliefs, being right, its fears, and wanting things to be different from the present, whether in people themselves or life's circumstances.

Chapter 25

Signs of Ego Mastery and Spirituality's Shadow

Signs of Ego Mastery

As you practice the awareness, tools, and techniques outlined here, you progress in your mastery of your ego and its shadow. When you gain greater mastery over your ego and shadow, it enables you to remember who you really are. When you both remember and trust who you really are as your higher self, you evolve in your spiritual growth. For those who align with a spiritual philosophy, you take another step towards awakening and enlightenment. There is no awakening or enlightenment unless realized through shadow and ego mastery. Signs of your growth and evolution here include:

- More accepting of others, even in their egoic behaviors, viewing them with more compassion
- Greater patience
- Less harshness and judgment of self and others

- Less interest in gossip, bashing others, or complaining
- Greater joy in everyday things
- Inner peace and contentment
- Accepting of life's circumstances without complacency
- Less interest in friends and associates who are focused on negative drama, superficial values, and objectives
- Greater enjoyment of nature, and just BEing, without having to be always doing something, and staying busy
- Have appreciation and gratitude for life
- Have more humility, seeing all as part of a whole without separation of *us* and *them* labels
- Become less interested in the ego's values and objectives:
  - ✓ Lose the desire to achieve the ego's definition of success
  - ✓ Lose the attachment to physical appearances
  - ✓ Lose the need to receive affirmations and admiration from others
  - ✓ Lose interest in acquiring things
- Lose the desire to climb to the top, or to participate in the rat race of societal expectations

Signs of Spiritual Shadow

If you look at the ego as a problem, as something to beat down, kill, eliminate, or even transcend, you could be inclined to blame, shame, and otherwise vilify the ego. This will, however, only result in more shadow, and not the compassionate detachment that is required for wholeness, integration, healing, and ego mastery. Instead, the ego and its shadow is something to be intimate with, understand, and move into the integrated, healed wholeness with the higher self in the lead. It is an equally problematic trap if you believe that if you do not stay at a constant higher-self state 24/7, your mastery or spiritual evolution *is less than,* or has fallen. If you get stuck, reactive, or have difficulties with emotions or thoughts, don't think you're not being spiritual, or that you've fallen off the wagon, no longer walking the path of mastery. We all continue to ebb and flow throughout life.

Part of the path of mastery is recognizing when, how and why we do continue to ebb and flow, as well as to learn more about how our ego and its shadow will also evolve to continue to try and stay in the lead. Think of the ego like an adolescent who evolves in his attempts at fooling the parent to sneak out at night to get what it wants. If your intention is to have mastery, have faith that you are still walking the path of ego mastery, advancing your higher-self consciousness, even when you see or experience an ebbing of consciousness state. Take confidence in the fact that, by virtue of your recognizing that you did ebb back into an egoic consciousness state, this awareness is an achievement, which is a critical part of ongoing mastery.

True mastery and spirituality allows the challenges, and uses them for further mastery, healing, growth, and evolution. If you use spiritual practices to avoid pain, or to avoid dealing with emotional wounds, unresolved pain, or developmental opportunities, this is just another method for suppression, which strengthens the shadow. You cannot eliminate the pain by bypassing it; however, pain doesn't have to cause suffering. This bypassing pain is commonly referred to as *spiritual bypassing.* True mastery and spiritual advancement embraces everything that presents in any given moment, including all the uncomfortable thoughts and emotions. Taking all as it comes and seeing it for what it is, is how it can be truly understood, mastered, healed, and integrated. Nothing is *bad*, but spiritual bypassing will label certain emotions, thoughts, and behaviors as *bad* or *wrong*. This is using the ego's tools of judgment, shame, and blame. Seeing these thoughts, emotions, or behaviors in themselves as *bad* or *wrong*, as well as seeking to suppress, ignore, or refuse to acknowledge their presence results in a deepening, widening, and strengthening of the ego's shadow.

This bypassing can surface as both a suppressing and condemning of these undesirable thoughts, emotions, and behaviors, such as anger, as well as overemphasizing and exaggerating being positive, vilifying signs of anger as *bad*. This produces a phobia of sorts of these thoughts and emotions, which induces people to avoid them at all costs and feel ashamed of them, instead of taking the time to explore them, and why they are there. There can be no healing or mastery when this avoiding, vilifying approach to any thought or emotion or behavior occurs. In many cases, people with this belief will falsely equate anger as incorporating ill-will or hostility, and they cannot see the productive use of balanced anger energies. This is another example of how the ego labels everything in either one pole or another without balance as an option.

When someone holds this anger phobia and a vilification of any thought type or emotion, they will be likely to have weak boundaries and will end up expressing their ego and shadow on the submissive side, subjecting them to victimization and allowing others to mistreat them, often in dysfunctional relationships. When this spiritual bypassing expresses itself submissively, the person will be internally bullying and judgmental to themselves with their thoughts and behaviors. This, in turn, will be likely to express towards others in a passive-aggressive nature of similarly bullying and judging others who are dealing with their own egoic reactions. Those who are spiritually bypassing will often bully others to "just drop your story", and delude themselves about their own superiority of their mastery and spiritual evolution. This is typical ego and shadow expressing as either aggressively or passive-aggressively. The caution here is that if someone does engage in this submissively or aggressively expressed spiritual bypassing, judging themselves for judging is just more of the ego's inner critic. Instead, we need to look at our spiritual evolution and ego mastery with the same perspectives, tools, and techniques just as we look at any other thought, emotion, and behavior.

We all have egoic challenges with shadow stories, triggers, and conditioning. None of that needs to be condemned. Instead, we want to become intimate with and investigate what we might consider to be our darkness. The more productive way to view our ego, shadow, and conditioning is to view it as our smaller self that is a wounded and fearful part of our whole being. To view our higher self and egoic self as our *light* and *darkness*, respectively, is, in my opinion, just more egoic polarization. Instead, I view it as just separated and broken off parts of ourselves that need to be integrated back together to achieve wholeness. We are a whole being, and we want to integrate all our parts in a way that is functional, healthy, healed, along with the more knowledgeable and sophisticated part of us—our higher self—in the lead.

Chapter 26

Conclusion

The most important thing to heed in your mastery evolution is to *trust the process*. Transformation and healing has its own schedule, and therefore know that it cannot be rushed. It takes time for the egoic lens of perception to be cleansed. Don't expect to be able to sustain the consciousness of your higher self 100% of the time. Instead, know that the consciousness of your higher-self state will come and go, alternating with the default programming of the ego. As your mastery increases, the time you spend in your higher self versus the egoic consciousness will increase. With your awareness of the egoic consciousness increasing, your ability to see how it expresses in you will become sharper. As you can call forth your higher self more often at will and know it as the truth, you will increasingly experience it. Have the intention to perceive yourself, others and life through the consciousness of your higher self, and it will occur more often.

Your awareness that a transformation is taking place is helpful, so just be patient with it, allow it, and continue working with the tools and techniques to continue moving along. Let everything BE as it is, surrender control and the need to know what, or when, something will happen. This surrender includes surrendering ideas of the future. This surrendering is not to be confused with surrendering the higher self's motivations and inspirations, which you will continue to pursue as those inspirations and motivations appear from your higher self.

When you are happy, you naturally feel love, gratitude, and compassion, which is the most natural expression of life. BEing loving is something anyone can do, and is what everyone really wants. Love and compassion is how you become empowered, happy, and turn negatives into positives, whether they be thoughts, stories, emotions, perspectives, behaviors, or experiences.

This is where I am compelled to make reference to our *soul*, and how that fits into this discussion, given the title. Throughout this book, I make reference to our true self as the higher self. My belief about the soul and the higher self is that the soul is the embryonic-like sack for a piece of the higher self to reside inside the human body. The higher self is far more expansive than what can fit into the human body, but the portion of our higher self that does reside in the body is encapsulated into our soul. For those who believe in reincarnation and the eternal life of the soul, it is this soul capsule that can become fractured from trauma, as well as stained and wounded from our human (and egoic) experiences, which can then be carried through to subsequent lives as our soul moves through an eternity of existence. Through this ego and shadow mastery and remembering who we truly are as our higher selves, we heal the fractures, wounds and stains of our souls, becoming whole once again.

Our souls are the bridges between our human selves and our divine, higher selves. It is our souls that enable us to, in fact, be Hu-Mans. *Hu* meaning our divine higher selves, and *Man* meaning our physical being with our egoic minds and bodies.[20] This ego mastery work is the bridge-repair that rebuilds our wholeness as both divine and worldly. This renewed wholeness, repair and integration, with our higher self directing the action through its consciousness state, is the perfecting of the soul. This perfected wholeness results in an unbroken presence of both the *hu* and *man* within us.

How we help others and transform the world.

Following your heart and BEing in your higher-self consciousness is the best way you can benefit others and this world. When you encounter others while in your higher self, you become a model for others for a way of living and BEing outside of the egoic consciousness. You can then become a catalyst for their growth. The more people living from their higher selves and following their hearts, the easier it is for others around them to do the same. Each person's growth isn't just about them, it's about the evolution of the collective, which grows as each person grows. When individuals stagnate and live in their egos, the collective also stagnates as a collective egoic consciousness and shadow. Conversely, as we each heal, we help heal the whole. This is the ripple effect of the sayings that *hurt people hurt people* and *healed people heal people.* By transforming our individual

---

[20] Many ancient civilizations and religions include the root, or name, of "Hu" in their references to the divine, from Egyptian to Sanskrit to ancient Arabic and more. There is much out there that discusses the roots of human, homo sapiens and the various derivatives. I invite you to explore your own research, heart and mind on this topic.

consciousness, we transform our values and, in turn, help to transform societal systems and structures around us.

As you see your ego and your higher self, you see the truth. This is when you begin your journey of mastery to become your own hero of your own life and take back your power. This is how we change the world . . . one ego and higher self state of BEing at a time. This is where you remember who you are as a divine, loving, compassionate, courageous BEing who is the hero of your own life. Welcome home, hero.

For illumination on how far you have advanced in your awareness, understanding, and knowledge about your own ego, shadow, and conditioning, please go to the *Companion Workbook, Section IV, Exercise 1* and answer the questions there.

Companion Workbook

Many of the exercises in this Companion Workbook have an Audio Companion to guide the reader through the exercises. These Audio files can be found at http://dawnely.com/perfecting-the-soul, organized by Section and Exercise as outlined here.

SECTION I

EXERCISE 1 - GUIDED: *The Difference between the Egoic Reaction and the Higher Self Response.*

Please access the *Companion Audio* for this *Section I* and go through the guided exercise. After completing the guided exercise in the Audio, please answer the following.

1. How did you think and feel differently about that situation before versus after the meditation?

    _____

    _____

SECTION II

EXERCISE 1: *Intention and affirmation [say three times earnestly from the heart with humility and with an adventurous, truth-seeking, accepting, and compassionate heart]*

I intend and affirm that I AM—and will continue to BE—open, alert, honest, willing, and courageous to see the underlying stories, limitations, and sabotaging beliefs and behaviors of my ego and its shadow that are overshadowing my higher self and hiding my lessons, growth, higher qualities, fractions of my true self, and my innate power.

I intend and affirm that I SHALL take back my power, integrate my full self in a balanced way, accept the lessons, heal the fractures, transcend the limitations, extend my growth, and step into my full and highest self.

EXERCISE 2: *Your Shadow Triggers*

1. What are the qualities in others that elicit the most rejection or condemnation from you and to which you have the most vehement objections or reactions:

_____

_____

a. Are there any emotions about yourself that you don't want to feel that come up for an instant before you criticize others or become defensive in hiding those uncomfortable feelings?

_____

_____

_____

b. Identify the emotions and reactions you have when you believe you're faced with these qualities from others:

_____

_____

_____

2. Are there particular scenarios that trigger your most extreme or intense distaste or resentment for any of these qualities listed above?

_____

_____

_____

a. Identify the emotions and reactions you have when you believe you're faced with these scenarios:

_____

_____

b. Are there any emotions about yourself that you don't want to feel that come up for an instant in these scenarios before your reactions to these scenarios and emotions about others?

_____

_____

3. Are there particular inquiries, questions or challenges made by others towards you that make you feel as if you're being attacked by them?

_____

_____

_____

a. Are there any emotions about yourself that you don't want to feel that come up for an instant in these scenarios before you criticize others or become defensive?

_____

_____

_____

b. Identify the emotions and reactions you have when you believe you're faced with these scenarios from others:

_____

_____

_____

4. What qualities, characteristics, or groups do you view as being part of a *them* in comparison to you in any way?

_____

_____

_____

a. Why do you view these groups to be a *them*? How are they different, and how do they reveal their differences?

_____

_____

_____

b. What qualities do they exhibit that you believe make them part of a *them* group? In what ways are you different?

_____

_____

_____

c. Identify the emotions and reactions you have when you believe you're faced with these *them's*:

_____

_____

_____

d. Are there any emotions about yourself that you don't want to feel that come up for an instant before you view others as a *them*, criticize them, or become defensive in hiding those uncomfortable feelings?

_____

_____

_____

EXERCISE 3 – GUIDED: EXPLORING THE SHADOW SIDE AND BALANCE

Please access the *Companion Audio* for this *Section II, Exercise 3* and go through the guided exercise. After completing the guided exercise in the Audio, please answer the following.

1. What physical body sensations did you feel when you were in the Shadow suppressive consciousness?

    _____

2. What physical body sensations did you feel when you were in the Shadow aggressive consciousness?

    _____

    _____

3. What physical body sensations did you feel when you were in the Higher-Self balanced consciousness?

    _____

    _____

4. Why did your ego feel a need to protect or fear that created your egoic shadow emotion or story?

    _____

    _____

5. How do you make peace with this emotion and story – what does it mean to you?

    _____

    _____

a. What is the real truth?

_____

_____

b. What is the positive progression that you can take forward?

_____

_____

6. How difficult or easy was this to work through in managing your emotions and stories in the moment, and what made it easy or difficult?

_____

_____

7. Can you think of something that you can do that can make it easier next time?

_____

_____

8. Other notes or observations:

_____

_____

EXERCISE 4 – YOUR EGOIC STORIES

1. What causes you the most suffering in your life?

    _____

    _____

    a. What belief about yourself, others, or life does this stem from?

        _____

        _____

    b. When/how did you come to this conclusion? (when do you recall the first time you felt or thought this)?

        _____

        _____

    c. What emotion or feeling comes to mind that under-lies or arises from this belief?

        _____

        _____

    d. [Question in Exercise 5]

        _____

        _____

    e. [Question in Exercise 5]

        _____

        _____

f.   [Question in Exercise 5]

_____

_____

g.   [Question in Exercise 5]

_____

_____

2.   What do you fear most in life or about yourself?

_____

_____

a.   What belief about yourself, others, or life does this stem from?

_____

_____

b.   How did you come to this conclusion that this was a real fear with real possibilities of what you fear occurring? When do you recall the first time you felt or thought this?

_____

_____

c.   What emotion or feeling comes to mind that underlies or comes forth from this belief?

_____

_____

d. [Question in Exercise 5]

_____

_____

e. [Question in Exercise 5]

_____

_____

f. [Question in Exercise 5]

_____

_____

g. [Question in Exercise 5]

_____

_____

3. What do you tell yourself about your success or failure in life? Do you consider yourself a failure at anything, or at life in general?

_____

_____

a. Why/why not?

_____

_____

b. When/How did you come to this conclusion (when do you recall the first time you felt or thought this)?

_____

_____

c. What emotion or feeling comes to mind that underlies or comes forth from this belief?

_____

_____

d. [Question in Exercise 5]

_____

_____

e. [Question in Exercise 5]

_____

_____

f. [Question in Exercise 5]

_____

_____

g. [Question in Exercise 5]

_____

_____

4. What do you believe is your worst quality?

_____

_____

a. Why?

_____

_____

b. When/How did you come to this conclusion (when do you recall the first time you felt or thought this)?

_____

_____

c. What emotion or feeling comes to mind that underlies or comes forth from this belief?

_____

_____

d. [Question in Exercise 5]

_____

_____

e. [Question in Exercise 5]

_____

_____

f. [Question in Exercise 5]

_____

_____

g. [Question in Exercise 5]

_____

_____

5. What do you believe you that you are lacking?

_____

_____

a. Why?

_____

_____

b. When/How did you come to this conclusion (when
    do you recall the first time you felt or thought this)?

_____

_____

c. What emotion or feeling comes to mind that under-
    lies or comes forth from this belief?

_____

_____

d. [Question in Exercise 5]

_____

_____

e. [Question in Exercise 5]

_____

_____

f. [Question in Exercise 5]

_____

_____

g. [Question in Exercise 5]

_____

_____

6. Do you believe that you are lovable or worthy of love?

    _____

    _____

    a. Why/why not?

        _____

        _____

    b. When/How did you come to this conclusion (when do you recall the first time you felt or thought this)?

        _____

        _____

    c. What emotion or feeling comes to mind that underlies or comes forth from this belief?

        _____

        _____

    d. [Question in Exercise 5]

        _____

        _____

    e. [Question in Exercise 5]

        _____

        _____

    f. [Question in Exercise 5]

        _____

        _____

g. [Question in Exercise 5]

_____

_____

7. Do you believe you can trust others?

_____

_____

a. Why/why not?

_____

_____

b. When/How did you come to this conclusion (when do you recall the first time you felt or thought this)?

_____

_____

c. What emotion or feeling comes to mind that underlies or comes forth from this belief?

_____

_____

d. [Question in Exercise 5]

_____

_____

e. [Question in Exercise 5]

_____

_____

f.   [Question in Exercise 5]

_____

_____

g.   [Question in Exercise 5]

_____

_____

8. Do you believe that you can trust life, or do you feel the need to guide it and have more control, so it comes out closer to what you want?

_____

_____

a.   Why/why not?

_____

_____

b.   When/How did you come to this conclusion (when do you recall the first time you felt or thought this)?

_____

_____

c.   What emotion or feeling comes to mind that underlies or comes forth from this belief?

_____

_____

d.   [Question in Exercise 5]

_____

_____

e.   [Question in Exercise 5]

_____

_____

f.   [Question in Exercise 5]

_____

_____

g.   [Question in Exercise 5]

_____

_____

9.   Do you believe you are worthy of respect?

_____

_____

a.   Why/why not?

_____

_____

b.   When/How did you come to this conclusion (when do you recall the first time you felt or thought this)?

_____

_____

c.   What emotion or feeling comes to mind that underlies or comes forth from this belief?

_____

_____

d.　[Question in Exercise 5]

_____

_____

e.　[Question in Exercise 5]

_____

_____

f.　[Question in Exercise 5]

_____

_____

g.　[Question in Exercise 5]

_____

_____

10.　Do you believe that you are often overlooked by others?

_____

_____

a.　Why/why not?

_____

_____

b.　When/How did you come to this conclusion (when do you recall the first time you felt or thought this)?

_____

_____

    c.   What emotion or feeling comes to mind that under-
lies or comes forth from this belief?

_____

_____

    d.   [Question in Exercise 5]

_____

_____

    e.   [Question in Exercise 5]

_____

_____

    f.   [Question in Exercise 5]

_____

_____

    g.   [Question in Exercise 5]

_____

_____

11. Do you believe that life is scary?

_____

_____

    a.   Why/why not?

_____

_____

b. When/How did you come to this conclusion (when do you recall the first time you felt or thought this)?

_____

_____

c. What emotion or feeling comes to mind that underlies or comes forth from this belief?

_____

_____

d. [Question in Exercise 5]

_____

_____

e. [Question in Exercise 5]

_____

_____

f. [Question in Exercise 5]

_____

_____

g. [Question in Exercise 5]

_____

_____

12. Do you believe that you are treated unfairly in life, whether by life or by others?

_____

_____

a.   Why/why not?

_____

_____

b.   When/How did you come to this conclusion (when
     do you recall the first time you felt or thought this)?

_____

_____

c.   What emotion or feeling comes to mind that under-
     lies or comes forth from this belief?

_____

_____

d.   [Question in Exercise 5]

_____

_____

e.   [Question in Exercise 5]

_____

_____

f.   [Question in Exercise 5]

_____

_____

g.   [Question in Exercise 5]

_____

_____

13. Do you believe you're a good person?

_____

_____

    a.   Why/why not?

        _____

        _____

    b.   When/How did you come to this conclusion (when do you recall the first time you felt or thought this)?

        _____

        _____

    c.   What emotion or feeling comes to mind that underlies or comes forth from this belief?

        _____

        _____

    d.   [Question in Exercise 5]

        _____

        _____

    e.   [Question in Exercise 5]

        _____

        _____

    f.   [Question in Exercise 5]

        _____

        _____

g. [Question in Exercise 5]

_____

_____

14. Do you believe you are a courageous person?

_____

_____

a. Why/why not?

_____

_____

b. When/How did you come to this conclusion (when do you recall the first time you felt or thought this)?

_____

_____

c. What emotion or feeling comes to mind that underlies or comes forth from this belief?

_____

_____

d. [Question in Exercise 5]

_____

_____

e. [Question in Exercise 5]

_____

_____

f.   [Question in Exercise 5]

_____

_____

g.   [Question in Exercise 5]

_____

_____

15. Do you believe you are a loving or compassionate person?

_____

_____

a.   Why/why not?

_____

_____

b.   When/How did you come to this conclusion (when do you recall the first time you felt or thought this)?

_____

_____

c.   What emotion or feeling comes to mind that underlies or comes forth from this belief?

_____

_____

d.   [Question in Exercise 5]

_____

_____

e. [Question in Exercise 5]

_____

_____

f. [Question in Exercise 5]

_____

_____

g. [Question in Exercise 5]

_____

_____

16. What do you believe is your best quality?

_____

_____

a. Why?

_____

_____

b. When/How did you come to this conclusion (when do you recall the first time you felt or thought this)?

_____

_____

c. What emotion or feeling comes to mind that underlies or comes forth from this belief?

_____

_____

d.　[Question in Exercise 5]

_____

_____

e.　[Question in Exercise 5]

_____

_____

f.　[Question in Exercise 5]

_____

_____

g.　[Question in Exercise 5]

_____

_____

17.　What do you believe you are good at?

_____

_____

a.　Why?

_____

_____

b.　When/How did you come to this conclusion (when do you recall the first time you felt or thought this)?

_____

_____

c. What emotion or feeling comes to mind that underlies or comes forth from this belief?

_____

_____

d. [Question in Exercise 5]

_____

_____

e. [Question in Exercise 5]

_____

_____

f. [Question in Exercise 5]

_____

_____

g. [Question in Exercise 5]

_____

_____

18. Are there any common emotions or feelings that you see in the above answers? If so, what?

_____

_____

EXERCISE 5

1. Pick one of the questions in Exercise 4 above to focus on and access the *Companion Audio* for this *Section II, Exercise 5* and go through the guided exercise. After the guided exercise, answer the following questions "d-g" in that question that you selected in Exercise 4 (and write your answers in that question in Exercise 4 above).

    d. What are the physical sensations when you think of this scenario?

    e. What are the hurts of others in this story?

    f. What compassion and forgiveness can you offer from your heart for the acts of others that may be involved in this story?

    g. How does your story here change now?

2. Do you see any patent lies or egoic self-sabotaging in any of the stories above in your questions in Exercise 4?

    _____

    _____

Homework: Work through a similar meditation, investigation, and assessment of each of the questions in Exercise 4 and answer the questions "d" through "g" and any observations in Exercise 5, Question 2.

EXERCISE 6

1. What do you typically do when things get difficult?

   _____

   _____

   a. Do you shut down?

   b. Do you become sad or angry?

   c. Do you seek a distraction or disengagement?

   d. Do you become depressed?

   e. Do you feel powerless, or do you try to take control?

2. When was the first time you enacted any of these behaviors, and what were the circumstances?

   _____

   _____

3. How did and does this behavior help you to cope with the difficulty?

   _____

   _____

EXERCISE 7 – BRINGING OUT YOUR HIGHER-SELF SHORTCUT

Please access the *Companion Audio* for this *Section II, Exercise 7* and go through the guided exercise. After completing the guided exercise in the Audio, please answer the following.

1. What is your shortcut?

2. Consider any of the questions you answered in Question 4 above and use your shortcut to get into your higher self to consider that question. Did anything change in your perspective on your answers in Exercise 4 after you considered it from your higher-self consciousness?

EXERCISE 8 – UNDOING THE EGOIC CONSCIOUSNESS

1. Identify a scenario about which you have been ruminating about (which will usually involve a lot about the "I," "me," "my," and "mine" perspectives) and access the *Companion Audio* for this *Section II, Exercise 8* and then answer the remaining questions in this Exercise 8.

2. How easy or difficult was it to break the trance of this thought-stream?

    _____

    _____

3. What bodily sensations did you feel during the thoughts?

    _____

    _____

4. How easy or difficult was it to make the choice to surrender those thoughts?

    _____

    _____

5. Was the act of choosing accompanied by any noticeable bodily sensations or feelings?

    _____

    _____

6. Were you able to make the choice to surrender them?

    _____

    _____

7. If you were able to make the choice to surrender them, how did that feel in the body?

   _____

   _____

8. What body sensations or feelings accompanied that choice?

   _____

   _____

9. What emotions came up during the pause and choice determination of whether to surrender or return to those thoughts?

   _____

   _____

10. What other attachments to your desire to think were present?

   _____

   _____

EXERCISE 9—HOW DOES YOUR INNER CRITIC SHOW UP?

1. My inner critic shows up when

   _____

   _____

2. My inner critic says to me

   _____

   _____

3. My response to my inner critic is

   _____

   _____

4. How my inner critic makes me feel

   _____

   _____

5. I feel smallest and least worthy when my inner critic

   _____

   _____

6. Who most reminds me of my inner critic is

   _____

   _____

7. How old I was when I first remember my inner critic

   _____

    a.   How old I feel when my inner critic is at its harshest is

_____

_____

    b.   Do you ever feel as if you revert to the thoughts and emotions and feelings of that age?

_____

_____

    c.   If the answer to "b" was yes, when does that seem to happen?

_____

_____

8.   I believe my inner critic is speaking truths to me when

_____

_____

EXERCISE 10 – FACING THE INNER CRITIC

Please access the *Companion Audio* for this *Section II, Exercise 10* and go through the guided exercise. After completing the guided exercise, answer the following questions.

1. Do you have a sense that the inner critic is still, or is no longer, in charge?

   _____

   a. Is the inner critic now more in the background?

   _____

   b. Do you still feel somewhat under the thumb of the inner critic?

   _____

2. How did your bodily sensations change between the beginning and end of the exercise?

   _____

   _____

Homework

1. Every time you notice the inner critic working up some comments, name it.

2. Shift your attention away from its comments and towards the physical sensations in the body at that moment

3. Have an intention to break the grip and impact of the inner critic

SECTION III EXERCISES

EXERCISE 1 – USING YOUR BODILY SENSATIONS TO GAUGE WHICH CONSCIOUSNESS YOU'RE IN
Access the *Companion Audio* for this *Section III, Exercise 1* and go through the guided exercise. After completing the guided exercise identify what are the bodily sensations you feel when you experience the following, as led through the audio guide on these.

1. Strength vs. Domination/Control

   Strength: _____

   Domination/Control: _____

2. Perseverance vs. Struggle

   Perseverance: _____

   Struggle: _____

3. Patience vs. Complacency/Disconnection

   Patience: _____

   Complacency/Disconnection: _____

4. Peace/Contentment vs. Agitation/Discontent

   Peace/Contentment: _____

   Agitation/Discontent: _____

5. Kindness vs. Resentment

   Kindness: _____

   Resentment: _____

6. Trust vs. Distrust

   Trust: _____

   Distrust: _____

7. Joy vs. Depression

   Joy: _____

   Depression: _____

EXERCISE 2 –THE DIFFERENCE BETWEEN FEELINGS AND EMOTIONS

Please access the *Companion Audio* for this *Section III, Exercise 2* and go through the guided exercise. After completing the guided exercise, identify what are the bodily sensations you feel when you experience the following as led through the audio guide on these.

1. Excitement/thrill:

   a. How does this differ from the bodily sensations of Joy?

   _____

   _____

2. Sadness:

   a. How does this differ from the bodily sensations of Depression?

   _____

   _____

3. Pride of Accomplishment:

   a. How does this differ from the bodily sensations of Strength?

   _____

   _____

4. Disappointment:

   a. How does this differ from the bodily sensations of Struggle?

   _____

   _____

5. Endurance

   a. How does this differ from the bodily sensations of Perseverance?

   _____

   _____

EXERCISE 3 –EXPLORING YOUR PERSONAL ANGER

1. What makes you most angry at:

    a. Yourself?

    _____

    _____

    b. Others?

    _____

    _____

    c. Life?

    _____

    _____

2. What do you usually do when you feel angry with someone?

    _____

    _____

3. When do you get extremely angry?

    _____

    _____

4. How did your parents deal with anger when you were a child?

    _____

    _____

a. How did that affect you?

_____

_____

5. Anger scares you when . . .?

_____

_____

6. If you strongly express your anger, what are you afraid of, or what scares you about doing that?

_____

_____

7. When does your anger turn to:

a. Aggression/venting?

_____

_____

h. Hostility or ill-will?

_____

_____

c. Downright hatred?

_____

_____

8. How does the child in you react to anger?

_____

_____

9. How is your ability to remain vulnerable while angry?

    _____

    _____

10. When do you turn your anger back on yourself?

    _____

    _____

EXERCISE 4 – EXPERIENCING YOUR ANGER

Please access the *Companion Audio* for this *Section III, Exercise 4* and go through the guided exercise. After completing the guided exercise, answer the following questions.

1. When you're angry, what happens to your hands?

    _____

    _____

2. When you're angry, what happens to your breathing?

    _____

    _____

3. Remember a situation when someone really angered you . . .

    a. How does it feel when you're in the situation when shut down?

        _____

        _____

    b. How does it feel when you breathe?

        _____

        _____

    c. How does your jaw feel, fists/hands?

        _____

        _____

EXERCISE 5 – GUIDED: EXPERIENCING YOUR PERSONAL ANGER EXPRESSIONS

Please access the *Companion Audio* for this *Section III, Exercise 5* and go through the guided exercise. After completing the guided exercise, answer the following questions.

1. Describe the physical sensations with anger expressed aggressively.

    _____

    _____

2. Describe the physical sensations with anger expressed submissively.

    _____

    _____

3. Describe the physical sensations with anger expressed in a balanced way.

    _____

    _____

EXERCISE 6 – GUIDED: AWARENESS AND HEALING TECHNIQUES

Please access the *Companion Audio* for this *Section III, Exercise 6* and go through the guided exercise. After completing the guided exercise, answer the questions below based on the different techniques of diffusing emotions after each technique in the Audio guided exercise.

A – Intimacy

1. How does the emotion feel and look when it arises?

   _____

   _____

2. How do you understand it?

   _____

   _____

3. What are you doing with this emotion?

   _____

   _____

4. Are you blaming it, venting it, repressing it, letting it mutate into a negative state such as hostility or other ill-will?

   _____

   _____

5. When are you triggered for this emotion?

   _____

   _____

6. What types of circumstances bring about this triggering?

    _____

    _____

7. Are you able to be empathetic towards the emotion or towards yourself?

    _____

    _____

B – Inquiry

8. What are the thoughts that created or contributed to this emotion?

    _____

    _____

C – Discourse

9. What is the emotion about? What does it have to say about what it is doing and why?

    _____

    _____

D – Combined

10. What are the common stories that your ego spins about others that produce anger in you about others? Use your intellect to analyze any common theme

    _____

    _____

11. What do these common theme(s) say about what your ego tells you that you *should* expect about/from others?

    _____

    _____

12. What are the flaws (and assumptions) in this these stories and/or expectations?

    _____

    _____

13. What are the common stories that your ego spins about you that produce anger about yourself?

    _____

    _____

14. What do these common theme(s) say about what your ego tells you that you *should* expect about/from yourself?

    _____

    _____

15. What are the flaws in these stories and/or expectations?

    _____

    _____

EXERCISE 7 – EXPLORING YOUR FEAR

1. What brings up fear most easily in you?

   _____

   _____

2. This fear is at its most intense when . . .

   _____

   _____

3. What do you notice most about your fear in such moments?

   _____

   _____

EXERCISE 8 – GUIDED: EXPERIENCING AND UN-
DERSTANDING YOUR PERSONAL FEAR (Intimacy–Inquiry–Discourse)

Please access the *Companion Audio* for this *Section III, Exercise 8* and go through the guided exercise. After completing the guided exercise, answer the following questions.

1. The feeling of this fear in your body (chest, belly, breath, and so on) is . . .

   _____

   _____

2. Where in your body do you most strongly feel your fear?

   _____

   _____

3. What do you notice about the movement of your fear in your body?

   _____

   _____

4. What happens as you move more closely to (become more intimate with) this fear?

   _____

   _____

5. How does your mind react to your fear and to your facing your fear?

   _____

   _____

6. How does it feel getting closer to your fear? Notice how it changes the closer/deeper you become with noticing and knowing your fear?

    _____

    _____

A – Intimacy

7. How does the emotion feel and look when it arises?

    _____

    _____

8. How do you understand it?

    _____

    _____

9. What are you doing with this emotion?

    _____

    _____

10. Are you blaming it, venting it, repressing it, letting it mutate into a negative state, such as hostility or other ill-will?

    _____

    _____

11. When are you triggered for this emotion?

    _____

    _____

12. What types of circumstances bring about this triggering?

   _____

   _____

13. Are you able to be empathetic towards the emotion or towards yourself?

   _____

   _____

B – Inquiry

14. What are the thoughts that created or contributed to this emotion?

   _____

   _____

C – Discourse

15. What is the emotion about? What does it have to say about what it is doing and why?

   _____

   _____

D – Combined

16. What are the common stories that your ego spins about others that produce anger in you about others? Use your intellect to analyze any common theme.

   _____

   _____

17. What do these common theme(s) say about what your ego tells you that you *should* expect about/from others?

   _____

   _____

18. What are the flaws (and assumptions) in this these stories and/or expectations?

   _____

   _____

19. What are the common stories that your ego spins about you that produce anger about yourself?

   _____

   _____

20. What do these common theme(s) say about what your ego tells you that you *should* expect about/from yourself?

   _____

   _____

21. What are the flaws in these stories and/or expectations?

   _____

   _____

EXERCISE 9 – GUIDED: EXPERIENCING YOUR PERSONAL EXPRESSIONS OF FEAR

Please access the *Companion Audio for this Section III, Exercise 9* and go through the guided exercises. After completing the guided exercises in the Audio, please answer the following, as guided in the Audio.

1. Describe the physical sensations with fear expressed aggressively.

   _____

   _____

2. Describe the physical sensations with fear expressed submissively.

   _____

   _____

3. Describe the physical sensations with fear expressed in a balanced way.

   _____

   _____

EXERCISE 10 – EXPLORING YOUR PERSONAL SHAME

1. When do you first recall feeling shame (as a child)?

   _____

   _____

2. What did you do with it (fight back, withdraw, feel bad about yourself, or so on)?

   _____

   _____

3. What or how did you feel from that?

   _____

   _____

4. How did you survive it then (what was your coping skill)?

   _____

   _____

5. Identify those thoughts, emotions, and feelings from your first encounter with shame.

   _____

   _____

6. Do you still handle your shame today the same way, or how is your reaction different?

   _____

   _____

7. When do you feel those emotions and feelings and think those thoughts you had as a child with shame?

   _____

   _____

EXERCISE 11 – GUIDED: EXPERIENCING AND REC-
OGNIZING YOUR PERSONAL SHAME

Please access the *Companion Audio* for this *Section III, Exercise 11* and go through the guided exercise. After completing
the guided exercise in the Audio, please answer the following.

1. How did the shame feel in your body?

    _____

    _____

2. Did your shame convert into aggressiveness/anger or sup-
    pressive-ness/withdrawal? If so, what did that feel like?

    _____

    _____

3. How did the body sensations and feelings change as your
    shame worked through different manifestations?

    _____

    _____

EXERCISE 12 – GUIDED: EXPERIENCING YOUR PERSONAL EXPRESSIONS OF SHAME—AGGRESSIVE, SUBMISSIVE, AND BALANCED USES OF SHAME

Please access the *Companion Audio* for this *Section III, Exercise 12* and go through the guided exercise. After completing the guided exercise in the Audio, please answer the following.

1. Describe the physical sensations with shame expressed aggressively.

   _____

   _____

2. Describe the physical sensations with shame expressed submissively.

   _____

   _____

3. Describe the physical sensations with shame expressed in a balanced way.

   _____

   _____

EXERCISE 13 – GUIDED: UNDERSTANDING YOUR SHAME USING DISCOURSE—INTIMACY–INQUIRY TO UNDERSTAND THE SHAME

Please access the *Companion Audio* for this *Section III, Exercise 13* and go through the guided exercise. After completing the guided exercise in the Audio, please answer the following.

A – Intimacy

1. How does the emotion feel and look when it arises?

_____

_____

2. How do you understand it?

_____

_____

3. What are you doing with this emotion?

_____

_____

4. Are you blaming it, venting it, repressing it, or letting it mutate into a negative state, such as hostility or other ill-will?

_____

_____

5. When are you triggered for this emotion?

_____

_____

6. What types of circumstances bring about this triggering?

   _____

   _____

7. Are you able to be empathetic towards the emotion or towards yourself?

   _____

   _____

B – Inquiry

8. What are the thoughts that created or contributed to this emotion?

   _____

   _____

C – Discourse

9. What is the emotion about? What does it have to say about what it is doing, and why?

   _____

   _____

D – Combined

10. What are the common stories that your ego spins about others that produce anger in you about others? Use your intellect to analyze any common theme.

    _____

    _____

11. What do these common theme(s) say about what your ego tells you that you *should* expect about/from others?

    _____

    _____

12. What are the flaws (and assumptions) in this these stories and/or expectations?

    _____

    _____

13. What are the common stories that your ego spins about you that produce anger about yourself?

    _____

    _____

14. What do these common theme(s) say about what your ego tells you that you *should* expect about/from yourself?

    _____

    _____

15. What are the flaws in these stories and/or expectations?

    _____

    _____

16. Were you able to let go any of the shame by the end of the meditation? Why, or why not?

    _____

    _____

SECTION IV EXERCISES

EXERCISE 1 – TAKING INVENTORY

1. What stories and beliefs about others or life changed by the end of the course?

    _____

    _____

2. What were the illusions or limitations you placed on yourself that you no longer believe define you?

    _____

    _____

3. What were/are your projections about which you now have greater awareness?

    _____

    _____

4. What qualities did you hide from yourself that you've discovered you actually have?

    _____

    _____

5. What have you discovered are your shadow's signs and go-to behaviors?

   _____

   _____

6. What are your shadow's messages to you?

   _____

   _____

7. How do you plan to handle your shadow's triggers?

   _____

   _____

8. What have you found to be the best technique(s) for you to put some distance between and stop identifying with your ego and shadow's thoughts and their resulting emotions?

   _____

   _____

About the Author

Dawn Ely is an inventor, entrepreneur, and accomplished C-level executive. She is experienced in assisting companies in their growth and operations, having managed multi-million and billion dollar business divisions of large and small, private and public companies both international and domestic. The founder of several companies with novel business models, she has held leadership roles in domestic and international community organizations. A frequent speaker and leader of domestic and international seminars on business, law, international trade and development, personnel management and development, conflict resolution, and women's empowerment. She has also been a radio host and contributing writer for community publications, and has been a featured guest on radio and podcast programs, both domestically and internationally, on business, international relations, hate speech, personal empowerment and ego management topics. She has also created and led comprehensive curricula on mastering the ego and conflict resolution that has facilitated transformation for many.

A graduate of the University of Virginia in Political and Social Thought (distinguished honors major) and English, she holds a law degree from Mercer University School of Law, and studies World Religions at Harvard University. She is a certified Stephen Minister, suicide hotline counselor, trained in shamanistic practices, a student of the Kabbalah, and studies with a Sufi healing order. Dawn recently founded the tax-exempt nonprofit, **Liberate from Hate, Inc.**, designed to liberate our individual and collective minds from hate and anger through practical tips on managing the ego to end *us versus them* narratives.

Made in the USA
Columbia, SC
12 November 2020

24365300R00293